International Political Economy Series
Series Standing Order ISBN 0–333–71708–2 hardback
Series Standing Order ISBN 0–333–71110–6 paperback
(*outside North America only*)

You can receive future titles in this series as they are published by placing a standing order.
Please contact your bookseller or, in case of difficulty, write to us at the address below with
your name and address, the title of the series and an ISBN quoted above.

Customer Services Department, Macmillan Distribution Ltd, Houndmills, Basingstoke,
Hampshire RG21 6XS, England

Public Policy in the Age of Globalization

Responses to Environmental and Economic Crises

Edited by

Helge Hveem
Department of Political Science and
Centre on Technology, Innovation and Culture
University of Oslo
Norway

and

Kristen Nordhaug
Department of Geography and International Development Studies
Roskilde University
Denmark

Editorial matter and selection and Chapters 1 and 8
© Helge Hveem and Kristen Nordhaug 2002
Chapters 2–7 © Palgrave Macmillan Ltd 2002

First published 2002 by
PALGRAVE MACMILLAN
Houndmills, Basingstoke, Hampshire RG21 6XS and
175 Fifth Avenue, New York, N.Y. 10010
Companies and representatives throughout the world.

PALGRAVE MACMILLAN is the global academic imprint of the Palgrave Macmillan division of St Martin's Press, LLC and of Palgrave Macmillan Ltd. Macmillan® is a registered trademark in the United States, United Kingdom and other countries. Palgrave is a registered trademark in the European Union and other countries.

ISBN 0–333–99848–0

This book is printed on paper suitable for recycling and made from fully managed and sustained forest sources.

A catalogue record for this book is available from the British Library.

Library of Congress Cataloging-in-Publication Data

Public policy in the age of globalization: responses to environmental and economic crises / edited by Helge Hveem and Kristen Nordhaug.
   p. cm. – (International political economy series)
ISBN 0–333–99848–0 (cloth)
   1. Environmental policy – Economic aspects – Developing countries – Case studies. 2. Economic policy – Developing countries – Case studies. 3. Globalization – Environmental aspects – Developing countries – Case studies. I. Hveem, Helge. II. Nordhaug, Kristen. III. Series.
HC59.72.E5 P83 2002
338.9'009172'4–dc21
          2002073540

10 9 8 7 6 5 4 3 2 1
11 10 09 08 07 06 05 04 03 02

Printed and bound in Great Britain by
Antony Rowe Ltd, Chippenham and Eastbourne

Contents

List of Tables

Notes on the Contributors

Benedicte Bull is research fellow at the Centre for Development and the Environment, University of Oslo. Publications include '"New" Regionalism in Central America', in *Third World Quarterly*, 1999.

Bernard Conte is senior lecturer in development economics at the Centre d'Etude d'Afrique Noire (CEAN) and the Centre d'Economie du Developpement (CED), both at the University

Montesquieu-Bordeaux IV. He has held positions in Togo, Côte d'Ivoire and Algeria. Among his latest publications is 'Côte d'Ivoire: Between Politic Reconstruction and Economic Adjustment', in Colin Legum (ed.) *Africa Contemporary Record*, 2001.

Helge Hveem is professor of political science and director at the Centre on Technology, Innovation and Culture, both at the University of Oslo. He was previously research director at the Faculty of Social Sciences, University of Oslo. He is a former research fellow of the International Peace Research Institute, research consultant with the UNCTAD Secretariat and former research director of the Centre for Development and the Environment of the University of Oslo. He has published and lectured widely, and is a member of several boards and committees both nationally and internationally. His books include *The Political Economy of Third World Producer Associations* (1978) and *Makt og velferd i det globale samfunn* ('Power and Welfare in the Global Society') (1996).

Sunghack Lim is research professor at the Center for International Studies and previously senior researcher at the Social Science Research Institute, Yonsei University. His published articles include 'The Politics of Economic Rise and Decline in South Korea' and 'Foreign Ownership of Korean Domestic Banks and Financial Reform'.

Alvaro López Mora is professor of political science at the School of International Studies, University of Heredia in Costa Rica. He has a doctorate from the University of Toulouse. He served as Costa Rica's chief negotiator of the country's accession to GATT and has since served as a consultant to several administrations as well as international organizations.

Chung-in Moon is professor of political science and currently Dean of the Graduate School of International Studies, both Yonsei University. He has published and lectured widely on international political economy and the development issues of East Asia, and is the author and co-author of several leading texts on the subject.

V.K. Natraj was formerly professor of development studies, University of Mysore and since February 2000, Director, the Madras Institute of Development Studies, Chennai. His major publications are *Regional Planning and National Development* (co-editor) and *Land Reforms in Karnataka* (co-editor).

Kristen Nordhaug graduated in sociology at the University of Oslo and holds a PhD in international development studies from Roskilde University. He is an associate professor in the Department of Geography and International Development Studies, Roskilde University and has previously worked as a researcher at the Centre for Development and the Environment, University of Oslo. Among recent publications are: 'Globalisation and the State: Theoretical Paradigms', *European Journal of Development Research,* 2002.

Alice Sindzingre is senior researcher, currently posted at the Centre National de la Recherche Scientifique (CNRS, Paris). Her research is focused on political economy and she has participated in the *World Development Report 2000* of the World Bank on poverty. She has also published: 'Crédibilité des états et économie politique des réformes en Afrique', *Economies et Sociétés,* 1998.

Larry A. Swatuk lectures in the Department of Politics at the University of Botswana. During the latter half of 2001 he was a senior research fellow at the Centre for Southern African Studies, University of the Western Cape, South Africa where he coordinated a research project on new institutions of water resource management in Zimbabwe.

María Fernanda Tuozzo was previously research fellow at FLACSO-Argentina (Latin American Faculty of Social Sciences) and visiting research fellow at Warwick University, UK.

Diana Tussie has been a senior research fellow at FLACSO-Argentina and CONICET (Argentina's National Council for Technical and Scientific Research). She was selected Distinguished Fulbright Scholar in 1996 and has published widely, including several books. She served as Undersecretary of State for International Trade Negotiations in the de la Rua administration.

Peter Vale is professor of Southern African studies in the School of Government, University of the Western Cape. His latest publication is a co-edited collection (with Larry Swatuk and Bertil Oden) entitled *Theory, Change and Southern Africa's Future* (2001).

List of Abbreviations

ACP	African-Caribbean-Pacific
ADB	African Development Bank
ADP	Alternative Development Paradigm
AI	Autonomous institution
ALIDES	Alliance for Sustainable Development
ANC	African National Congress
ANFE	Association for Economic Growth (Asociación Nacional de Fomento Económico)
BCEAO	Central Bank of the West-African States
BEAC	Bank of the Central African States
BJP	Bharatiya Janata Party
BOAD	West African Development Bank (Banque Ouest Africaine de Développement)
BWI	Bretton Woods institutions
CACM	Central American Common Market
CADEXO	Chamber for Costa Rican Exporters (Cámara de Exportadores de Costa Rica)
Caistab	Price stabilization fund for coffee and cocoa (Caisse de Stabilisation)
CBI	Caribbean Basin Initiative
CBRA	Caribbean Basin Recovery Act
CDI	Council for the Defence of Institutionality (Consejo para la Defensa de Institucionalidad)
CEFSA	Consejeros Economicos y Financieros
CENPRO	Center for Promotion of Export and Investment (Centro para la Promoción de las Exportaciónes y las Inversiónes)
CEAO	West African Economic Community (Communauté Economique de l'Afrique de l'Ouest)
CEDEAO	Economic Community of West-African States (Communauté Economique des Etats de l'Afrique de l'Ouest.
CEPICI	Centre for Investments Promotion in Côte d'Ivoire

CET	Common External Tariff
CFA	Communauté Financiére Africaine
CINDE	Costa Rican Coalition for Development Initiatives (Coalición Costarricense de Iniciativas para el Desarrollo)
CITU	Centre for Indian Trade Unions
CNCE	Comision Nacional de Comercio Exterior
CODESA, Costa Rica	Costa Rican Development Coalition
CONNEP	Conference on New National Environment Policy
CPM	Communist Party of India, Marxist
CTE	Committee on Trade and Environment
DPG	Domestically Prohibited Goods
ECOWAS	Economic Community of West-African States
EDF	European Development Fund
EMCCA	Economic and Monetary Community of Central Africa
ENJF	Environmental Justice Networking Forum
ESAF	Enhanced Structural Adjustment Facility
FDI	Foreign Direct Investment
FIPB	Foreign Investment Promotion Board
GATT	General Agreement on Tariffs and Trade
GSP	General System of Preferences
HDI	Human Development Indicator
HIPC	Heavily Indebted Poor Countries
ICE	Costa Rican Electricity Institute (Instituto Costarricense de Electricidad)
ICCO	International Cocoa Organization
ICO	International Coffee Organization
ICT	Costa Rican Tourism Institute (Instituto Costarricence de Turismo)
IDB	Inter-American Development Bank
IDBI	Industrial Development Bank of India
IEA	International Enviornment Agreement
IFI	International Financial Institution
INBIO	National Institute of Bio-diversity (Institutio Nacional de Bio-Diversidad)
INRO	International Rubber Organization
ISO	International Organisation for Standardisation
KEB	Karnataka Electricity Board
MEA	Multilateral Environment Agreement

MERCOSUR	Latin American Southern Common Market (Mercado Común del Sur)
MINAE	Ministry of Environment and Energy
MINEX	Program for Exports and Investment (Programa de Exportación e Inversiones)
MIRENEM	Ministry of Natural Resources, Energy and Mines
MNC	Multinational Company
MSEB	Maharashtra State Electricity Board
NEERI	National Environmental Engineering Research Institute
NEP	New Economic Policy
NGO	Non-Governmental Organizations
NRI	Non-Resident Indians
OCAM	African and Mauritian Common Organization
ODA	Overseas Development Assistance
OECD	Organisation of Economic Co-operation and Development
OHADA	Organisation for Harmonising Business Law in Africa
PIL	Public Interest Litigation
PLN	National Liberation Party (Partido Liberación Nacional)
PPA	Power Purchase Agreement
PSE	Public Sector Enterprise
PUSC	Social Christian Unity Party (Partido Unidad Social Cristiana)
SAP	Structural Adjustment Programme
SEB	State Electricity Board
SETENA	National Technical Secretariat for the Environment (Secretaría Técnica Nacional Ambiental)
SICEDA	System of Integration of Central America (Sistema de Integración Centroamericano)
SINAC	National System for Areas of Conservation (Sistema Nacional de Areas de Conservación)
SME	Small- and Medium-sized Enterprise
SS	Shiv Sena Party
SSA	Sub-Saharan Africa
Stabex	Stable export earnings program

TRIM	Trade-Related Investment Measure
TRIP	Trade-Related Intellectual Property Right
UCCAEP	Union of Chambers and Private Enterprise Associations (Unión de Cámaras y Asociaciones de la Empresa Privada)
WAEMU	West-African Economic and Monetary Union UEMOA
UNCED	United Nations Conference on Environment and Development
UNCTAD	United Nations Conference on Trade and Development
UNDP	United Nations Development Programme
USAID	The United States Agency for International Development
WCED	World Commission on Environment and Development
WTO	World Trade Organization

Preface

This book analyses the way in which six developing countries have responded to demands for adjustment to globalization processes in the last couple of decades. It reports on a project that grew out of a concern that the academic discourse on adjustment needs and policies after the Uruguay Round on trade and the Rio conference on sustainable development needed a deeper understanding of the political economy of adjustment in the developing world. It is our hope that this collection of country case studies contributes to that understanding. They cover a period up to the turn of the millennum. Developments after that date have been marginally referred to.

The project is part of a research programme, International Production and Trade, Environment and Development, carried out at the Centre for Development and the Environment, University of Oslo. The country chapters have nearly all been contributed by researchers outside the Centre, all of the contributors having special competence in their respective fields. Their participation was made possible by a special grant from the Royal Norwegian Ministry of Foreign Affairs. The editors wish to express their gratitude to all our research colleagues for their contributions, and to the Ministry for its generous financial support. The contents of the book and the conclusions drawn are obviously not the responsibility of the Ministry, but those of the authors themselves.

H.H.
K.N.

1

Introduction: National Institutions and the Politics of Adjustment to Globalization

Helge Hveem and Kristen Nordhaug

1997 was a hard year for Indonesia. Plantation companies had started forest fires in Sumatra and Kalimantan to clear new land. Now these fires had got out of control. During autumn the fires had developed into environmental disasters which destroyed enormous land areas, and polluted large tracts of Indonesia and Southeast Asia. Meanwhile, Indonesia was badly affected by the currency and financial crisis that hit several of her neighbouring countries. The exchange rate fell and the country's foreign debt escalated. Agriculture was also affected by a major drought. On top of these problems a political succession crisis broke out as the ailing President Suharto declined to nominate a successor.

The Suharto regime was clearly not able to address these political, environmental and economic problems. Its inability to handle the financial crisis escalated the political crisis of 1998. The government was highly recalcitrant when it came to implementing the kind of reforms demanded by the IMF in return for supplies of new credit. It was severely punished by the international community of investors for its inability to take forceful action. The *rupiah* continued to fall and Indonesia's foreign debt mounted accordingly. The reforms demanded by the International Monetary Fund (IMF) included banking reforms and anti-monopoly reforms – which went against the economic interests of Suharto's family and close associates – as well as a number of other sensitive reforms, such as removals of subsidies on food and fuel. The opposition capitalized on exposing the cronyism and nepotism of the regime in a time of national hardship, while the government's brief attempts to heed the IMF's call for a removal of subsidies triggered political turmoil and growing opposition against the regime. As the anti-Suharto demonstrations and riots increased in intensity, divisions within the regime surfaced. On 21 May 1998, Suharto was forced to resign from his presidency as it became apparent that he was unable to summon a 'reform cabinet' to win time.The fall of Indonesia's long-time dictator was a result of the inability to steer between domestic-political constraints and the international market in a situation where Indonesia's economy had become heavily dependent on the confidence of international investors. The renewed forest fires in early 1998 also indicated that Indonesian authorities were unable or unwilling to go against the well-connected plantation companies despite strong pressures against Indonesia from affected neighbouring countries and the transnational and international communities.

Indonesia's problems are, with all their dramatic aspects, not unique. Several developing countries have been or are struggling with more or less success to cope with the challenges of a new and globalized world economy. This brings with it international and bilateral demands for liberalization of trade and foreign investment, and international pressure for environmental improvements in ways which do not go against the imperatives of domestic growth, stability and political legitimacy. Inability to handle these challenges may have severe economic, social, political and environmental effects, as the Indonesian case demonstrates.

International challenges

One general feature of the situation since the 1980s is that the number and the variety of international policy prescriptions and recommendations have increased quite radically, in fact almost exponentially. They range from the adjustment requirements of the Structural Adjustment Programmes (SAPs), via expectations of political liberalization measures linked to development assistance disbursement, to resource and environment protection policy recommendations made by the World Commission on Environment and Development (WCED) as well as the UN Conference on Environment and Development in Rio in 1992 and in the negotiations that followed it. In the 1990s, a vast range of policy prescriptions adopted by the protracted but finally successful Uruguay Round negotiations in GATT, the General Agreement on Tariffs and Trade, have been added. They are contained in the Final Act setting up the World Trade Organization (WTO). The establishment of the WTO on 1 January 1995 also confronted members and would-be member governments with a large agenda of issues and demands to be further negotiated. After the aborted ministerial meeting in Seattle in

December 1999, the meeting in Doha in November 2001 may have put the negotiation machinery back on track and initiated a new round of negotiations. As it coincides with China's entering the WTO, the new round, sometimes referred to as 'the development round', will present developing countries with new challenges and probably a set of new policy prescriptions.

Most if not all policy prescriptions imply in some sense and to some degree a regulatory activity. Market actors are thus supposed to be regulated under the codes of conduct administered by the WTO and other multilateral institutions as well as semi-public institutions such as the International Standardisation Organisation (ISO). At the same time, partly because such institutions do not cover all issues of interest to economic actors, and partly because these regulations occasionally may impede vital interests, market actors develop their own rules and procedures, including informal regulation of competition (for example, cartels, price leadership). They can or will develop international alliances by which local domestic interest groups may undermine or circumvent public regulatory efforts that change the established position of such groups.

Over the last few years, as far as environmental policy is concerned, a range of policy recommendations with regulatory goals has been introduced. Several International Environment Agreements (IEAs) contain provisions for the regulation of trade: and some of the multilateral trade agreements referred to above contain provisions for environment protection. These institutional developments take place in parallel with the liberalization of international foreign direct investments, with growing short-term capital movements and with foreign trade deregulation.

Our research focuses on these changes from the point of view of countries with different historical trajectories of political-institutional and socio-economic development. We assume that such differences also provide the countries concerned with differing flexibility and institutional capacity for adjustment. We focus in particular on countries which for various reasons are less endowed in terms of such capacity: in international parlance, the so-called low- and middle-income countries.

The contributions in this volume investigate the implications of international system change for national decision-making institutions and for policy. The focus on national institutions is a deliberate choice. It is premised on an assessment of contemporary research efforts. National institutions may be viewed as positioned in the interface between private economic agents and the international system. Their role in that respect varies from case to case and is thus multifaceted. One role that national institutions may play – and which is focused on in the reports – is that of transmitting domestic group ideas and interests to the international level and vice versa. Studies of the role of these institutions within processes of international change are still relatively undeveloped. Most studies of international regime change focus: (a) on international negotiating processes; and (b) on the outcomes of these processes in terms of rules and procedures established at the international level. They also look at such things as the interrelationship of sectorial regime-building – such as trade liberalization in the GATT/WTO on the environment – or the effects of the environmental agreements on free trade rules.

The focus in the present volume is on *processes and practice* of policy implementation. It is not assumed that national institutions more or less automatically adjust to international change once policies or rules according to which change is to take place have been set down through some internationally negotiated rule or principle. Experiences with non-compliance during the first generation of SAPs represent one important illustration of this. It also represents one important reason why the IMF entered into more active monitoring and supervision of the SAPs in what is called the second generation. To assume automatic compliance would be even more questionable in another context – that of international environmental policies. We do not assume that these are implemented in an atmosphere of harmony. This scepticism, which is empirically supported by other research contributions, is warranted because *inter alia* nation-states should not be viewed as unitary actors which behave completely rationally and always reach compliance with international agreements – even those which they have signed as the (most) rational option to pursue.

The project assumes, on the contrary, that the implementation phase is one of the most problematic. Nation-states are normally complex and pluralistic entities. Their capacity to implement is a function both of the specific national socio-political conditions and the role of institutions in society. This capacity may vary considerably from one country to another according to its political culture, historical background, phase of development, and, not least, according to the shape of its state-society relations. Capacity also depends on the nature of relations with international actors and agencies. These observations, made rather briefly and sketchily in the present context, call for a research strategy that focuses on the interplay between international and domestic national political processes and the interaction between state and private agencies.

Adjustment, negotiation and institutions

The political economy of national adjustment to international trends and demands has become a central issue since the introduction of SAPs at the beginning of the 1980s. Research in the area has covered various subjects, all of which are complex and many of which are controversial. There is practically nobody who argues that adjustment is not (sometimes and in some form and degree) a necessity. Rather, debate is on the form and content of such adjustment, about how fast and how radically adjustment should be executed and about who should take part in deciding on and implementing it.

One simple distinction that may be drawn is that between macroeconomic and microeconomic forms of adjustment and their contents. Macroeconomic adjustment aims at re-establishing the balance of payments and at stabilizing prices. It is based on measures such as devaluation and tight fiscal and monetary policies. A microeconomic oriented mode of adjustment aims at structural adjustment of the economy through rationalization of the domestic production sector and distribution of resources as well as strengthening of the export sector. This adjustment process takes place through measures such as industrial restructuring, banking reforms, foreign economic liberalization, privatization and deregulation.

Debate on the degree and timing of adjustment centres primarily on whether or not it should take place for *all* policy areas at once (such as in the 'Big Bang' executed for the liberalization of the financial sector in a number of 'transition economies') or take place *gradually*. The argument for gradualism is one which states that the appropriate institutions should be in place before adjustment takes place. Or, to put it differently and concretely: adjustment of regulatory institutions must precede adjusting to the conditions of competitive markets.

The issue of who should decide on and implement adjustment is a question of the balance between efficiency and legitimacy of decision-making. Simplifying reality a little, efficiency is the assumption underlying the argument of those who are in favour of letting international expertise, in practice the Bretton Woods institutions – the World Bank and the International Monetary Fund (IMF) – design adjustment policy packages and also take part in implementing them. As long as society matters and social capital is important, this will not suffice to legitimate decisions and their implementation. There has to be basic societal support in order for decisions to be sustainable. Although transnationalization has gone a long way in establishing transnational networks that have broad societal bases, in most cases, in the present world, only national polities can muster such support. The role of national political institutions and processes in decisions on adjustment policy therefore remains crucial.

Adjustment to environmental policy demands may for many purposes be analysed along the same lines as the above. But in some respects these pose particular challenges for decision-makers – and not only because they sometimes represent interests opposite to those promoted in the market economy. Environmental problems are not as readily calculable as economic ones, a fact which partly explains why the issue of internalizing environmental costs in calculations of economic growth, product prices and so on is so important. Moreover, some environmental issues, such as that of clean drinking water at the local level or controlling climate change at the global level, deal with issues that are perceived as public goods. That perception, or construction, was a major factor behind the relatively fast and successful conclusion of an international climate policy regime, the most recent manifestation of which was the Kyoto Agreement. But the construction of environmental policy as a public good is contested by at least two groups: first, those who believe that such policy may or will jeopardize what they see as a more important public good, a freely competitive market, and, secondly, those who calculate that they themselves stand to lose in relative terms from an enforceable definition of a concrete environmental problem.

A further complication may lie in the possibility that economic policy and environmental policy domains are differently structured as a result of exogenous factors. In other words, it may be argued that economic liberalization, by the very nature of the issues, may be left more to market forces and the principle of self-regulated markets than may the environment domain. It may also be argued that the regulatory activity associated with these processes has to do with substituting general rules for discretionary government action. Environmental policy, then, because of its character as a public good domain, naturally demands more public intervention, including more discretionary government action.[1]

The argument probably exaggerates the difference between the two policy domains. In fact, there are probably more important elements of 'global governance' – by, for example, multilateral agreements in the economic sector – than in environment. Implementing these economic agreements means that the state abdicates some of its previous case-by-case handling of market access and so on; whereas, handling environmental issues is still very much concerned with particularistic local projects that demand a case-by-case approach. On the other hand, the process that started at the Rio conference in 1992 and resulted in the Kyoto agreement in 1997 is proof that a corresponding trend is visible even in the environmental domain.

There are in other words both theoretical arguments and indeed empirical evidence to support not using a method of difference too literally in comparing the two domains. Both are open to 'free-riding': private actors may seek protection from the competitive market while others are left to carry the costs of competition; and they may avoid internalizing environmental costs and at the same time have competitors carry them. In addition, institutional developments such as the advance of industrial and environmental standards under the International Standardisation Organisation (ISO) and decisions by corporate managers to invest in environmentally-friendly production as a strategy to gain advantage over polluting competitors are empirical proofs that private regulatory activity can move the environment policy domain in the direction of more sustainable development.

These counter-arguments, however, are not a rejection of the case for differentiating between regulatory institutions in the two domains. So far it is probably fair to say that environment policies in developing countries have been implemented on a case-by-case basis. Economic liberalization may have reduced the scope for rent-seeking[2] and corrupt behaviour in that domain (although there certainly also are examples of countries where the sum of these vices is a constant irrespective of economic policy regime), yet the opposite trend may be evolving in the field of environment and pollution management as agreements such as the Kyoto agreement on emissions and trade in carbon quotas takes hold.

Finally, it may be useful to define adjustment in a wider sense. A distinction may be drawn between *direct* adjustments, as discussed above, and *compensatory* adjustments. Compensatory adjustments are aimed at making the initial adjustments politically feasible by measures which neutralize or dampen short- or long-term economic, social, political or environmental problems caused by these adjustments.

The discussion so far has focused on external demands for adjustment, but adjustment may also result from other sources of demand than external ones. Thus environment regulations may come in response to domestic demands put forth by groups affected by the problem concerned. In terms of external demands, trade deficit – as for example resulting from a crisis of import substitution – may provoke a government to undertake trade and foreign investment liberalization without any pressure from foreign actors. Furthermore, these kinds of adjustment may also be anticipatory in order to prevent future problems. The first issue that is raised and will be discussed throughout this volume is what type and degree of interplay between external and internal pressures for adjustment is found. The second, related issue to be discussed, is how domestic reactions to external demands arise and are organized. External demands are filtered through an institutional setting that includes and indeed links domestic and international processes both in bargaining over the agreement and in implementing it.

Institutions are 'relatively stable collections of practices and rules defining appropriate behaviour for specific groups of actors in specific situations' (March and Olsen, 1998, p. 948). Institutional arrangements may be viewed as ways of providing security by reducing risk and uncertainty and of solving collective action problems to those members in the community whom they serve, or are supposed to serve. This definition of institutions is a broad one, which applies to a variety of institutions. Regulation can take place through or by various types of institutions – public, private non-profit (NGOs) and profit organizations (firms). A variety of non-public institutions, such as transnational corporations, non-governmental organizations or other civil agents, play a great role in the adjustment process. In this volume we have, therefore, given public institutions a place of prominence in the discussion. A focus on state institutions is defined by one or several among three different, but partly related perspectives, as follows:

1. that public and in particular state institutions are recognized by international convention and indeed law as the legitimate holders of the right of jurisdiction over a defined territory, function or sector of public policy;
2. that they therefore are the foci of demands from foreign actors and requirements by international institutions to adjust policy to the priority of such sources; and
3. that they are supposed to act as 'transmission belts' or bargaining channels between such priorities and the priorities of domestic interests.

International negotiation and adjustment

The 'transmission belt' perspective underrates the potential for autonomous and planned action by public institutions. Two relatively new analytical approaches offer better opportunities in that respect. One is the *double-edged diplomacy* approach; this builds on previous analytical models of the interplay of international and national level in shaping foreign policy, but expands such models to cope with the outcome of simultaneous negotiation processes at the inter-state level and within the state. In this model, the nation-state is viewed as a unitary actor, represented by a 'chief negotiator' who needs to cope with a double-edged problem of mobilizing support from both foreign partners and domestic constituencies in order to sign up to the agreement. The outcome that optimally guarantees a cross-national alliance to carry through the agreement is the 'win-set' (Putnam, 1988; Evans, Jacobson and Putnam, 1993).

The two-level game approach may be too state-centric. Jeffrey Knopf (1993) has modified this approach by abandoning its assumption of a unitary state, and emphasizing the role of non-government actors in policy-making. This allows him to distinguish between three types of cross-border alliances: (1) transnational alliances between non-state actors: (2) transgovernmental alliances between government segments; and (3) 'cross-level alliances' between state actors in one country and non-state actors in another country.

The logical implication of these models is that the extent to which broad national support of the agreement is achieved and is supported by various types of cross-national alliances that include powerful actors within and outside the state, is equivalent to the extent to which post-agreement implementation can be expected. It goes almost without saying that in addition the exercise of power helps to achieve agreement and its implementation. In other words, when a great power is party to international negotiations and they themselves are salient to it, one may also assume that the probability of success is considerably enhanced. The effect of power should not and cannot, however, always be taken for granted. Experiences with the Structural Adjustment Programmes (SAPs) indicate that even in a relationship characterized by highly asymmetric power – such as the IMF versus a poor developing country – the latter may move the outcome a considerable distance from what the former would have wanted (Kahler, 1993). Even in cases where bilateral agreements are produced, the process of 'involuntary defection' may obstruct implementation after agreement has been made. Defection takes place either because domestic interest groups mobilize, or groups originally in favour of the agreement change their mind and oppose it during the implementation process.

The Executive thus confronts a great variety of demands, expectations, timing problems and codes of behaviour when they attempt to mediate between sources of conflicting interest articulated in the process of not only setting up, but implementing and maintaining an international agreement. The purpose of the present project is to investigate whether and how institutions in countries at different levels of economic development and stages of political development are able to handle this complex adjustment task. Priority is given to the role of state institutions, but the analysis of the state will be supplemented by research on the role of other institutions.

Adjustment represents no problem if or when there is harmony of interest and everybody expects to realize a collective good through adjusting to international rules, standards or procedures. Such harmony is found only in rare cases at a rather general level of policy agreement. Areas such as climate policy, preventing dumping of radioactive nuclear waste and some others may be cases in point here. In most cases policy goals may be partly or totally in conflict with one other. This is often the case when industrial policy confronts environmental regulation. Behind particular goals are found particular interests. According to neo-realist or structuralist theory, the capability of these interests to carry through their preferred policy is a function of their relative power. If several and conflicting interests enjoy equality in power, the outcome may be a straight clash of interests with either stalemate or hard bargaining as the ultimate implication. But there may also be a compromise of interests. In the case of unequal distribution of power the outcome may be determined by parties adopting positional strategies, and in the extreme case by domination of one interest over the other.

Structuralist theory is, however, far from the only valid and useful approach to the analysis of policy processes. As was suggested above, the conventional double-edged diplomacy model overrates the importance of the 'chief negotiator' and underrepresents the possibility that non-state agents may create cross-national alliances to compensate for, or in other ways alter, the power structure prevailing domestically. In addition, and in a more 'benign' perspective on conflict of interest, parties may deliberately seek co-operative solutions even when a confrontational approach appears more rational. The reason may be that they go through a learning stage which make their priorities converge – a *reflectivist* explanation of outcomes. They learn by reiterating the bargaining game (Axelrod, 1984). On the other hand, they may commit themselves *a priori* to resolving conflicts through negotiations, the outcome of which are automatically binding on parties – an *institutionalist* explanation.

Finally, interest articulation in the bargaining process may be embedded in ideologies which provide a certain degree of consensus and also favour some outcomes and interests over others. This social *constructivist* perspective is particularly salient with regard to another question which is addressed in the present project: the impact of the international transformation from a Cold War ideology to an ideology of economic and political liberalism epitomized by the term 'globalization' and the impact of this change in developing countries. The idea of the self-regulating market has been a strong factor over several years. Has it achieved ideological hegemony, and what would be the consequences of such an ideological hegemony (Cox, 1987)? According to one view, this would marginalize important societal demands and environmental protection concerns. Another view would be that these kind of demands are not marginalized *in toto*, but they must now be represented in terms of the neoliberal discourse in order to be influential. For instance, environmentalist demands for tradeable emission quotas are more likely to be heard than demands for non-tradeable restrictions. Others would argue that neoliberalism is still contested and may have to compromise with societal or environmental concerns in the way the Bretton Woods Institutions did when they constructed a post-war system based on what Polanyi (1957/44) may have had in mind and which a student of his refers to as 'embedded liberalism' (Ruggie, 1984). These questions warrant concrete understanding of whether and how new ideas circulate internationally and transform policy thinking nationally.

Summing up these observations, neorealist or structuralist accounts do matter, but do not suffice to account for adjustment to international change. Liberal institutionalist and constructionist contributions also matter. But developing countries do not simply bow to the will of the great powers, nor do they automatically follow the rules set by powerful international finance and trade institutions. Domestic politics and the capacity of domestic institutions to modify or withstand external demands are crucial. The task we face is therefore to study how national institutions in different political and socioeconomic settings handle the problem of adjusting to international demands to implement new policies in a variety of issue areas.

Adjustment at the national level

There has over the past few years been a strong call from the donor community for democratization as well as market liberalization in developing countries. The argument is that the two are twins and that the one will not be firmly established without the other. It is an argument that is often heard and it has a strong intuitive backing.

But do democratic regimes allow for the kind of political flexibility and capability which is needed for undertaking structural adjustment reforms – or in our case trade reforms that also take into account environmental concerns? There is little empirical evidence in favour of a clear-cut relationship between regime form and state capability. It is however sometimes argued that specific varieties of authoritarianism, mainly in East Asia, have raised the adjustment capacity of the state (Sørensen, 1991, 1993). The uncertainties on the role of authoritarianism reflect widely diverging opinions in the debate on what kind of state-society relations facilitate economic relations.[3]

One model of state–society relations focuses on achieving *complementarity* or convergence between public and private agencies acting independently of each other, emphasizing clear delimitation between the public and private spheres. Public and private actors work at arm's length towards the same policy or practice by practising some division of labour among themselves. This is largely consistent with the idea of the self-regulating market, as well as liberal parliamentary democracies with a strong emphasis on the judicial.

Another model focuses on state autonomy and the state's power over private actors. Here it is assumed that there is considerable state capability for action if or when the state is relatively unrestricted by particular interests. State institutions, either the executive or the bureaucracy, are insulated from the processes of interest articulation, and the state has access to a number of policy instruments which enable it to 'discipline' the private sector (Amsden, 1989, 1992). State autonomy is sometimes related to regime forms as it is held that authoritarian regimes are more autonomous than democratic ones. They are not only unrestrained by interest group pressures, but also parliamentary institutions, the media, and independent judiciary, and so on.

Objections may be raised that in this view of an autonomous authoritarian state there is too much focus on the state's ability to make and remake policies and a neglect of implementation. Even the executive of authoritarian states – with a nominal power to make and remake policies – is normally dependent on the support of strong interest groups in order to implement these policies and may have to offer concessions to such groups (Haggard and Webb, 1993). Compared with authoritarian regimes, the plurality of organized interest articulation and the complicated decision-making procedure in democratic-pluralist systems may be strong obstacles to policy change. Yet once a policy shift has taken place according to democratic procedures of consulting, it has a strong binding power in terms of legitimacy. Thus, there may be a trade-off between authoritarian capability to make swift decisions and democratic capabilities to actually implement those decisions that result from the tortuous and long-drawn out process of decision-making in those democracies.

A third model represents neither authoritarian state autonomy nor the rule of the market, but a situation whereby state institutions are *embedded* in society. The government and social actors are not posited at arm's length, but have a relational position towards each other through institutional arrangements.

The *embedded autonomy* model represents in some way a compromise, a mediating position between the thesis on authoritarian state autonomy and the embeddedness thesis (Evans, 1995). It assumes a state that is attentive to society and to societal needs, thanks to institutional ties with broad societal interest groups, yet it does not let itself be bound by them. State institutions, political leaders and above all the bureaucracy, preserve a high degree of autonomy over policy matters. They manage to do so by maintaining both freedom of manoeuvering in setting policy and through the appropriate organizational capability to carry policies through.

The three views that are presented here focus on state-society relations, but they also have implications for the organizational capability of the state. They all tend to focus on the need for bureaucratic organization as a prerequisite for organizational capacity. The technical capabilities to plan and implement new measures, for example, the enforcement of environmental standards, will to a large extent depend on the qualities of bureaucratic agencies with regard to expertise, efficient procedures for information collection, a well-developed organization, sufficient financial foundation *inter alia* to prevent corruption and the cohesiveness and continuity over time of the personnel involved. The political system's perception of economic problems, environmental problems, international pressure and the need for major reforms is directly affected by the sophistication of the technocracy (Callaghy, 1989, p. 120).

The qualities of (technocratic) bureaucratic agencies depend on the larger political-administrative system in which the bureaucracy is embedded. Thus, a prerequisite of bureaucratization is a high degree of state autonomy from societal interests with regard to recruitment and allocation of resources controlled by a domestic civil service (Rueschemeyer and Evans, 1985; Shefter, 1977).

The organization of the state apparatus should moreover be decomposed. Some bureaucratic agencies may be more insulated than others by strong political protection, financial independence, and so on. Thus, state capabilities may be raised within 'pockets of bureaucratic efficiency', new or refashioned state agencies which under the protection of the political leadership have been allowed to develop bureaucratic autonomy while the overall state apparatus is based on clientelist ties (Evans, 1995).

Related arguments have also been applied to the inclusion of organized labour and agriculture in corporatist arrangements, as seen in some European countries. For Katzenstein, 1985, these arrangements, integrated into democratic systems of governance, produced an efficient system for adjusting to international change. Those countries that belong to the 'democratic corporatist' systems, according to him, lived with the need to adjust by compensating for it internally. He also finds that they managed to adjust well even during the 1980s and early 1990s (Katzenstein, 1996). While Katzenstein's account finds much support, Weiss correctly modifies the 'optimism' expressed in his view by arguing that in one of the success stories, Sweden, welfare policies that are so prominent in the 'Scandinavian model' were not supported by a development policy that took care of the need for industrial restructuring (Weiss, 1998). The problem was not, as neoclassical economists argue, that welfare policy had gone too far, but that industrial policy did not follow suit. Even in the case of Norway, which did not face the same kind of economic set-back as Sweden, one may argue that lack of industrial innovation and restructuring is an underlying problem which is covered over by Norway's continued revenues from oil extraction (Hveem, 1994). The 'optimistic' view of adjustment capacity is therefore not sufficiently aware of the problems encountered by the North European 'success stories' during the 1980s and early 1990s (Mjøset, 1987 and Mjøset *et al.*, 1994).

Here the question might be posed whether the North European countries represent a special case that cannot be generalized to, for example, developing countries. Senghaas and Menzel offer a well-argued set of conditions for using elements of the historical experience of the North European cases to 'model' development strategies for postwar development in the global 'periphery' (Senghaas, 1985; Menzel, 1985, 1992). Their studies indicate that equality in terms of distribution of various assets (land, income, education, etc.) is an important factor in promoting effective adjustments to changing world market conditions in small export-economies. This issue has also been discussed in more state-centred frameworks where it is argued that 'developmental states' require an equitable distribution of income which reduces the extent of unproductive forms of rent-seeking and allows for enhanced state autonomy (Amsden, 1992).

Intuitively, it appears likely that there is a positive correlation between country income level and institutional capacity. As for bureaucratic capacities, these will depend on the bureaucracy's access to financial resources. Furthermore, encompassing corporate associations within industry will also require a certain degree of economic development. We may therefore assume that there is a rough positive correlation between average income level in a country and institutional adaptive capabilities, although there certainly may be great variation in terms of the ability of countries to convert their wealth into institutional capabilities.

What sort of adjustment is actually the optimal one? Again, there is no universally applicable best model, but approximations to the ideal-type set out above. Contributions in this volume therefore will come up with varying accounts of what is optimal. Individual chapters do not focus on the conditions of utopian 'technically perfect' economic adjustment, but rather on economic adjustment in the complex and sometimes 'muddy' world of politics. They attempt to pursue a research methodology which is sensitive to shifts in political-institutional arrangements and accepts that there always will be some discrepancy between the imperatives of power politics in real world policy-making and 'optimal' adjustment policies in a technical sense. Economic adjustments along with other economic policies are seen as instruments in political power struggles and alliance formation in ways which frequently lead to 'sub-optimal' policies and decisions according to 'technical' standards (Moon and Prasad, 1994), although some political-institutional arrangements and power constellations certainly may be more favourable than others to reaching a state of optimization.

The empirical study: country comparisons

The problems that are discussed in the empirical studies that ensure contain at least three elements. The first part is a general survey of what demands are being addressed and registered by state or private national institutions in the countries under study and from which sources, international or domestic, they come. The second element, to which emphasis is given, is the study of the implementation process and its outcome. Fiscal demands are filtered through a complex network of institutions. The end result could be non-decisions – using the 'garbage can' in the March/Olsen terminology (1976) – or positive decisions. The third and final element of the study is the concluding part where the situation with respect to how adjustment was actually handled in the respective countries is summarized and an explanation of the outcomes is sought.

Our cases include Argentina, Costa Rica, India, South Korea, Ivory Coast and South Africa. No strict comparative designs have been applied for the selection of the countries chosen for this study, but we have attempted to follow some rules of thumb. One criterion has been that two countries be selected from each of the continents: Latin America (Costa Rica, Argentina), Africa (the Ivory Coast, South Africa) and Asia (India, South Korea). A more important criterion is level of economic development. The World Bank rank India and the Ivory Coast as low-income economies, Costa Rica as a lower-middle-income country, South Africa and Argentina as upper-middle-income economies and South Korea as a high-income-economy. The latter 'graduated' to become a member of the Organisation for Economic Co-operation and Development (OECD) in the mid-1990s, but was hit by a financial crisis in 1997 that automatically downgraded her rating as a high-income country. This explains why it was kept as a case in the present study. (Statistical details are given in Table 1.1.)

The study has aimed at including a selection of countries with various degrees of inequality according to distribution of assets and standards of human welfare to see how these variables would affect the countries' adjustment capabilities. One indicator may be the difference between a country's ranking in terms of GNP per capita and its ranking on the list of UN Human Development Indicators (HDI). A higher HDI ranking than GDP per capita ranking among the countries listed on the HDI (Human Development Indicator) Index may be seen as an indicator of a profile of equal distribution and relatively high welfare, while a HDI ranking below the GDP per capita ranking would indicate a pattern of unequal distribution and relatively low welfare. According to these criteria, the Ivory Coast and South Africa come out as poor performers in terms of welfare and distribution relative to their income level (rank difference ÷ 9 and ÷ 15 respectively). Costa Rica, Argentina and South Korea come out as good performers (rank difference + 28 and +11 and + 6 respectively), while India come out close to the middle (rank difference +1).

A third criterion for selecting cases has been whether or not they have been subjected to radical exogenous or endogenous pressure amounting to economic or political crisis. To focus on adjustment during or after a crisis is a methodological choice that has certain implications and potential dangers for generalizing objectives (Lijphart, 1977; Ragin, 1987). But it also has some advantages. Two such advantages are likely to be: during what are generally perceived as crisis times, interests are becoming more explicit in the political process; and the alternative policy options are also being more clearly presented (Gourevitch, 1986). In a sense, all the cases selected found themselves in some sort and degree of 'crisis' during the 1980s and/or 1990s. In particular, Argentina and South Africa were obvious choices (for partly different reasons), whereas South Korea, originally meant as a 'control case' of a developing country having in fact 'developed', appeared as a crisis case only after the project had been initiated.

These crises were also associated with varying degrees of pressure for economic and environmental adjustment of the economy from external agents, although it is important to bear in mind that these 'external agents' are frequently allied with influential domestic groups. The nature of such influence is yet another criterion for selecting cases. In India, outside pressures were limited. In South Africa, it may be more appropriate to talk about *influence* through NGO networks on environmental issues, rather than pressure. One indication of why these differences should be expected is found in the way and extent of economic integration into the international economy. Here (see Table 1.1, above), export dependency, the importance of foreign direct investments (FDI) in the economy and exposure to foreign debt were chosen as indicators. There is a fairly clear difference between the highly integrated case of Costa Rica and to a lesser extent the Ivory Coast, the medium integration cases of South Africa and Argentina, and the less integrated cases of South Korea and above all India.

South Korea, Costa Rica, Ivory Coast and Argentina were exposed to various mixtures of multilateral pressures through GATT-WTO, IMF, the World Bank and OECD and bilateral pressures, especially from the United States. While most of these external agents favoured some variety of neoliberal reform, there was nevertheless a great disparity between cases of unitary and fairly well co-ordinated pressure (Costa Rica, South Korea) and diverging and conflicting demands (Ivory

Coast, Argentina). As a result, the degree of the leeway of the governments exposed to the pressure varied among countries and over time.

The cases have also been selected according to regime form. Among the countries studied, Ivory Coast can still be said to have a semi-authoritarian form of rule, while the other countries have democratic governments. South Korea, Argentina are relatively newly democratized countries, India and Costa Rica are long-established democracies.

In terms of the characteristics of public bureaucracies and government-business interaction, the federal civil service of India has relatively high bureaucratic capabilities with long roots back to the British colonialism. The effectiveness of the economic policy-making of this federal bureaucracy has however been restricted by its strong autonomy from business, its small size and the amount of red tape (Evans, 1995). At the local state level, bureaucratic capabilities are generally lower, there is 'embeddedness without autonomy' between government and business which frequently have led to unproductive forms of rent-seeking, that is, seeking favours from government.

South Africa and South Korea both had state forms strongly oriented to geopolitical tasks with a high degree of autonomy from business interests and other organized non-state interest groups. In the South Korean case, security interests were however strongly linked with developmental interests. South Korea under Park Chung Hee (1961–79) is frequently viewed as the classic developmental state with strong mercantilist state interventionism. It started out as a highly autonomous state, but gradually moved towards embedded autonomy, tight government-business relations administered by an effective bureaucracy. It is frequently argued that the classic South Korean developmental state was dismantled by the combined impact of democratization and pressure from business and external groups for liberalization during the late 1980s and the 1990s. South Korea may then partly have moved in the direction of a liberal model, and partly towards 'embeddedness without autonomy'. The South African security regime was less 'developmental' than the South Korean. Democratization and the transition to black rule implied a move towards a state form which included liberal features as well as political clientelism that weakened the effectiveness of the public sector.

Until the debt crisis of the early 1980s, the Ivory Coast has had a fairly successful public administration based on the legacy of the French colonial administration. Public administration existed along with a state enterprise sector which was used for various kinds of unproductive rent-seeking by political elites. The economic crisis of the

1980s and the ensuing lack of funds for the administration weakened bureaucratic capabilities, while privatization of public enterprises allowed for new kinds of self-enrichment by political elites. Thus the Ivorian crisis and the ensuing policies of austerity and liberal reform weakened the existing locus of bureaucratic autonomy and capability, while rent-seeking by political elites reappeared in new forms.

Costa Rica and Argentina both had strong traditions of corporatist interest group representation of labour and capital coupled with policies of import substitution (in the Costa Rican case 'import substitution' refers to the regional level within the Central American Common Market). In Argentina this corporatist legacy was based on the semi-authoritarian order of Peronism, while Costa Rica had a well-established democratic system. Costa Rica also had a well-institutionalized public bureaucracy, while the Argentinian bureaucracy was relatively weak as it was permeated by political clientelism. The Argentinian military governments of the 1970s attempted to dismantle the corporatist framework, but various kinds of 'embeddedness without autonomy' based on clientelist and corporatist government-business relations remained. Organized labour allied with the Peronists re-emerged as a political force after the end of the military government in 1983. As discussed by Diana Tussie (with Fernanda Tuozzo), President Carlos Menem (1989–) has managed to draw on his Peronist credentials to weaken the corporatist framework and labour influence. The Argentinian political system, then, appears to have been moving in a pro-business liberal direction in the 1990s, possibly with some remaining clientelist government-business relations. As for Costa Rica, its previous social democratic corporatist order has also been moving in the direction of liberal arm's-length economic policies.

The cases chosen for the present study can also be expected to display considerable variety in the ways by which they react to exogenous influences. Sometimes national adjustment efforts were reactions to major economic crises, in other cases they were anticipatory in that they aimed to protect against potential future economic problems. These types of 'domestic' reactions were often influenced by perceptions of necessity and a feeling of destiny, by international pressure or by hegemonic ideas.

But in other cases exogenous agency or international factors were limited, or they were present but had limited effect. Pressure for adjustment in these cases came from *within* the country. One particular purpose of the study is to explore whether environmental policy change in developing countries, often said to be subject to domestic constraints and thus mainly an effect of exogenous influence, is in fact also a bottom-up process in those countries. Change may, on the other hand, be partly triggered and thus indirectly explained by contextual factors such as, in India, the crisis in her current account at the end of the 1980s. In other cases domestic pressure for change is partly a reflection of previous influence from hegemonic ideas. This is particularly true in the case of South Africa, but there are indications that it may be true for some of the others as well, perhaps even to represent a general feature in all the cases. If South Africa really stands out on this point, this may be partly explained by its comparative isolation from international currents up until the beginning of the 1990s.[4]

As will be seen, sometimes the pressure for adjustment has been bilateral, consisting of particularist and targeted pressure from strong powers with economic and political leverage. In other cases the main pressure came from multilateral agencies applying carrot and stick strategies, but also, primarily, communicating through ideas and prescriptions. In yet other cases, both these sources of pressure or prescription were operating simultaneously and, as we have indicated above, even co-ordinated. The workings of the so-called 'Washington consensus' and the institutions most directly linked to it, Wall Street, the US government and the International Financial Institutions (IFIs), are cases in point.

The saliency of these external policy prescriptions varied, depending on the degree of coherence or disunity among influential external agents, but also on the capability of these agents to exercise influence and the priorities they gave to influencing the country concerned.

Notes

1. The point was made by John Martinussen in his comment as a discussant at a seminar in Oslo on 22 April 1999.
2. In the present discussion the term rent-seeking loosely refers to the act of individuals or corporations seeking special economic favours from governments.
3. This is an elaboration of Evans, 1998, Ch. 7.
4. The fact that it is being emphasized in the case of South Africa may be due to the authors of that case study being particularly sensitive to this factor. Since strictly comparative data are not available here, caution should be applied when drawing conclusions at this point.

Table 1.1 Indicators of industrial organization and global market integration

	Argentina	Costa Rica	Ivory Coast	India	South Korea	South Africa
Manufacturing as % of GDP (1997)[5]	24.8	17.1	17.6	19.5	25.7	23.9
Inward foreign direct investment (FDI) stock in % of GDP, 1990	5.3	25.3	9.9	0.5	2.3	8.6
1996	10.2	35.5	8.6	2.6	2.6	9.9
Inward FDI flows as % of gross capital formation 1986–91	5.3	11.7	5.1	0.3	1.3	-0.2
1996	9.7	24.7	1.6	2.9	1.3	3.5
Total debt/GDP (1997)[6]	32.4	37.2	171.8	24.8	34.9	19.5
Total debt/GDP (1976)[7]	18.1	40.8	39.2	15.2	–	–
Manufactures as % of total exports 1980[8]	23	34	n.a.	59	90	39
Manufactures as % of total exports 1993[9]	32	33	17	75[10]	93	74
Exports as % of GNP	8.3	31.4	39.8	9.3	28.1	23.8
Imports as % of GNP	8.2	41.9	34.7	13.4	29.7	21.6

Table 1.1 Indicators of industrial organization and global market integration *contd.*

	Argentina	Costa Rica	Ivory Coast	India	South Korea	South Africa
Average tariff level[11]	13.5	11.2	23.5	34.9	7.9	22.0
Member of GATT/WTO[12]	1967	1990	1963[13]	1948	1967	1948
Acceded to ISO[14]	1960	1994	1960	1947	1963	1947

Source: 5. Country statistics: URL: http://www.worldbank.org/data/countrydata/countrydata.html; 6. Country statistics: URL: http://www.worldbank.org/data/countrydata/countrydata.html; 7. Country statistics: URL: http://www.worldbank.org/data/countrydata/countrydata.html; 8 *World Development Report 1997*, Table 15, 'Exports and imports of merchandise'; 9 Same source as footnote 4, above. Table 15 in *WDR 1997*; 10. In the case of India, figures are not from 1993, but 1992; 11. Studies of the countries' trade policies are done individually by the WTO's Trade Policy Review. Average tariff level is based on TPRs for Argentina (1998), Costa Rica (1995), Ivory Coast (1995), India (1997), Korea (1994) and South Africa (1988 – GATT tariff study). Methodologically some studies are based on applied tariff rate, while others are based on bound rates in the respective country's list (India, South Africa). The last mentioned are probably higher than the actual applied rates; 12. WTO (1996) *GATT Activities 1994–95*, Annex IV; 13. It has applied the General Agreement since 1947, first of all as a French Overseas territory and since 1963 as a contracting party (TPR, 1995); 14 Norges Standardiseringsforbund (NSF, Norwegian Standardization Organization).

2
Shooting for Reform. The Interplay of External and Domestic Constraints in Argentina

Diana Tussie with María Fernanda Tuozzo

Introduction

In the context of a global order where markets are more open and inter-dependent, the policy revolution in developing countries can be looked upon as an adaptive process whereby countries have grappled to extract the best of the new economic conditions. Starting in the late 1980s and into the 1990s, Latin America also took on this policy revolution and suc-ceeded in obtaining a measure of stabilization unknown in its recent history. Although the timing and degree of the policy revolution has dif-fered, the direction has been the same. The implementation and success of reforms, however, have been uneven. In some cases (Argentina being an example) economic achievements were short lived. The temporary success of economic reforms has been dampened since 1995 by several international crises that hit the Argentine economy, leading to lower levels of growth, increasing recession and soaring unemployment. By December 2001, Argentina's 'convertibility success story' was crushed by one of its most severe economic and political crises.

Argentina's particular situation is, to a large extent, a result both of the reforms undertaken and the way that the political class imple-mented them. Political and economic reforms in Argentina were carried out in a somewhat disjointed way; the over-emphasis on eco-nomic reforms during the 1990s understated the political implications and helped to foster widespread corruption as well as non-transparent decision-making that lead to a gradual loss of legitimacy and credibility in the system and its leaders. Many of the neo-liberal economic reforms reviewed in this chapter were taken on in a rather short-sighted fashion with little consideration for long-term political and social consequences. Short-term opportunism characterized not only a highly self-serving and self-perpetuating political class who sought external cooperation and approval, but also rent-seeking interest groups – that is, those seeking favours from government. Liberalization and adjustment, then, did not deliver the expected results and left a legacy of patchy reforms, highly unequal distribution of gains and losses, an unprecedented steep increase of vulnerable sectors and social fragmentation, and a highly weakened and unpopular political system.

Within this wider context of reforms, this chapter maps out some of the most important reform policies in Argentina between 1985 and 1998 and briefly introduces some of the tip of the iceberg that eventually led to the collapse of the country's economy. The chapter also describes the role played by international financial institutions (IFIs) in shaping the Argentine policy agenda within the first phases of reform. This influence was mainly exercised through conditionality packages. Policy-based finance is one of the principal means used by IFIs to promote change. Financial support is offered contingent upon taking measures the international community favours; conversely, the withdrawal of funds is threatened if a government is not ready to go along with these policy alternatives. Conditional finance, in this way, becomes a form of pressure, and at times it can touch raw nerves in domestic politics. While in principle these are the most transparent and effective means of IFI influences, there are, however, several other ways through which IFIs' influence is exercised. Sowing the ground with suggestions for policy alternatives and courting key opinion leaders, although more subtle, may be nonetheless as effective in structuring the domestic agenda or in inciting influential business lobbies. In most cases, all these mechanisms are present in combination and usually as a country progresses to achieve one goal so does the thrust of conditionality – leaping forward towards a new target. This continuously expanding scope of external creditors has turned adjustment into a moving target, as IFIs move from macro management and trade liberalization to reform of labour markets, social security, health policy, legislative support and judicial reform, the so-called 'second generation of reforms' and good governance.

The reform package is so overarching that all the components cannot be adequately covered in a single chapter. This contribution takes trade liberalization[1] as its starting point. Trade liberalization was an economic landmark in at least three ways. First, it was the beginning of policy-based lending in Argentina. Second, it became a *cause célèbre* in the relations between the World Bank and the IMF because the former circumvented the IMF and granted the loan without the customary seal of approval. Lastly, trade reform was a trend-setting instrument which paved the way for full-scale transformation. Moving beyond the opening of trade, the chapter then looks at the political setting in which these reforms germinated and temporarily thrived. It also looks at the ensuing institutional adaptation that accompanied growing social and economic demands, issues which are not only home-grown but also now closely related to the most recent agenda of external creditors.

To better understand and explain the general policy shifts, attention should be focused on the interaction between external and domestic factors (Putnam, 1993; Evans, 1993). International conditions changed the character of domestic constraints. As domestic actors received rewards for their reforms, preferences were adapted. In turn, the movement of domestic politics opened up new possibilities for furthering policy reform. Changing domestic political and institutional conditions explain both the sequencing and the intensity of reforms. As the process unfolded the international and domestic dimensions of the new agenda have become closely entangled. It is no longer possible to clearly separate what national authorities are genuinely forced to assume (as an external demand) from what they project of their own preferences on external actors. On many occasions authorities chose to tie their hands externally in order to increase their domestic room to manoeuvre. While national authorities have amply emphasized external conditions, new international linkages now interlock external and internal actors.

Implanting reform: the interaction of external and domestic factors

The Latin American debt crisis in the 1980s introduced economic reform as an imperative issue in these countries' agenda. As pointed out by a United Nations report, one of the most important consequences of this debt crisis was to bring about a radical change in the economic philosophy:

> In contrast to the external shocks and crisis of the 1930s, which had led to a switch away from *laissez-faire* towards a strategy of import substitution, and provided for a greatly enlarged role for the state, the shocks and crisis of the 1980s led to exactly the reverse movement, towards an outward-oriented development strategy based on deregulation, liberalisation, and privatisation. (UNCTAD, 1995, p. 73)

Given credit rationing at the time, it became apparent to Latin American countries that, in order to stabilize their economies, the financial assistance and support of IFIs was indispensable. In the late 1980s and early

1990s economic reforms began to be introduced in most of the countries of the region; governments made efforts to reduce fiscal deficits, to liberalize trade and exchange rate regimes, and to generally expand the role of market forces and the private sector (Acuña and Smith, 1994). At the time, in order to reduce budget deficits, a rush toward privatization took place. This urgency in implementing structural changes largely resulted from the need to gain access to financial flows that seemed contingent on the adherence to orthodox economic policies, both short and long term.

The breath and depth of external pressures, however, was not limited to mere access to official finance at a time of scarce private flows. As Haggard and Maxfield point out (1996), developing countries also received political pressures to liberalize their economies and these were played out at a number of different levels, from the formulation of the agenda at the GATT to the offer of hemispheric negotiations. The first agreements with the IMF immediately after the debt crisis were mainly aimed to raise a financial package in order to reschedule debt servicing. They never went beyond the customary macro targets of improving budget and current account balances and combating inflation. But starting with the launching of the Baker Plan in 1985 which attempted to streamline the structural adjustment programmes, the World Bank gradually became a key participant in the determination of the flow of funds and in the shaping of conditionality. Argentina was going through very particular circumstances at the time. On the one hand, Argentine democracy was nascent and fragile; the administration of Raúl Alfonsín, inaugurating democracy after years of dictatorship, first tried Keynesian reactivation policies. By the time the authorities became aware that their diagnosis was not appropriate vis-à-vis the depth of the crisis and the lack of financing, domestic confidence had been lost. The business establishment and trade unions turned to systematically harassing the government and thus undermined its resolve to pursue adjustment. The fragility of the domestic scenario was aggravated by the fact that indicators of Argentine creditworthiness were the worst amid the bigger debtors. Argentina was thus placed as a weak link in the stability of the international financial system.

The World Bank became heavily engaged in the reform programme. So much so that for the first and probably only time, the World Bank stepped in with a policy-based loan for trade reform without the IMF's seal of approval in 1988. It was an unprecedented step for the World Bank insofar as both IFIs were tied, by a tacit working agreement, that the World Bank's policy loans had to go in tandem with IMF monitoring of macro variables. Although the division of labour between the twin institutions had become blurred at times on account of the World Bank's incursion into policy reform, their strategies had never been confronted as they were on this occasion. Without a stand-by loan from the Monetary Fund, the World Bank and the IMF found themselves played off against each other. One of the main justifications put by the World Bank to get involved without IMF support was that an early indication of external support was essential for domestic credibility:

> there was an urgent need for visible and prompt international assistance to Argentina, so that the government's efforts would not falter. The hope of the Bank management, supported by the Board, was that this good faith action by the Bank would have a strong catalytic effect on other financial agents. (Tussie and Botzman, 1990, pp. 400, 01)

The 'well-intended' scheme devised by the Bank, however, failed. External support and endorsement wavered as the macroeconomic variables failed to deliver the expected results and financial support from the Bank was not backed up by an IMF stand-by loan. Eventually the financial package raised was insufficient, there was a run on the currency, and the World Bank was forced to suspend disbursements. The government lost the external support that had so far helped it to uphold its programme. Without external aid, the socio-economic policies of the administration were doomed to failure. After a severe hyperinflation crisis, followed by violent supermarket lootings, the government lost all credibility and found itself cut-off from its middle-class constituency. In July 1989, the government, having lost first external and then internal support, was compelled by circumstances to withdraw from power in tatters, six months before its term was over.

The experience, however, was not lost on Argentina. The international negotiations with the World Bank during Alfonsín's government played a key role in the 'economic mindset change' that gradually took place in the country (Palermo and Novaro, 1996). Key gurus were assiduously courted and an ample array of economic diplomacy tactics were displayed to urge business groups and raise their interest in the need to transform the economy. It is a known fact that the World Bank has always been dextrous at selling models of successful adjustment and good behaviour. This capacity to exhort and make 'influential declaratory statements' (Woods, 1997) can often end up being more important than narrow conditionality itself. For instance, the experience of New Zealand was amply expounded in Argentina with repeated visits from the former prime minister of New Zealand, Ruth Richardson, a leading ambassador of comprehensive reform. To many opinion leaders, politicians and policy-makers, it became evident that Argentina could not hope to be both successful and remain out of the reform fold.

The Peronist Party was able to win the elections easily thanks to the vote of the working class, its historical class support base, but Carlos Menem was acutely aware that if the party stuck to its traditional class appeal his government would face mounting obstacles. As soon as he took office he courted and succeeded in forging links with the reform-minded business establishment. Thus a powerful, albeit tacit, coalition between the lower and upper classes emerged and Menem's pro-business economic programme, clad in populist discourse, allowed the new government to spearhead the reform programme. The new administration managed at once to represent both the lower classes and the business establishment. The composition of this alliance, however, gradually expanded as convertibility won over larger sectors from the middle class who firmly clung to the benefits provided by a horizon of economic stability. The elements of a consensus for reform in the 1990s were also the result of the dramatic economic crisis produced by the unleashing of hyperinflation during 1989. The political crisis, a crumbling economy, and the generalized deterioration of public management had worn out all resistance. By then, public opinion and organized labour had become more tolerant towards swallowing the bitter pill of policies that had been adamantly rejected in the past.

Receptivity of public opinion was, no doubt, a necessary condition for reform. But, at the same time, the agenda was given a mantle of legitimacy by calling in the IFI once again. After the fiasco produced by their experience of competition, the World Bank and the IMF had worked out a broad agreement for reform – brought together as the so-called Washington Consensus – and had also hammered out new working arrangements. Enhanced cooperation between the World Bank and the IMF, with the addition in early 1990s of the Inter-American Development Bank (IDB), strengthened the role of conditionality in the reform process and its influence vis à vis domestic agents. The new government's strategy was to deflect the influence of external restraints. It decided to lean heavily on the joint action of the IFI as a way to increase its own room to manoeuvre in relation to domestic opposition or vested interests. Conditionality packages linked to adjustment loans were chosen as a transmission link of a new economic paradigm. The domestic setting thus proved to be the enabling element which affected the timing and degree of change.

Trade policy and its spillovers

Trade policy reform had been initiated as part of the conditionality package of the late 1980s, and it played a complex and changing role. It was the first powerful engine that effectively set in motion the tide of structural adjustment. In the initial steps, when the culture of import substitution was still strong, trade conditionality gave Alfonsín's weak administration the external technocratic support required to confront vested interests and to take up the reform of the system of incentives. In such circumstances it may not be possible to distinguish between what countries want to assume by way of commitments for domestic political reasons and what they are obliged to accept by way of strict conditionality.

The reform was later accelerated when new international conditions again provided an enabling environment. From 1991, the drastic fall in interest rates created a new surge in international liquidity which allowed the Menem administration new fuel to push further. In 1991, the Convertibility Act was passed restricting the Central Bank from printing local currency without a one-to-one backing in foreign currency. The rationale behind convertibility was the use of the exchange rate as an anchor to obtain price stability. By then trade conditionality was not seen as an external imposition but as a way of unblocking external finance to put together a Brady deal.[2] Trade liberalization proceeded without much opposition, with tariffs falling from an average of nearly 30 per cent to 18 per cent; dispersion also progressively reduced. In early 1991, specific duties were eliminated and the share of manufactures covered by quantitative restrictions dropped from one-third to approximately 5 per cent. At that point three tariff levels were established: 22 per cent for final goods; 11 per cent for inputs and zero for commodities and food products. Cars and electronics were the only exceptions. The average tariff in 1991 reached 9.7 per cent. Export duties, extensively used in the past to reduce the cost of inputs produced by the primary sector for local industry, were severely cut. Export subsidies were also either abolished or drastically cut.

Trade liberalization had spillover effects in other fora. It led Argentina into a more active participation in the Uruguay Round of GATT. The Uruguay Round negotiations were important trend setters. In sharp contrast to previous GATT rounds, developing countries, in general, were exceptionally active. Argentina, too, was alert to the challenges and opportunities offered by the Round, having been one of the countries most severely penalized by the historical exclusion of agriculture from the

GATT-regulated system. Policy-makers, therefore, displayed an active negotiating strategy based on the assumption that the country had much to gain from the promise of agricultural liberalization in the context of the Uruguay Round. As Argentina undertook adjustment and trade liberalization simultaneous to the Round, it used its opening both as a goodwill gesture and as a moral argument to push for increased access to markets. (Tussie, 1993). It joined forces with Australia and other members of the Cairns Group, the group of 18 agricultural exporting countries formed in 1986, and played in this context an unprecedently active role throughout the Uruguay Round and beyond.

In parallel to unilateral and multilateral initiatives, another forward-looking enterprise gathered momentum: the creation of MERCOSUR, a customs union with Brazil, Paraguay and Uruguay, in 1991. MERCOSUR gave a regional anchor to the process of liberalization. From 1991 until 1995, the so-called transition phase of MERCOSUR, the regional liberalization programme consisted of automatically progressive duty reductions across the board, and the elimination of non-tariff restrictions as well as other trade impediments. In 1995, MERCOSUR was effectively implemented as a free trade area when intra-trade was fully liberalized, with the exception of sugar, cars and an assortment of several other sensitive products. As a result, nearly 90 per cent of intra-regional trade was freed. The remaining tenth, covering the so-called 'adaptation regime' and the automobile and sugar sectors, was scheduled to be liberalized by 2000. However, by the end of 2000, MERCOSUR had established a common regime only for the automobile sector.

To start progress towards the customs union, a common external tariff (CET) was established, covering nearly 85 per cent of extra-regional trade, based on 11 tariff levels, ranging from 0 per cent to 20 per cent. Rules of origin were also established for goods not covered by the CET. The exceptions to the CET are varied: they include capital goods, telecommunications, computers, cars and sugar in all four members; in addition, lists of national exceptions are allowed for each country up to a maximum of 300 products (399 for Paraguay). These lists of national exceptions should be eliminated by 2000 (2005 for Paraguay). The CET on capital goods is expected to converge at 14 per cent – in 2001 for Brazil and Argentina, and in 2006 for Paraguay and Uruguay – telecommunication goods and computers are scheduled to converge at 16 per cent in 2006.

Spurred by integration, Argentine exports to MERCOSUR were growing at a rate that far surpassed the growth of total exports (36 per cent as against 15 per cent annual growth rate in the period

1991–1995, respectively). Argentine exports to MERCOSUR increased from $1.8 bn in 1990 to nearly $8 bn in 1996, representing at that time one-third of total exports. Brazil has become the first destination of Argentine goods, taking over one-third of total exports, and MER-COSUR has become the only region with which Argentina holds a surplus. In the process, Argentina's trade has become less dependent on traditional markets: that is Europe and the US. However, imports were also buoyant and Argentina suffered a trade shortfall from 1991 to 1994. The external deficit at the macro level seemed to jeopardize the maintenance of the fixed exchange rate; and on the other, at the micro level, the buoyancy of Brazil's industrial exports added severely to the pressure points on business. The new competitive environment had several effects. Some firms were able to take advantage of duty free access to capital goods to introduce new and modernized technology. Many small- and medium-sized enterprises (SMEs), unable to face the challenges, therefore lost business. Unemployment surged to levels unknown to Argentine people as many firms succumbed to the new competitive pressures that they faced with scant public support, and the private sector shed thousands of jobs.

In 1995, when the *tequilazo* (the crisis in Mexico) drove Argentina into severe recession, unemployment reached 18.6 per cent in the economically active sector of the population. This situation increasingly stimulated the debate on trade and industrial policies, considered to have a direct effect on employment levels. On the one hand, orthodox economists proposed to de-regulate labour contracts to allow markets to be cleared. On the other hand, others thought that the way forward was for the state to undertake active trade and industrial policies aimed at promoting those sectors more capable of creating jobs (Casaburi, 1997). The administration chose to steer a middle course, countering only some of the worst macro and micro pressures, a role that will be expanded upon below. The effects of 1994, however, were not easily overcome and the ensuing crisis in Asia (1997) and devaluation in Brazil (1998) greatly affected Argentina's already stagnant economy, creating more recession, deflation and unemployment and leading the country into a new crisis that belied the success of the economic model and the reforms.

Steering through: institutional capabilities

The administration of Raúl Alfonsín had failed to secure support from labour and business as well as to ensure legislative support. Opposition paralysed the government politically; hyperinflation led it into a downward spiral of economic turmoil. At this point, when the new Peronist government was sworn in, it had the upper hand. It confronted a tamed socio-political and economic environment – a clean slate on which a new plan for reform could be displayed.

Although Argentinian trade policies depended mainly on decisions taken and implemented by the Ministry of Economy, they had to be negotiated both with big business conglomerates and with labour. To continue with trade reform and make it palatable to the firms that had grown quite cosily under the culture of import substitution, the administration resorted to dangling carrots in front of the big conglomerates. The carrots came in the form of promises to ease access to the forthcoming privatization contracts. But privatization depended on passing legislation so it was conditional on the acceptance of a congressional majority that would endorse it. Thus trade reform became part of a much wider compact, all of which hinged directly or indirectly on the capacity of the Executive to mobilize congressional majorities and neutralize the trade union movement. A divide and rule strategy was deployed over the unions; and their representation in the party and Congress severely curtailed. The institutional capacity of the new administration to manage these sources of opposition and to gain civil society consensus was crucial to the success of policy reform.

The ability to gain the support of Congress emerged as a key factor in enabling the rapid progress of the policy agenda. The Executive was able to exercise command and obtain congressional approval for two major laws that became the master keys to reform, the Economic Emergency Act and the State Reform Act. Both of these Acts allowed the Executive to steer the new policies following the mere sanctioning of decrees and without the need to go through Congress. Armed with this legal cover, the Executive was able to increase its hold over the decision-making process and deal with policy reform in an expedite and unilateral way. Ferreira Rubio and Goretti (1996) calculate that between 1989 and 1994, Menem issued 308 decrees without prior congressional authorization, in contrast to only 25 under all the preceding constitutional regimes taken together. The logic of personalist decision-making was not new in Argentina. Moreover, one could argue that further concentration on the Executive only built on an embedded pattern of unilateral and verticalist decision-making. The fact that the lead was in the hands of the Peronist party, rooted in a populist tradition, and the trade union movement, meant that the most intensive negotiations were internal to the party. The populist tradition also enabled some disguising of the rough edges of structural adjustment (Gerchunoff y Torre, 1996). Every time specific objectives were endangered, the government resorted to the creation of on-the-spot alliances and neutralized opposing fractions in order to maintain the reform course. Indeed, the Menem administration was successful in keeping together warring members of the party and rallying political support for a remarkably long period. It even succeeded in reforming the Constitution in order to allow re-election when the presidential term was over in 1995.

The radical reform programme was sustained by other signs of compromise such as a major overhaul in the pattern of international alignment such as withdrawal from the Non-Aligned Movement, dismantling of the nuclear programme and political rapprochement with the United States. This international and domestic 'U-turn' revealed the President's pragmatism. His somewhat shaky record of standing up for principle was another indicator, features which, alternatively, increased his short-term hold over power, but ultimately haunted the Peronist party. The President's preference for such a mixed menu came to be caricaturized as 'pizza (a long-time staple in the Argentine diet) with champagne'. Although the class division had been circumvented, as by-elections loomed once more, conflict within the party became rife, pitting a revamped old guard against the new Menemists, many of these being either newcomers or not even real 'card-carrying' members. While the government had succeeded in bridging the historical class divide, it became increasingly unable to rule its own party incumbents. Politics became a match of mud-slinging, different factions exposing each other's evils and corrupt practices, taking each other to court over fraudulent deals in the administration and finally threatening to kill the goose that laid the golden eggs.

Moreover, these very rapid transformations were obviously socially very costly. As the competing import sector and the privatized firms shed jobs, the rate of unemployment surged to unprecedented levels, unknown to countless generations of Argentines. In 1995, unemployment reached almost 19 per cent, a rate which must be contrasted to the historical 4 to 5 per cent. Different sectors of the Argentine society, middle and working classes, SMEs and trade unions, were severely affected by the shock policy. Dissatisfaction mounted as economic reforms proceeded and privatizations escalated. Since 1996, the country has seen rising waves of protest and demands for government intervention that have outlived the Menem administration. The social cost of adjustment has posed a complex challenge to the chosen policy path and one that may prove to be unsustainable. By the end of 1998 unemployment levels were again on the rise, reaching 15 per cent in 2000, and Argentina seems to be in the midst of a much more severe economic crisis (*The Economist*, 2000, p. 89).

The first compensatory policies were introduced to assuage the negative effects of trade liberalization. Government intervention was a result of the pressures received from business associations and industrial groups with enough lobbying capacity to produce policy modifications. The government resorted to the introduction of trade management policies in order to slow down the pressures of import competition. Subsequently, as by-elections loomed, it was impossible for the government to neglect any further the demands of its constituency. As it continued with its reform of health, labour and education polices, the government also started to work on a compensatory agenda for the unemployed and the 30 per cent of the people living below the poverty line. These people constitute its natural power base and will ultimately determine the result of elections. These efforts, however, were not enough to assuage the deep social crisis and the growing economic stagnation and in 1999 the Peronist party lost the elections. The heritage they left proved to be very complex for the winning coalition of Radicals and dissident Peronists whose intrinsic weakness made it ill-fitted to cope with the messy scenario. Higher interest rates, a soaring external debt, recession, unemployment and increasing social fragmentation submerged Argentina at the turn of the twenty-first century in a profound crisis that led to default, devaluation and political and social chaos.

Sustainability: trade management beyond conditionality

As business demands flowed in during the early 1990s, authorities faced the urgent need to invigorate their dwindling capacities to manage the arising conflicts. The first institutional response was chiefly centralized in the Ministry of Economy. The Ministry contracted loans from the World Bank and the IDB, underwent modernization, carried out a wide voluntary retirement scheme, hired specialized and better paid technocrats and created new agencies within its aegis of managing the sources of pressure.

After the trade policy loans from the World Bank were fully disbursed and the adverse effect of trade opening with a fixed exchange rate began to be felt, the authorities inaugurated a battery of pragmatic and selective interventions. These were compatible with international commitments; both conditionality and consolidation in the Uruguay Round had only set across-the-board and ceiling binds at 35 per cent thus allowing, some room to manoeuvre. In 1992, Argentina passed law no. 24 176 to adhere to the 1979 Tokyo Round agreements on anti-dumping (AD) – i.e. the prohibiting of exports at prices below domestic production costs; and subsidies and countervailing (CV) duties.[3] In 1994 Argentina adhered to the Uruguay Round agreements which included fresh versions of accepted international practices for countervailing and anti-dumping duties.

Intervention first aimed to relieve fiscal pressure on business. Burdensome and distorting taxes were eliminated and direct incentives to the tradable sector were provided. The aim was to reduce domestic costs and improve the relative price of tradables. Effective return to exporters was further improved by granting tax reimbursements equivalent to tariffs on imports. Thus, the weighted average of rebates increased from 3.3 per cent to 6.3 per cent of the total value of exports. Subsequent to the fiscal interventions, classic trade instruments were phased in to promote exports and restrict imports. At the end of 1992, an across-the-board tax on imports under the guise of a 'statistics levy' was increased from 3 per cent to 10 per cent. In the second half of 1993, import quotas were imposed on some food and paper products. Specific duties were applied to a number of textile goods; this raised tariffs up to an average of 36 per cent, especially hitting imports from China. In some tariff items the tariff equivalent reached 100 per cent. The footwear industry was also granted special protection with specific duties against imports from China and Indonesia. As a result of these changes, average nominal protection increased to 18.6 per cent, doubling the rate at convertibility's starting point. In order to reduce production costs, capital goods were allowed duty free treatment, albeit for a short-lived period. Two years later, under renewed fiscal pressure after the so-called *tequilazo*, all duty free entry was eliminated, including capital goods, computers and telecommunications goods.

Subsequently, a new device was designed for goods that were considered to be particularly 'sensitive'. Textiles, garments and footwear, mainly flowing from China, were required to provide a special additional certificate of origin to obstruct, or at least significantly slow down, the flow. China, not yet being a member of the WTO, has been unable to file a formal complaint. In the footwear sector, the application of specific duties above set levels triggered a reaction from American firms (e.g. Reebok and Nike) who were established in China and Indonesia. In this case, the firms involved chose to use their industrial clout from their home base rather than from the host country and managed to get the United States to raise a formal complaint in the WTO.

To tackle the pressures of import competition the government accompanied trade reform with institutional reforms. In 1994, the Comision Nacional de Comercio Exterior (CNCE) was created to handle petitions from business against unfair foreign practices affecting the local market. The Comision is in charge of the analysis, investigation and regulation regarding the determination of 'injury' caused to domestic producers by unfair competition from abroad, either in the form of dumping or subsidies. It also implements the safeguard measures that can be put in place in the case of 'sharp and substantial' import increases of certain products.

The request to open an investigation must be presented by the injured industry, or by a representative segment of it on its behalf. The request must be supported by sufficient evidence of the existence of dumping or subsidies, the damage caused, and causal relation between the foreign practice, and injury to domestic production. The petition is presented to the Subsecretaría de Comercio Exterior. Subsequently, while the Subsecretaría, for its part, must examine the actual existence of dumping or subsidies, whichever is the case, the Comision must study the actual damage posed to local industry. Jointly, both agencies then submit a preliminary report to the Secretaría de Comercio e Inversion. On the basis of this report the Secretaría decides whether to open an investigation. Should it be necessary to avoid further damage during the investigation, provisional measures can be applied. Definitive measures must await the final report which must be presented to the Ministerio de Economía within 120 working days from the adoption of preventive measures, or one year from the opening of the investigation if these measures were not applied. Following WTO rules, the final measures can last up to 5 years, with annual revisions, and they can be retroactive.

With the implementation of these new institutional procedures, organized business, under growing pressure of competition from abroad in its home market, has become quite adept at submitting petitions. This resort to *ad hoc*, case-by-case petitions for protection is a novelty in the management of trade policy. The result has been a strikingly sharp rise in the resort to anti-dumping and countervailing duty action against imports. Indeed, while only 9 cases had been opened to investigation in the period 1986–90 (GATT, 1992), 70 cases were opened between 1991 and 1995 (CNCE, 1996). In a similar fashion, while just one case was finally found to require a punitive duty between 1986–90, 54 cases were subject to punitive duties between 1991 and 1995. Anti-dumping and countervailing action has become the cutting edge of Argentine trade management. The highly concentrated steel sector was especially active in 1992, moving very quickly to counter the effect of a declining market share and stave off competitive imports. By 1996, Argentina was second at anti-dumping action, equalling the European Union, with 23 cases in hand.

The countries against which most complaints were raised were Brazil (with 25 investigations opened and 20 measures taken), followed by China (with 11 and 10, respectively). The twin pressures of advancing regional integration in the context of bilateral exchange rate disequilibria explain the frequency with which Brazil was targeted between 1991 and 1995. These twin pressures were particularly intense between 1991 and 1994, when, on the one hand, MERCOSUR was moving ahead but not yet fully completed; and, on the other, exchange rate misalignment between the two countries was most severe. Imports from Brazil increased from $718 m in 1990 to $4 bn in 1994. After the Plano Real was inaugurated in mid-1994, the bilateral exchange rate was corrected. Moreover, the trade deficit was reversed and Argentina has been in surplus with Brazil since then.

In any case, the start of the customs union in January 1995 has precluded the easy option of to further anti-dumping and countervailing duty action against regional trading partners. Claims against Brazil, which must now be resolved by negotiation, fell drastically. As complaints against Brazil subsided, those against Asia, particularly China, jumped. Imports from China rose from $12 m in 1990 to $728 m in 1994 and $607 m in 1995. The effect of imports from China is obviously negligible at the macro-level; but not so at the micro-level.

The pressure of Chinese imports is deeply felt by producers of consumer goods: tyres for bicycles, pocket lighters, pencils, bicycles, motorcycles, microwave ovens, among others; but textiles, garments and household goods in particular, all long-established import competing producers for which anti-dumping action has been quite active. Overall, the Ministry of Economy has gradually improved the performance of the state in order to resolve conflict. However, corrupt practices were not yet buried and indeed are seen to have increased, albeit under the new mantle of modernization. Corruption has distorted results and jeopardized the monitoring capacity of the state apparatus, something which is crucial for the long-term success of any support policy (Casaburi, 1997).

Sustainability through second-generation reforms: the new face of conditionality

By the mid 1990s, unemployment increased the relative and absolute number of people living below the poverty line, and posed a new set of challenges to the Peronist government, bent on retaining power as elections loomed ahead. Policy redress and amendments required not only political bargaining but also resources in order to create a social safety net. Unable to finance compensatory strategies through a politically unpalatable tax reform, the Menem administration, like other governments in the region, turned once again to IFIs for financial support – now with a new agenda.

The IFIs have responded to these new challenges in a creative way that opened new spheres of action to them and has prompted a wider thrust of their conditionality. The interpretation of their mandates has been gradually broadened. Social and institutional issues began to command closer attention from the World Bank, the IDB and the IMF: the 'second generation' of reforms under the supporting hand of the IFI was born, comprising social, political and institutional issues. Conditionality has now moved beyond macro-economic fundamentals to address issues of corruption, transparency, environment and poverty. Indeed, to cope with this new agenda, the presence of IFIs in Latin America has grown steadily in the last decade: both the Word Bank and the IDB have doubled their commitments in Latin America, up from $3 bn to $6 bn each per year. The expansion of the IFIs' agenda in Argentina was reflected in the overarching scope of lending portfolios, which now extends from social programmes to judicial reform. Their sphere of influence has also expanded with new adjustment loans for subnational units, directly negotiated with provincial authorities and municipal governments.

Conditionality has also changed. Since the 1990s, the IFIs have acquired a new role providing conditionality that acts as a trigger or catalyst for reform processes already in place. Major reforms in Argentina and the region were largely settled with the collapse of state planning experiments that were inspired by the communist world and the adoption among decision-makers of the Washington consensus. This event indicated a novel cooperative turn in IFI-government relations that has affected the nature of policy-based lending and conditionality ((Tussie and Tuozzo, 2001). IFIs now act as an 'ancillary intelligentsia' of governments and have become key players in domestic politics beyond the field of macro management (Casaburi *et al.*, 2000, pp. 512–5).

Moreover, IMF missions began to discuss the distributional aspects of reform with government representatives and began to require the identification of measures that could help cushion the possible adverse effects of policies on vulnerable groups. A large part of World Bank lending since the mid-1990s has been directed at strengthening and creating social safety nets to assuage the thrust of reform. Most second-generation loans have come to include both reform and compensatory components. The IDB also conveyed a particular emphasis on equity and growth and expanded microcredit programmes for vulnerable groups. The changes in all three institutions have been more or less simultaneous, and although there is an attempt to keep a division of labour, overlapping is frequent.

In addition to this social dimension, a second source of concern relates to institutional reform: increasing the legitimacy of the government, enhancing its regulatory capacity, promoting active participation by those directly affected by reform, creating a capable and honest civil service and a decentralized system of policy implementation that generates accountability in the whole system. Put together, these new conditions have become increasingly packaged under the catch-all word 'governance' (Cassaburi *et al.*, 2000, p. 495). In Argentina, the IMF's involvement in governance issues has been modest, given its strict guidelines on good governance and has been related to aspects regarding the surveillance over macroeconomic policies such as the transparency of government accounts and the effectiveness of public resource management. The World Bank has been the one mostly responsible for furthering public sector management reforms and governance issues. During the 1990s, the World Bank destined approximately two billion dollars to this type of lending (World Bank, 2001) that stretches from reform of the national administration and civil service, to decentralization and judicial reforms. Governance-related conditionalities and reforms have had far-reaching impacts for World Bank and IMF operations. Governance entails a bundle of reforms and initiatives that are highly problematic for their traditional lending practices, given their apolitical and technical mandate and their economic and financial expertise. It is an unprecedented move in the history of the World Bank and the Fund since it is leading them to set foot in grey areas bordering on highly sensitive political domestic issues. For borrowers such as like Argentina, good governance has emerged as yet another requirement to earn the World Bank's and the IMF's seal of approval, although the precise weight of these soft criteria relative to macro targets remains unclear.

Sustainable development: the floundering environmental policies

A missing link in Argentina's reform agenda has been a proper and systematic consideration of the environment. A Secretariat to regulate and enforce legislation was created but the commitment to 'sustainability' still wavers. In 1995, a World Bank study on pollution and environmental performance in Argentina revealed that the most serious restriction to improve pollution management was the absence of clear institutional responsibility and effective mechanisms of enforcement. The state institutions responsible for the design of environmental policies are weak and they are formed by a network of state agencies with overlapping responsibilities at the national, provincial and municipal level. This scenario is worsened by the unusually complex legal and regulatory framework that has eventually led to the unclear and unequal application of the regulations that result (World Bank, 1995). In order to improve the country's environmental performance there is a striking need to change the current regulations and to use adequate enforcement mechanisms.

From a general perspective, public policy still needs to recognize that there is a trade-off between the increase in environmental degradation and the economic benefits deriving from the expansion in trade. This trade-off expresses the strategic dilemma between the short-term need for export earnings and the increased degradation of natural resources. Openness to trade has tended to encourage exports of goods which are intensive in terms of natural resources, with growing and sometimes unsustainable pressures on the environment (Gutman, 1998). There is evidence in Argentina that intensification in the use of natural resources is taking place at high rates. Public policies in agriculture, forestry, fishing and mining are absent. With strong budgetary constraints as well as low levels of public awareness, authorities have attached greater priority to growth than to environmental conservation. In the absence of strong public policies for the protection of the environment, it is likely that economic growth associated with a resource intensive export pattern will aggravate environmental damage, which in turn will compromise growth in the long run.

In recent years, openness *per se* has favoured some environmental upgrading in industry. Although public policies do not yet exist, environmental standards are making slow progress with the helping hand of markets. The environmental requirements of foreign markets have forced some national producers to comply with international environmental regulations in order to expand or maintain their market share. The adoption of voluntary rules – such as the ISO 14.000 series – as well as technological upgrading to respond to outside standards, are seen by local exporting firms as a way of retaining access to international markets. However, export-oriented environmental protection has serious loopholes. As Argentine industrial exports are mainly destined to non-OECD markets, not all exporters feel the need to upgrade. Moreover, the impact of widely dispersed inward-oriented smaller firms, which cannot be reached by consumer preferences abroad, is left untouched. The individual contribution of small firms to degradation is minute, but when considered in the aggregate, their impact on environmental quality is greater, thus posing by far the greatest challenge. Last but not least, upgrading to gain or retain market access follows consumer preferences in the main markets, leaving behind local priorities which remain either neglected or overshadowed.

All in all, incorporation of environmental sustainability is still not considered an important dimension of public policy. Internalization of environmental externalities more often than not are missing as a result of monitoring costs and the scarce development of institutional capacities and administrative skills. Direct estimates of abatement costs are as rare as in other developing countries. Enforcement of existing regulations is also often limited by poor functioning of judicial and governmental procedures. A World Bank loan to finance research activities on environmental pollution granted to the Secretariat for Environment remains undisbursed.

Environmental education and social awareness are essential so that both producers and consumers can appreciate the benefits of a less polluted environment; these are also still very weak. Environmental pollution has only recently become a topic of national debate and civil society action tends to be fragmentary. A clear example of this has been the relative lack of action against the construction of the Yaciretá dam on the Parana river. Despite the extensive problems this dam has brought – resettlement of large sectors of population because of floods, corruption and misuse of public funds – complaints from civil society have been remarkably weak, almost inexistent, as has been press coverage. The Yaciretá issue only gained attention when the World Bank and the IDB, which had partially funded the dam, were compelled to initiate an investigation in 1997 under pressure from Friends of the Earth, an NGO with global connections. Friends of the Earth supported a small local NGO from Paraguay to file a claim under the Inspection Panel mechanism. The focus on this debate, however, was very brief, and shows that country-environmental awareness in Argentina is only beginning. The lack of demands from civil society on the policy agenda shows that environmental resources are still not genuinely perceived as public goods over which rights can be exercised collectively.

Conclusions

Some scholars argue that the introduction of economic reform, structural adjustment and trade liberalization in many developing countries was due to the expanding influence of international agencies. True, in the case of Argentina, external actors lent a supporting hand; the government programme has been closely intertwined with conditionality and the policy agenda of the IFIs. But this is only half the picture. As the agenda progressed, much of it has become domesticized and in many cases a symbiotic relationship between external and internal actors has grown. In these circumstances it is difficult to distinguish between what authorities want to assume as 'international commitments' for the sake of domestic political reasons, and what they are obliged to accept by way of strict conditionality.

These second generation reforms are a case in point. They have become – both for external creditors and the national government – the way to make adjustment gains sustainable, and to illustrate newly formed linkages. This involves highly politicized and complex issues intimately related to a domestic policy agenda but it provides a needed public good. External creditors have thus adopted an ever-widening agenda, which seems both to forge new links with domestic civil society at large and increase their weight as public guardians of borrowing governments. Even though, in a world of rapidly multiplying international finance, their grip on international capital markets is much reduced, their new role as guardians of good governance has given the IFIs a new lease of life. Their radar screen has become broader as the thrust of conditionality leapfrogs towards new targets and incorporates new loan recipients, the judiciary, the legislature, subnational units, and so on. This ongoing internationalizing socio-political and institutional agenda is surely one of the most significant features of the new international context that many developing countries now face. The governance agenda (and within it judicial reform) will most probably become a new landmark of institutional change in Argentina, intertwining, yet again, the foreign and domestic agendas on to increasingly new fields.

Acknowledgement

Generous comments from Carlos Acuña and Gabriel Casaburi are gratefully acknowledged.

Notes

1. The paper draws on FLACSO/Argentina's research on the World Bank and the Inter-American Development Bank's reform lending with case studies of Argentina, Peru, Paraguay, Brazil, Colombia and Mexico. For more on this subject see *Global Governance*, vol. 6, no. 4 (2000).
2. The term Brady deal is named for US Treasury Secretary Nicholas F. Brady.
3. When these agreements came into being in 1979, the legacy of import substitution was still alive and quite strong. Argentina chose not to join the GATT codes because countries were required to undertake a commitment to phase out subsides in exchange for the injury test in foreign markets. By 1992, subsidies had already begun to be phased out; but it was also clear that Argentine exports to the US market, which, growing rapidly, and excluded from the right to use the injury test in the US, had become vulnerable to US countervailing action. Thus, belatedly, the injury test became obtainable as progress was made to dismantle domestic subsidies.

References

Acuña, Carlos and William Smith (1994) 'The Political Economy of Structural Adjustment: the Logic of Support and Opposition to Neoliberal Reform', in *Latin American Political Economy in the Age of Neoliberal Reform*, (New Brunswick and Oxford: Transaction Publishers).

Argentine Republic, Comisión Nacional de Comercio Exterior (1995). *Informe Anual 1994*, CNCE.

Casaburi, G., M.P. Riggirozzi, M.F. Tuozzo and D. Tussie, 'Multilateral Development Banks, Governments and Civil Society: Chiaroscuros in a Triangular Relationship', in Diana Tussie (ed.) (2000) 'Special Issue on Civil Society and Multilateral Development Banks', *Global Governance*, (Boulder, CO: Lynne Reinner).

Casaburi Gabriel (1997) 'Comparative Study of East Asia and Latin America', CEPAL project mimeo.

Chudnovsky, Daniel, Fernando Porta, Andrés López and Martina Chidiak (1996) *Los límites de la apertura. Liberalización, reestructuración productiva y medio ambiente*, (Buenos Aires: CENIT – Alianza Editorial).

Evans, Peter (1993) 'Building an Integrative Approach to International and Domestic Politics: Reflections and Projections', in Peter B. Evans, Harold K. Jacobson and Robert Putnam (eds) *Double Edged Diplomacy. International Bargaining and Domestic Politics*, (Berkeley, CA: University of California Press).

Ferreira, Rubio Delia and Matteo, Goretti (1996) 'Cuando el Presidente Gobierna Solo. Menem y los Decretos de Necesidad y Urgencia hasta la Reforma

Constitucional (Julio 1989–Agosto 1994)' *Desarrollo Económico. Revista de Ciencias Sociales*, vol. 36, no. 141, 443–74.

GATT (1992) *Trade Policy Review Mechanism: Argentina*, GATT.

Gerchunoff, Pablo & Juan Carlos Torre (1996) 'La Política de la Liberalización en la Administración de Menem', *Desarrollo Económico. Revista de Ciencias Sociales*, vol 36, no. 143, 733–68.

Gutman, Graciela (1998) 'Agriculture and the Environment: the Challenge of Trade Liberalisation', in Diana Tussie (ed.) *The Environment in North-South International Trade Relations* (London: Palgrave Macmillan).

Haggard, Stephen and Sylvia Maxfield (1996) 'The Political Economy of Financial Internationalisation in the Developing World', in Robert O. Keohane and Helen Milner (eds) *Internationalisation and Domestic Politics* (Cambridge: Cambridge University Press).

Palermo, Vicente and Marcos Novaro (1996) *Política y poder en el gobierno de Menem* Bogotá: Grupo Editorial Norma.

Putnam, Robert D. (1993) 'Diplomacy and Domestic Politics: the Logic of Two-Level Games', in Peter Evans, Harold Jacobson and Robert Putnam (eds) *Double Edged Diplomacy. International Bargaining and Domestic Politics* (Berkeley, CA: University of California Press).

The Economist (2000) 'Argentina's Struggle for Confidence and Growth', 18 November, p. 89.

Tussie, Diana and Mirta Botzman (1989) 'Sweet Entanglement: the IMF and the World Bank', *Development Policy Review*, vol. 8, no. 4, 393–409.

Tussie, Diana (1993) 'Bargaining at a Crossroads: Argentina', in D. Tussie and D. Glover, *The Developing Countries and World Trade: Policies and Bargaining Strategies*, (Boulder, CO: Lynne Rienner).

Tussie Diana (ed.) (1997) *El BID, el Banco Mundial y la Sociedad Civil: Nuevas Formas de Financiamiento Internacional, FLACSO* – Oficina de Publicaciones del CBC.

Tussie, D. and M.F. Tuozzo (2001) 'Opportunities and Constraints for Civil Society Particiaption in Multilateral Lending Operations: Lessons from Latin America', in M. Edwards and J. Gaventa (eds) *Global Citizen Action*, (Boulder, CO: Lynne Reinner Publishers).

UNCTAD (1995) *Trade and Development Report 1995*, UNCTAD.

Woods, Ngaire (1997) 'Governance in International Organisations: the Case for Reform in the Bretton Woods Institutions', Paper prepared for the G-24 Technical Group, mimeo.

World Bank (1995) *Argentina. Managing Environmental Pollution: Issues and Options*, Environmental and Urban Development Division , Washington, DC.

World Bank (2001) www.worldbank.org/sprojects/.

3
The Limits to Liberalization: Adjustment, the Environment and Political Reaction in Costa Rica

Benedicte Bull and Alvaro López Mora

Decision-making on issues related to trade and the environment has presented the Costa Rican political system with serious challenges since the mid-1980s. The Costa Rican debt crisis of the early 1980s intensified the problems of the old state-led development model, and left Costa Rica vulnerable to pressure to join the international free trade regime. From the early 1980s, Costa Rica has undergone a profound process of liberalization of the economy, but it has at the same time established a framework for the development of environmental policies. However, the process of adjustment has not occurred without resistance, most profoundly expressed through the opposition against the third structural adjustment programme (SAP III) and the massive protests against the privatization of the national energy and telephone company, ICE, in April 2000.

In this chapter, we trace the national responses to global regime changes through in-depth case studies of three inter-linked processes. The first is the extension of benefits to Costa Rica from the US Caribbean Basin Initiative (CBI) in 1983, which led directly to membership in the General Agreement on Tariff and Trade (GATT). The second is the adoption of three structural adjustment programmes (SAPs) supported by the World Bank and the Inter-American Development Bank (IDB) between 1985 and 1995. The result of these processes was a shift from a development model, based on export of primary products and import-substituting industrialization under the Central American Common Market (CACM) framework, towards an export-oriented model focused on non-traditional goods. The third process is the shift in environmental policies emerging in connection to the location of the Earth Council headquarters to Costa Rica after the Rio Summit.

These processes have been paralleled by institutional inventions of two kinds. First, a series of new organizations and institutions have been established with the aim of voicing new issues such as environmental protection and liberalization, often with significant international support. The clearest example is the establishment of the 'parallel state-institutions' in the mid-1980s with support from USAID, the United States Agency for International Development. These institutions have in turn become important players in the continued formulation and implementation of policies concerning environment and development. Second, new institutions have been established that are aimed at incorporating new issues and interest groups into the democratic process. However, these Costa Rican institutions have not been able to prevent the development of an elitist approach to decision-making on environment and development-related issues, privileging the private sector's access to decision-making processes. Currently, this fact is met with increasing public resentment in Costa Rica, something which is a key to understanding the recent public resistance to further liberalization.

Thus, this chapter puts forward two general arguments. First, that it is often misleading to draw a sharp distinction between international influence and domestic responses. We argue that in small, vulnerable states, such as Costa Rica, domestic institutions themselves are often the result of external pressure or transnational alliances. Our second argument is that in countries with democratic traditions, again, such as Costa Rica, there is a limit to liberalization growth if it is not conducted with inclusion of large segments of the population. Thus, what we currently see in Costa Rica may be interpreted in the Polanyian sense as a 'second movement': society is reacting against nearly two decades of increasing domination of the market. Society demands a restoration of some of the state institutions that were of core importance to the establishment of Costa Rica as a peaceful and relatively prosperous country.

Before we develop these points further through the case studies, we provide an introduction to the Costa Rican development model and its institutional structure.

The debt crisis and challenges to the Costa Rican democracy and development model

The short civil war of 1948 and the initiation of the second republic that followed in 1949 is often viewed as the starting point of Costa

Rican modern history. The 1949 constitution provided the basis for abolishing the military, providing the conditions for the stability and democracy that Costa Rica has enjoyed since. What is less well known is that the constitution also provides the foundation for an extensive role of the state in economic development and as provider of the welfare of the citizen.[1]

The starting point of the founders of the second republic was a typical primary product-producing economy: 90 per cent of export earnings came from coffee and bananas (later, when sugar was added to the list of export goods, Costa Rica received the nickname 'the dessert economy'). The group taking power after 1949 had emerged around the National Liberation Party (Partido Liberación Nacional (PLN)) and the Center for the Study of National Problems. It initiated a two-track development model. On the one hand, it was focused on strengthening and modernizing the traditional sectors: banana and coffee production. On the other hand, it aimed at industrialization through an import-substituting model. The introduction of the Industrial Production Law in 1959 and the entering into the Central American Common Market (CACM) in 1963, marked the beginning of the industrialization model. CACM was based on the world's highest levels of protectionism of the common market of the five Central American countries, combined with fiscal incentives for national industries (López, 1995). The result of this policy was unprecedented economic growth (averaging 6 per cent annually between 1950 and 1975) and a strong growth of the share of industry in the BNP (increasing from 13.8 per cent in 1960 to 19.7 per cent in 1973) (Barahona Montero, 1999).

The role of the state in Costa Rica's industrial sectors was paralleled by increased state activity in the production of welfare for its citizens. Through the establishment of a number of autonomous institutions (AIs), the state took on responsibility for the development of infrastructure, education, health, insurance, and so on. The result of these policies is that Costa Rica has achieved a privileged position with respect to all indicators of human welfare compared to other Latin American countries as well as countries within its income group worldwide. Its infant mortality rate (14 per 1000 live births) and life expectancy (76 years) as well as literacy rate (95.3 per cent)[2] are comparable to those of developed countries (UNDP, 2000).

In the 1970s, a changed and deepening of the role of the state in the economy took place, described as the change from the 'intervening state' to the 'business-man state' (Cerdas, 1979).[3] With the establishment of the Costa Rican Development Coalition (CODESA) the state became a direct participant in various enterprises, either as a majority or minority investor or by giving cheap loans or guarantees. The consequences of these actions meant an increased role for politicians in terms of business activity and increasing tensions between the state and private business groups.

Private business has always occupied an ambiguous position in relation to the state. A large part of the Costa Rican business sector emerged around autonomous institutions and the CODESA enterprises as sub-contractors, suppliers, and so on or the CACM protectionist scheme. These actors have traditionally been represented by the Chamber of Industry. At the same time, there were groups who, for ideological reasons or due to objections against the 'crowding out' of private investments, opposed increased state involvement. These groups joined in the Chamber of Commerce (Cámara de Comercio) and the more ideologically based interest group, the National Association for Economic Growth (Asociación Nacional de Fomento Económico (ANFE)),[4] both of whom opposed the Chamber of Industry. Thus, when economic crisis struck in the early 1980s, the seeds of tension of the old model had already been sewn.

Partly due to the expansion of the public sector, the Costa Rican external debt had increased by 27 per cent a year between 1970 and 1980. In terms of per capita debt, it increased from US$320 in 1976 to US$1,200 in 1981, one of the largest per capita debts in the world. The cost of servicing the debt rose from a manageable US$60 m in 1977 to US$510 m in 1982. At the end of the 1970s, three other developments added to the burden. First, the Sandinista takeover in Nicaragua in 1979 caused the CACM to disintegrate and closed the only viable market for domestically produced manufactured goods. Second, the price of oil imports soared and caused the index value of the country's terms of trade to decline from 114 in 1978 to just 69 in 1983 which meant that the capacity to import goods and services declined by almost 40. Third, the price of coffee declined.[5]

In order to resolve the crisis, the then President, Rodrigo Carazo Odio of the Partido Coalición Unidad (later PUSC, see below), signed two agreements with the IMF. First, a stand by agreement in February 1980, and second, in May 1981, an extended service agreement worth US$300 m and valid for three years. The main goal of the IMF agreements was to reduce the fiscal deficit (Salom Echeverría, 1992). Carazo attempted to adjust taxes, the domestic price of oil products, and the international exchange rate of the national currency, the Colon, but attempts were repeatedly blocked by the Legislative Assembly (Wilson,

1998). Finally, in complete frustration, Carazo attempted to bypass the Legislative Assembly by using his decree power to devalue the currency. This was challenged by parliamentary deputies, and was found unconstitutional by the Supreme Court.[6]

The IMF responded to the Carazo government's failure to continue the reforms and its unwillingness to address the rapidly growing deficit by ending the loan disbursement and ceasing negotiations with the Costa Rican government. In 1981, Carazo became so frustrated with the IMF demands that he expelled the IMF's Costa Rican mission, and declared a unilateral debt moratorium, several months before Mexico sparked off the 'debt-crisis' by doing the same.[7]

The main policy shift came in the succeeding government, that of Luis Alberto Monge (1982–86) (the PLN). Monge's government chose a less confrontative line towards the IFIs and led a turnaround in the Costa Rican development model. He signed a standby agreement with IMF in December 1982, leading to an agreement with the Paris Club in 1983, an informal grouping of official creditors, mostly governments of industrialized countries, seeking solutions for debtor countries facing payment difficulties. Subsequently, he introduced a freeze on government expenditure and tax increases, and a change from production to consumption taxes. By 1983, the fiscal deficit dropped to 3.4 per cent after having reached its peak at 14.3 per cent in 1983. However, popular protest increased and after 18 months of austerity measures, President Monge sided publicly with the protesters and argued that the austerity measures were the result of IMF conditionality and were undermining the social fabric of the country (*La Nación*, 20 December, 1983, quoted in Wilson, 1998, p. 117). He subsequently refused to sign a new IMF standby agreement, ended some austerity measures, and increased social spending.

The other part of the adjustment process, the shift towards export orientation and non-traditional products, turned out to be a smoother process than the fiscal reforms. Costa Rica was the first of the Central American countries to shift the policy towards export diversification and markets outside the region, primarily to the USA and the EU. There are two dominant views on the reasons for the policy change towards liberalization and privatization. Some see it as a result of outside pressure, primarily from the United States (through USAID) and the IFIs (Sojo, 1992; Echeverría Salmon, 1992; Honey, 1994). Others see it as a consequence of internal developments, particularly the changing orientation by dominant groups within the PLN (Wilson, 1994, 1999). What we will do in the following section is not so much to take a stand in this debate, but rather to examine the *processes* through which the policies have been introduced in Costa Rica, how they have been determined by the existing political institutions, but also how the processes have come to threaten their legitimacy. First, let us give a brief preview of the main feature of the Costa Rican institutions.

Costa Rican institutions in transition

As shown above, in the early period, the characteristics of Costa Rica's political system and its constitution would leave its mark on adjustment to external pressure. The 1949 constitution includes a strong role for the legislature and a relatively weak presidential role compared to other Latin American systems. The presidential power to issue decrees is limited, and international loans can be contracted only through approval by the Legislative Assembly. Grants from donors, on the other hand, may be accepted without approval from the Legislative Assembly.

Both the President and the deputies are elected by direct elections and are then prohibited from seeking re-election. This ruling has, among other consequences, an effect on the party discipline. The President, after election, is effectively a lame duck, and the deputies group around the presidential candidates for the upcoming elections. Thus, in both parties, but perhaps particularly in the PLN, the deputies tend to take different political positions from those of the official party. Attempts by former president Oscar Arias Sánchez (1986–1990) to change the constitution in order to allow for presidential re-election, have not succeeded.

For the last 20 years, Costa Rica has basically had a two-party system. In the first period after the civil war, the social democratic party (PLN), established by the winning forces, dominated completely. The conservative opposition, which included the old coffee elite, appeared under various weak parties, but established the Social Christian Unity Party (Partido Unidad Social Cristiana (PUSC)) in 1983. Since then, PUSC has alternated in power with the PLN. The communist party has recently emerged in a modernized version under the name the Democratic Force (Fuerza Democratica) and gained 2 representatives in the 1998 elections. It has adopted an environmental agenda and it is against liberalization and privatization. The most recent addition to the political landscape is the Libertarian Movement (Movimiento Libertario) that was established in 1994 and gained 1 representative in the 1998 elections on a pro-liberalism platform.[8]

However, the main changes in the political landscape over recent years have occurred within the PLN rather than between different parties. A significant fraction within PLN has, since the mid-1980s, embraced market-oriented policies (Carriere, 1991; Wilson, 1994). This has led to an ideological rapprochement between PLN and PUSC. An example of the change in the situation is that the 'Alan Greenspan of Costa Rica', the highly respected liberal economist, Eduardo Lizano Fait, has served undergovernments of both parties as the President of the Central Bank.[9]

In addition, the AIs are a significant element of the political institutions in Costa Rica. The role of many of them is established in the constitution, a matter which has limited the room for manoeuvre of the government in several cases of liberalization. For example, did the constitutionally established monopoly of the Costa Rican Electricity Institute (Instituto Costarricense de Electricidad (ICE)) in the telecommunication sector hinder the government from signing the telecommunication agreement under GATT in 1998? The degree of autonomy of the AIs differ, but for all of them autonomy has decreased since in the mid-1970s. The argument then was that the President had too little power since a large part of the state apparatus was constituted by autonomous institutions with a high degree of independence with respect to priorities and management. Thus, a series of laws were introduced that gave politicians a higher degree of control, through new budget procedures and through new rules for the appointment of the board and the Presidents of the AIs.[10] These changes have made the AIs prime instruments for distributing spoils for Costa Rican governments. The resulting politicization has been pointed to as one main reason for the declining performance of some of the AIs. Another political function of the AIs has been to be institutional 'safety valves' (Schifter, 1978). Whenever a new political pressure group has appeared on the scene, a new AI was established as a 'pseudo solution' to incorporate demands. This is an option that basically has been closed off over the last 15 years, when structural adjustment programmes have limited the possibilities for new spending.

Lately, two institutional innovations have appeared which have changed the political game to a certain extent. In 1992, a new AI, the Public Defender/Ombudsman (Defensor de los Habitantes) was established to investigate wrongdoing by public officials. If the ombudsman's investigation finds the accusations against the state to be credible, he or she has three options: to facilitate the search for redress by publicly denouncing the actions; to ask the Legislative Assembly to establish an investigative commission; or to take the case to the Fourth Court (Sala IV). Sala IV is the second institutional invention. It was established in 1989 as a branch of the Supreme Court to handle the increasing use of the courts by individuals and groups challenging the constitutionality of various laws and regulations. The intention of both institutions is to deepen the democracy and rule of law in Costa Rica and they have become a significant political instrument for interest groups, government agencies and individuals.

In sum, the Costa Rican constitution is highly democratic and in order to avoid any weakening of this democracy, there is an ongoing process of adaptation. Nevertheless, there is increasing talk of a democratic deficit and a crisis of confidence in the political system (Cerdas, 2000). The state apparatus has gone from a situation of having a relatively high degree of autonomy from the political parties to one where it is more closely connected in what Eduardo Lizano has called the GPP system: 'Guildsim', Paternalism and Populism (Gremialismo, paternalismo y populismo) (Lizano, 2000). A third feature of present-day Costa Rican politics is the frequently referred to crisis of direction; a lack of direction in economic reform and policy.

These problems have caused increasing frustration among groups who do not see themselves as any longer represented by the political system, and it has caused a partial standstill in the reform agenda. The clearest expression of this was the demonstrations against a proposal which would open the national markets for electricity and telecommunications to competition and allow ICE to enter into strategic alliances with private companies. The labour unions had for years opposed any opening for private actors in these sectors, but when the decision was finally made they were joined by large groups of civil society. Among the key organizations in mobilizing support was the Council for the Defense of Institutionality (Consejo para la Defensa de Institucionalidad (CDI)) established by former President Rodrigo Carazo. In additition, university students and environmental organizations played key roles. A key issue for the students was the opposition against becoming 'customers' rather than 'citizens' with a right to services. The environmental organizations emphasized parts of the proposed law that would threaten the management of water resources and protected areas. Together they mobilized against the liberalization proposal and thus managed to bring the whole country to a standstill through the largest demonstrations since the Civil War. The end of the story was that the civil society groups were included in a commission in the Legislative Assembly that formulated an alternative proposal, rejecting any opening of the markets (Representación Social, Comisión Especial Mixta del ICE, 2000). In November 2000, the proposal was accepted in an agreement with the government which blocked further liberalization. The network established during these events, has since attempted to establish itself as a permanent political alternative, connected to the Democratic Force Party and the PLN- defector, Ottón Sollís.[11]

Adoption of liberalization and adjustment programmes

In the following section, we will examine the processes of national adoption of liberalization and adjustment programmes in order to shed light on how this situation emerged.

The Caribbean Basin Initiative and GATT entry

At the beginning of the 1980s, US President Ronald Reagan sent what has become known as the Caribbean Basin Initiative (CBI) for consideration by the US Congress and GATT. CBI denominates a series of US laws that unilaterally extend trade preferences to countries around the Caribbean Basin. The original Caribbean Basin Recovery Act (CBRA) was passed by the US Congress in 1983 and was approved by GATT soon after. It represented a clear departure from the US tradition of supporting exclusively multilateral liberalization efforts. The aim was to promote growth and diversification of the Caribbean Basin economies by promoting export-oriented production in the region, especially in the non-traditional sectors. However, the political motives were clear: it was intended to provide leverage for the US to push for market-oriented policies and discourage any protectionist measures (Bulmer-Thomas, 1994). It has been used as a political tool in a series of bilateral disputes between the US and signatory members.[12] The signatories, such as Costa Rica, were also required to become members of the GATT within a 'reasonable' time limit. Before this, the only country in the region that had joined GATT was Nicaragua.

The immediate reaction to the CBI by Costa Rica's elite – economic experts, politicians and the business community – was positive.[13] The crisis of the CACM had become a major problem for Costa Rican exporters, and the balance of payments plummeted. Thus, although industry representatives had not been part of the CBI negotiations, they enthusiastically welcomed the inclusion of Costa Rica in the scheme. Their enthusiasm increased as the exports from Costa Rica to the US expanded rapidly. This was especially true for 'non-traditional products' such as ornamental plants, flowers and metal items (López and Aguilar, 1985). The CBI was soon promoted to a General System of Preference status in GATT to become the access route to products entering the US market. In the end, Costa Rica became one of the main beneficiaries of the scheme. Its share of US imports under the CBI program increased from 11 per cent in 1984 to 25 per cent in 1999 (IDB, 2000), and it became the largest exporter to the US under the scheme.

In 1984, the first year that CBI was in effect, the Costa Rican government applied for observational status in GATT, a status which was agreed almost immediately. However, the decision to join GATT took the general public by surprise. It had been made by a small group of politicians with participation by individual representatives from business, but without any prior public debate or participation from organized interest groups.

The perception that GATT membership was a 'done deal' with the US before the public was informed, spurred a large public debate. Experts and technocrats of government were divided over what exactly would be the costs and benefits of GATT membership, and it was obvious that the business community and politicians who had initially been positive to CBI had not in fact understood the magnitude of the compromises it entailed. They had previously only had experience of the General Treaty of Central American Integration and its protocols, a Treaty which is much less encompassing than GATT.

It was not until after the government had made its decision to join GATT that the business sector began to realize the scope of the compromises. It subsequently got involved in the process of negotiation through a technical committee that included public and private sector actors. However, business did not participate with a single voice as there were significant differences between sectors. The Chamber of Industry feared the consequences for production subsidies, whereas the Chamber of Commerce welcomed increased imports competing with domestic production that up until this point had been covered by the protectionism of the CACM. Within the political parties, the debate cut the governing party, PLN, in two: the majority favoured CBI and GATT, but a significant minority opposed the recently adopted market-oriented policies.

However, the debate did not stop Costa Rica from joining GATT. In a strategy to win time, the government applied for provisional participation that did not cover tariff negotiations in 1985. In June 1987, Costa Rica was accepted as a member of GATT according to GATT Art. 33, providing for full tariff negotiations.[14]

One significant outcome of this process was the institutionalization of a new practice; namely the participation of private sector groups in negotiations over international agreements. In the initial phases, the private sector did not participate in any structured and formal way, although certain individuals close to government were influential. However, following membership, the business sector was gradually included in consultation groups formed by the government. At the end of the 1980s, during the negotiations in Geneva, private sector participation was considerable, and when Costa Rica signed the Protocol of Adhesion in 1990, it was with the full support of the private sector. The practice of private sector participation continued in later trade negotiations: for example, the negotiations over the Free Market Treaties with Mexico and Chile.

This change in practice cannot be related only to the nature of the new international negotiations. They were also highly affected by institutional changes occurring under the auspices of the USAID programme for industrial conversion. This was introduced at the height of the conflict in Nicaragua in order to establish Costa Rica as a bulwark of democracy and market-economy in the region, and it would have consequences for future policy-making in Costa Rica.

USAID, institutional change and the changes in the Costa Rican development model

Under the leadership of its powerful director, Daniel Chaij, USAID understood early that in order to introduce real changes in the Costa Rican development model, prior institutional changes were indispensable. With the approval of the Costa Rican government, USAID financed an evaluation of the institutional framework for formulating and implementing market-oriented policies, in particular in the export sector. Teodoro Moscoso, ex-Director of the export promoting institution, Fomento Económico de Puerto Rico, was hired, together with Leopoldo Suslov, to direct the evaluation and come up with recommendations for changes in the Costa Rican institutional structure. Moscoso had also been advisor to President Kennedy in the establishment of the Alliance for Progress in 1961.

The report of Moscoso and Suslov was the background for the establishment of a series of new institutions of importance for the further course of events. One of them was the Chamber for Costa Rican Exporters (Cámara de Exportadores de Costa Rica (CADEXCO)), established to represent the interests of the new exporters, and to be a counterweight to the Chamber of Industry which had come to be associated with the old import substituting policies.

Among the most important outcomes of the report was the establishment of the Costa Rican Coalition for Development Initiatives (Coalición Costarricense de Iniciativas para el Desarrollo (CINDE)). This is a non-profit organization devoted to encouraging investment in non-traditional sectors, enhance productivity, employment and exports of non-traditional goods to third markets. The initiative to form CINDE was taken in 1983 by two businessmen, Ernesto Rohrmoser and Richard Beck, together with Daniel Chaij and Jorge Manuel Dengo (then consultant for the Inter-American Development Bank (IDB)). This group formed CINDE with a grant from USAID. CINDE later became a main driving force behind the change of development model in Costa Rica.[15]

The third main institution established with USAID support was the Programme for Exports and Investment (Programa de Exportación e Inversiones (MINEX)). The programme was established by President Luis Alberto Monge in 1983, with the task of developing and executing new policies for the promotion of export to third markets. From the start, MINEX was funded by USAID and it worked in close coordination with CINDE. Co-founder of CINDE, Jorge Manuel Dengo, became later the Coordinator (with rank of a minister) of MINEX. All the issues with respect to administration of CBI and GATT was placed in the portfolio of MINEX, and due to its dynamism it was later transformed into the Ministry of Foreign Trade.

The recommendations by Moscoso and Suslov also included other minor institutional changes. Among them were the re-structuring of the Center for Promotion of Export and Investment (Centro para la Promoción de las Exportaciónes y las Inversiónes (CENPRO))[16], the creation of a National Investment Council and the Foreign Trade Promoter (PROCOMER), and re-structuring of the Free Trade Zones (Zonas Francas de Exportación). The above mentioned institutions form the foreign trade sector.

It is important to point out that the people who occupied the high-level positions in these institutions were the same people who had negotiated CBI and GATT. Many of them have also occupied government positions, been members of the Legislative Assembly and held top positions in the private sector. For example, among the associates of CINDE were Mario Carjaval, Luis Diego Escalante, Federico Vargas, Fernando Naranjo, and Eduardo Lizano. Mario Carjaval became the first coordinator with ministerial rank of MINEX, followed by Jorge Manuel Dengo. Luis Diego Escalante became Minister of Foreign Trade, and Fernando Naranjo and Federico Vargas became Ministers of

Finance. Naranjo had been Executive Director of the CINDE and was Minister of Foreign Affairs in the Figueres government (1990–94). Many of the above are currently associates of the major economic think-tanks in Costa Rica, CEFSA (Consejeros Economicos y Financieros) and Academia Centroamericana.

In conclusion, the shift towards export-oriented policies entailed two kinds of institutional shifts, both of which favoured private sector elites. First, it institutionalized a practice of the participation of organized business in free trade negotiations. Second, and perhaps more importantly, under the auspices of the USAID programme, a set of new institutions to promote export orientation was established. With these as a springboard, a small free trade-oriented elite established itself as a political force, occupying various influential positions. This elite would also represent the core in the coming controversy over the structural adjustment programmes.

The structural adjustment programmes: external pressure and institutional limitations

Immediately before entering negotiations with the USA on obtaining beneficiary status in the CBI and joining GATT, Costa Rica started negotiations with the World Bank over the first Structural Adjustment Programme (SAP I), and, in April 1985, the first agreement was signed with the World Bank facilitating credits up to US$80 m.[17]

On several accounts SAP and not GATT may be viewed as a primary cause for the emergence of an open market. For example, the tariff level agreed upon in the 1990 GATT Protocol regarding Costa Rica's accession, is higher than the one that was negotiated in the SAP (60 per cent compared to 20 per cent). The impact that these programmes had in Costa Rica was large, but differed from one programme period to the other. We shall therefore review the three programme periods separately.

The main focus of the first Structural Adjustment Programme (SAP I) was to achieve macroeconomic stabilization through economic reactivation and reduced fiscal spending. The programme called for policy changes in five major areas: (1) change in policy towards export, trade and industrialization; (2) reforms of the financial system; (3) reforms in agricultural production; (4) improvement of public administration and control with public expenses; and (5) 'economic democratization', meaning, primarily, privatization but also access to property for new social groups (Mideplan, 1987).

SAP I thus included both 'negative measures': reduction of tariffs and removal of benefits for producers of traditional products directed towards traditional markets, and 'positive measures': incentives for production of non-traditional exports directed towards third markets. Among the main measures were continuation of a flexible exchange rate policy; reduction of tariffs; elimination of export taxes; encouragement of non-traditional exports to third markets through reduced income taxes on profits; and exceptions on import taxes for goods to be used in production designated to be exported to third markets. In addition, a series of the measures directed towards the public sectors had an impact on the patterns of production and exports: the policy of privatizing CODESA that had been agreed with USAID in March 1985 was also included as a condition for SAP I (Sojo, 1995; Evans, Castro and Jones, 1995; Mideplan, 1992).

However, the progress of the reforms was slow, and in order to increase the pace, President Oscar Arias of PLN (1986–90) initiated a new structural adjustment programme in 1988. The World Bank issued a loan of US$100 that was approved of in the Legislative Assembly in October 1989.[18] In addition, the government signed a convention with the Japanese Overseas Economic Cooperation Fund for the same amount. SAP II included measures to further commercial openness, reform the financial system, limit governmental controls on agricultural prices, and improve in the administration of the public sector (Barahona Montero, 1999). Reforms in trade policy continued, and new reforms were introduced in order to improve financial performance and agricultural prices.

Many of the people involved in negotiating SAP II were the same as the ones who had promoted CBI and GATT and who now occupied core positions in the foreign trade sector. Jorge Manuel Dengo, now vice-president of the Republic, Eduardo Lizano (President of the Central Bank), Fernando Naranjo, now Minister of Finance, were among the people in charge, along with a number of officials who shared their liberal economic ideas.

They saw SAP as an effective way of binding the country to liberalization policies in the short term, whereas GATT entry would be a long-term solution. The two agreements had essentially the same goal: to open the economy to the international market and to introduce mechanisms to ensure competition in the domestic market. However, the intention of the adjustment programmes was to make short-term compromises and also to secure a loan. Meanwhile, accession to GATT would be a lasting commitment. Thus, the tariff ceiling agreed upon with the World Bank was lower than the one agreed upon with GATT. The plan was to leave the country with sufficient room for manoeuvre in case the financial circumstances should change. This would allow changes in economic policies without risk to the negotiated tariffs.

The negotiation of the two first SAPs was much less inclusive in terms of the number of negotiators than the GATT negotiations had been. The decisions were made by the government without participation either from the business sector or the labour unions. Particularly in the negotiations over SAP I, the public debate was close to absent. SAP I was known to the public primarily as a loan that the country needed.

Before the subscription of SAP II, there was some public debate between the private sector,[19] the President of the Central Bank, Eduardo Lizano, and the government, represented by Fernando Naranjo. However, the main critique raised by the private sector related to the lack of transitory regimes that would mitigate the costs of adjustment for their own sectors. In general, private sector leaders declared their support for the programme, and argued that the conditionalities connected to the US$200 m loan were necessary for the country. They considered that SAP II would help in modernizing companies and in promoting exports and investments.

Both SAP I and SAP II passed relatively easily through a disciplined Congress, where a majority of members belonged to the governing party. The most vocal opponent of the programme was the Minister of Planning, Ottón Sollís, but he was rapidly replaced by a minister whose views were in accordance with the team of negotiators. In the end, the business community passively accepted the conditions imposed upon it by SAP I and II.[20]

In 1990, a new PUSC government, led by Rafael Angel Calderón, took office. Soon after it announced its intention to negotiate a third SAP. This signified a deep change in the Costa Rican political landscape. Calderón had been in opposition to the two preceding PLN governments (Monge 1982–86 and Arias 1986–90) who initiated the first two programmes. By proposing a SAP III, he did not only continue the preceding government's policies, he did so with many of the same technocrats among his advisors. Most importantly, he kept Eduardo Lizano as President of the Central Bank. The brains behind the third programme were of the same group of liberal economists, technocrats and business people who had promoted membership in CBI, GATT and the two former programmes. A new elite constellation had emerged around neo-liberal economic polices and export promotion, that had no regard for partisan boundaries.

However, SAP III met with opposition during both the negotiation and implementation phases. Within the business sectors, there were certain critical voices. Members of the Chamber of Industries, as well as CADEXCO, wanted an evaluation of SAP II before starting yet another structural adjustment programme. They feared that the already substantial opening of the market and consequent increase in foreign competition would drive small and medium businesses into bankruptcy, something which in turn would cause increased unemployment. However, the President of the Chamber of Industries argued in favour of SAP III: that it would facilitate regional integration through a convergence of macroeconomic policies between the different Central American countries. However, this time the private sector wanted to be active participants in the negotiations, expressed thus by the President of the Chamber of Industries: 'We want to be actors and not spectators in the negotiations with the World Bank over SAP III' (*La Republica*, 6 February 1991, p. 6A). To this end, the Union of Chambers and Private Enterprise Associations (Unión de Cámaras y Asociaciones de la Empresa Privada (UCCAEP)), a private sector umbrella organization, established a so-called Unification Commission with Calderón's government. Some of its proposals were added to the negotiation agenda that was presented to the World Bank. In general, the private sector expressed the desire to play an active role in the SAP III negotiations.

Meanwhile, there was general social unrest and a series of strikes against the measures of SAP II. In the Legislative Assembly, the protest against a new programme was fierce, led by former Minister of Planning, Ottón Sollís (*Reporte Politico*, No. 59, June 1991). The opposition to the reform programme focused especially on public sector downsizing that was targeted to a reduction of 25 000 employees, privatization plans and the demonopolization of the insurance and petrol markets. The PLN did not oppose signing a SAP III, but argued that the proposed programme was too 'neo-liberal'. They pushed for changes such as measures to reduce unemployment, establishment of a programme for disabled workers, revision of import tariffs, improvement in public services and the dropping of privatization plans for certain state institutions.

There were also splits within the government with respect to the adjustment measures. In November 1991, President Calderón announced changes to the budget by adding US$12 m to the budget for the four State Universities, suspending the programme to cut the number of public employees, and dropping plans to privatize a series of public enterprises. This revamped version of the SAP was named SAP 'á la Tica' (Tica is a nickname for Costa Rica). These changes caused the main neo-liberal ideologue in the government, the long-term ANFE associate, Thelmo Vargas, to resign (Reporte Político, No. 6, November 1991).

This was the first time that a structural adjustment programme had been the subject of a nationwide debate. All social classes in Costa Rica engaged in the discussion, seemingly regardless of the knowledge they might have had about the contents. Nevertheless, in the end, the Calderón government signed agreements with the IDB and the World Bank for a total of US$350 m to support SAP III (see Table 3.1).

There was a huge list of partially crossed conditionalities – implying coordination of the conditionality demands by the World Bank and the IDB – attached to the loans, most of which were directed towards state reform (Lizano, 1994). The total SAP III programme depended on the passing of 17 different laws in the Legislative Assembly. The passing of legislation went far from smoothly, and even Eduardo Lizano criticized the structure of the programme and its heavy dependence on new legislation.[21] Due to initial conflicts and troubles with the passaging of these laws, neither of the loan agreements had entered into effect when the PLN government of José Maria Figueres took office in 1994. SAP III had been the main issue in the 1993 election campaign and Figueres won the election essentially on an anti-SAP platform. During the election campaign, which has been described as one of the dirtiest in Costa Rican history (Furlong, 2000), the real consequences of SAP became lost in the

Table 3.1   SAP III: structure and resources

Component	*Area*	*Source of finance*	*Amount in US$ (000 000)*
Third structural adjustment loan	Reform of the public sector	World Bank	100
Public sector adjustment programme	Reform of the public sector	IDB	80
Sector investment loan	Reform of the financial sector	IDB	100
Multi-sector investment loan	Productive transformation	IDB	70

Note: In the strict sense, SAP III refers to the first two loans. However, because they are related to the structural adjustment process, it is common to talk about all four as a bloc and as integral parts of the SAP III.
Source: MIDEPLAN, 1993.

political rhetoric. The private sector was divided, with one side support-ing the campaign of PUSC and the other supporting that of the PLN.

The new government re-negotiated the World Bank part of the agree-ment in order to make it more in tune with its own policy. However, due to various disputes, the government was not able to pass the neces-sary legislation to make the agreement effective and ensure the first disbursement. The World Bank granted four extensions, but finally cancelled the agreement in March 1995. The IDB loans were disbursed, but the conditionalities were heavily modified. Consequently, the last stage in the reform process in Coasta Rica was never really adopted.

In sum, it seemed as if both the political and institutional limits to liberalization had been met. The Ticos had reacted against what had come to be viewed as an elitist and exclusivist style of making develop-ment policies, and the Legislative Assembly had used its constitutional right to stop the approval of international loans.

The partial failure of the third structural adjustment programme must be viewed against the background of the developments on a different field, namely the environmental one. The 1990s saw an increased concern, both by the elites and by general society, with the serious envi-ronmental problems the country was facing. This led to the adoption of measures to protect the environment and the establishment of a series of new institutions. However, it also led to the emergence of opposition groups and of new alternative elites. These in turn have been core actors in the opposition against further liberalization of the economy. In the fol-lowing section we turn to this part of the adjustment process.

The Rio Summit and the 'ecology boom'

Environmental policy making in Costa Rica may be divided into three periods: 19490–60, 1960–90, and 1990 up to the present.

In the first period, environmental legislation was essentially non exis-tant. However, certain laws intended to ensure national security or promote economic growth provided for environmental protection as well. The 1949 Constitution gives the state of Costa Rica full jurisdiction over the environment and certain natural resources. It states, for example, that water resources, coal deposits and oil are state property and cannot be privatized. Moreover, the ICE is vested with the responsibility to protect water resources, and the 1955 Tourism Law, establishing the Costa Rican Tourism Institute (Instituto Costarricence de Turismo (ICT)), provided the legal foundation for establishing national parks in proximity to volcanoes. However, most of the laws passed in this period are characterized by leaving environmental concerns as a secondary priority.

In the second period, Costa Rica signed a number of agreements, treaties, conventions and protocols aimed at environmental protection.[22] Simultaneously, all international treaties which regulate regional and global environmental protection levels were adopted into the Costa Rica legislation. Accordingly, a large number of environmental protection laws were passed that regulated specific issue-areas, such as the use of land. The Ministry of National Planning and Financial Policies was put in charge of planning and coordinating environmental policies. These institutions and laws demonstrate a certain awareness about environmental concerns. However, there was neither a systematic and integrated approach to environmental problems nor any strategic vision. There was also a lack of legal sanctions and the institutions required for proper application of the laws.[23]

In the 1990s and up until the present, Costa Rica has undergone a legal and institutional modernization process providing the country with a framework for linking environmental needs with developmental problems. The process started with the establishment, in 1990, by the Calderón government of the Ecological Commission. However, the real breakthrough with respect to the understanding of environmental issues, both in the government and the general public, occurred after the Rio Summit (Salazar, Cabrera and López, 1994).

The invitation to participate in the Rio Summit was first treated with little political attention in Costa Rica, and it was assigned to a marginal office in the Ministry of Foreign Affairs. The people in charge had practically no competence in the issue-area. Consequently, they had to engage professionals who had the required competence, among whom figured the prominent scholars of the National Institute of Bio-diversity (Institutio Nacional de Bio-Diversidad (INBIO)), Dr Rodrigo Gámez Lobo and Dr Alfio Piva Mesén.[24] Through a bureaucratic process, the Minister of Foreign Affairs, Bern Nihaus Quesada, took the initiative to form an Ecological Commission and invited the Minister of Natural Resources, Energy and Mines (MIRENEM) to participate. This enabled the country's active participation in the preparatory sessions of the United Nations Conference on Environment and Development (UNCED) and in the negotiations on Climatic Change and Biological Diversity signed by leaders during the Earth Summit. Together with the Costa Rican Ambassador to the United Nations, the participants in the Ecological Commission ensured that Costa Rica was designated as the host of the Earth Council in the chapter written on institutions as part of Agenda 21.

The formation of the Ecological Commission led to various initiatives to link developmental and environmental issues. Costa Rica has engaged in environmental certifications, and in carbon trading, through an agreement with the Norwegian government.[25] A further consequence of the success in locating the Earth Council headquarters in Costa Rica was the initiative for the Alliance for Sustainable Development (ALIDES) signed between the Central American countries in August 1994. The idea of the Alliance was further developed during Figueres' administration; it obtained bipartisan support and was made public only three months after Figueres took office.

ALIDES constitutes the basis for a national and regional development strategy uniting financial, political, social and environmental needs.[26] However, so far, it has brought few tangible results. There have, for example, been no relevant compromises on how to accommodate labour or environment concerns with trade. Currently it seems as if the System of Integration of Central America (Sistema de Integración Centroamericano (SICA)) is unable to do much more than accelerate the pace of economic liberalization (Bull, 1999).

Another outcome of the Rio Summit was the creation of a National System for Sustainable Development. This idea had been born at the Rio Summit as a national counterpart to ALIDES and it was carried out by the Figueres administration (1994–98) under the leadership of René Castro. He headed the Ministry of Environment and Energy (MINAE) which in 1994 had replaced the Ministry of Natural Resources, Energy and Mines (MIRENEM). The new ministry was much more specifically aimed at environmental protection than the old MIRENEM, and one of its main achievements was the adoption of a General Environmental Law. Furthermore, it established two important agencies: the National System for Areas of Conservation (Sistema Nacional de Areas de Conservación (SINAC)), which undertakes studies of national parks and offers environmental education, and the National Technical Secretariat for the Environment (Secretaría Técnica Nacional Ambiental (SETENA)), which is responsible for environmental impact assessments.

During this period the participation from Costa Rican NGOs was minimal. Participation was practically limited to INBIO which is a semi-governmental institution. However, after the Rio Summit, Costa Rica experienced what may be called an ecology boom with a virtual explosion of NGO participation. This happened parallel to a process of what we may call 'elite co-optation': the emergence of alternative elite networks which over time have merged in with more traditional elites. This will be the topic of the next section.

Civil society activity and elite co-optation

During the 1980s and 1990s the number of NGOs in Costa Rica concerned with environmental issues increased, according to some estimations, from approximately 50 to close to 1000. Moreover, considerable civil society activity is carried out outside the NGOs. Municipal organizations, known as Local Committees, contribute to enforcement of the environmental protectionist laws by either putting pressure on federal bodies or by influencing the Ministry of Environment and Energy. Any Local Committee may report violations of the environmental protection law in any province to an office of the MINAE. Such crimes may also be reported to the local municipality, to the Fiscal Ecological Agencies of the Judiciary, or to the Public Defender. The local committees have, for example, been active in reporting violation of environmental laws connected to tourism developments.[27] Currently, considerable effort is put into the establishment of Regional Councils by integrating the local committees.

The challenges relating to the environment initially brought about different reactions among the traditional elites. The Chamber of Industries, the Chamber of Commerce, and CADEXCO set up a study commission on the environment, following the example of the WTO, in an attempt to institutionalize routines for dialogue on environmental subjects. Nevertheless, the business community's attitude to environmentalism may be described as modest and uneven. There is an acknowledgment of issues concerned with, for example, labelling and packaging, and there is support for the 'green flag' – an award given to companies that display environmental awareness. However, these measures carry little risk for the companies involved and allow them at the same time to look 'trendy'. On more profound topics, such as including environmental issues in the trade agenda, the business community has demonstrated a failure to make far-reaching compromises. CADEXCO has shown a greater interest in the subject than the others, perhaps due to their hands-on experience with exports.

At the same time as environmental issues caused some changes among the political elites, members of various civil society organizations and environmentally concerned academics began to reach important positions in government. This led to a rapid growth in ecological awareness. The above mentioned Minister of Environment and Energy,

René Castro Salazar, is only one example of an academic who has taken up a government position. A number of other scholars, in particular university professors, have taken up positions in the central administration and in various environmental NGOs.[28]

However, as the example of the Carazo brothers (discussed below) shows, these groups are also closely connected to traditional elites. The two sons of former President, Rodrigo Carazo, have both been active in work towards environmental protection. Mario Carazo Zeledón is a distinguished member of PUSC and chairman of the AMBIO Foundation. His brother, Rodrigo Alberto Carazo Zeledón, used his position as Public Defender to file complaints about violation of environmental laws. For example, he contributed to halting controversial tourism developments in Golfo de Papagayo and Aurora del Pacifico due to accusations of violations of Law 6043 that regulates the maritime zone (Zona Maritime Terrestre) (Bull, 1996). The ex-president himself has also been active in promoting environmental issues through the CDI.

Although environmental issues have entered elite politics, there are still clear differences in budget resources, rank, prestige and political influence between those governmental institutions handling environmental issues and those handling financial and economic issues. Advisers, ministers and vice-ministers have different degrees of influence, allowing them to investigate issues and lobby the president. Even though legal experts have questioned the position of the Ministry of Foreign Trade, Economy and Finance, its political weight is probably double that of the Ministry of Environment and Energy. These differences have at various occasions tipped the scale in favour of the former. For example, did the then Minister of Environment and Energy, René Castro, propose that environmental issues were included on the agenda for the Summit of Central American Presidents in Panama in April 1997. However, the Minister of Foreign Trade, José Manuel Salazar, protested on the grounds that conditions were not yet ready. When repeated attempts were made to bring environmental concerns to the table of the Government Council, the foreign trade sector applied all their leverage to prevent it from happening.[29]

What we see therefore is a process of elite co-optation in which the Costa Rican institutions have incorporated environmental policies in a rather narrow way onto the traditional development agenda, and where alternative elites have been included in the old elites. As shown above, the 'alternative elites' to a large extent emerged out of the traditional ones. Policies that profoundly differ from traditional approaches had still not achieved their institutional expression, and in the eyes of the majority of Costa Ricans, development policy was still run by a small elite, excessively influenced by neo-liberal ideas.

Conclusion

Costa Rica has, in the course of the last two decades, been through a thorough transition from a state-led development model. As we have argued in this chapter, the foundation for this transition was laid by the policies of USAID in the 1980s, in alliance with significant segments of the national private sector. The institutions established in this early phase have been instrumental in the further moves towards liberalization. In the 1990s, a second major change occurred with the introduction of an environmental agenda, and the emergence of new elites promoting environmental issues. The democratic institutions have been adapted, and new institutions have been added, in order to incorporate new groups and issue areas into the democratic process.

In spite of this, since the debt-crisis, policy making in Costa Rica is increasingly elitist, including, primarily, members of the two major political parties (PLN and PUSC), private sector representatives and a small group of intellectuals. Although Costa Rica has an active civil society, the political institutions have failed to include the demands of many of these groups in the development policy-making process. Recent reactions that have led to a halt in the reform process should be understood against this background. Both the dismantling of SAP III and the recent blockage of telecommunications and electricity reform, must be viewed as expressions of long-term frustration over the dismantling of the Costa Rican state without the consent or participation of the population. If this stasis is to be overcome, there is a need for the incorporation of new voices in the increasingly rigid and elitist political system.

.

Notes

1. Its article 50 reads: 'The state shall secure the welfare of the population, organize and stimulate production and ensure appropriate distribution of wealth'.
2. This is the literacy rate for adults age 15 and above. For youth (age 15–24) the rate is 98.2 per cent.
3. In Spanish: 'Del Estado Intervencionista al Estado Empresario'. These terms have later entered into the vocabulary of politicians and academics in Costa Rica.
4. ANFE counts a series of prominent businessmen and it has often been pointed out as one of the most powerful groups in Costa Rica (Arias

Sánchez 1971) and a main source of market oriented ideology in Costa Rica. For a position contending this view, see Wilson (1998).

5. Causes and consequences of Costa Rica's debt crisis are well discussed elsewhere. See for instance Rovira Mas (1986).

6. It was not only lack of support in the Legislative that hinderened compliance by Carazo. According to several authors Carazo himself was by no means convinced of the virtues of the IMF/World Bank medicine (Rivera, 1982; Salóm Echeverría, 1992). Carazo never really intended to comply with the agreeements, in spite of what he argued to be a coalition of pressures from local and external forces, referring to on the one hand small but economically powerful internal groups and on the other to the IMF and the World Bank (interview quoted in Salom Echeverría, 1992, p. 33).

7. This led to serious internal discontent with the president, and, according to later accounts by the president, plans to overthrow him. One of the reasons why this never happened was probably the upcoming presidential elections in 1982 (Salom Echeverría, 1992).

8. In the same elections, PLN gained 23 representatives and PUSC 27. There are also two additional minority parties in the current congress: Partido Integración Nacional and Partido Renovación Costariccense. They both have one representative in the Congress, but they have had a much lower profile than Movimiento Libertario and Fuerza Democratica.

9. He became President of the Central Bank for the first time in 1984 during a cabinet reshuffle in the government of Luis Alberto Monge that signified the opening for a new group of neo-liberal technocrats entering power.

10. The most important of these were the 'Law of 3/4' saying that the boards of the AIs shall be composed by 4 members of the current government and 3 members of the opposition, and the Law of the Executive Presidents, adding a new layer of management to the AIs that is to be politically appointed.

11. See http://www.red-ice.co.cr for information on further activities by this group.

12. As an example: When the Costa Rican constitutional court found the operations of the US company Millicom to be unconstitutional and decided it had to seize its operations in the country, the US Congress threatened in return to withdraw the benefits under the CBI (*La Nación* 18 April 1995).

13. This section draws on interviews conducted with a series of people involved. (See list in Reference Section).

14. For the first time in diplomatic and commercial history, the USA conducted two investigations into subsidies and dumping practices in Costa Rica. The first related to subsidies of cement exports from Costa Rica to Puerto Rico, and was made after Costa Rica had applied for observation status to GATT. The second investigation was made after the application for 'provisional participation' had been sent in 1986, and it related to subsidies and dumping of Costa Rica's flower exports (carnations, short carnations and chrysanthemums) to Minnesota, USA.

15. For a thorough account of the role of CINDE in Costa Rican development policies, see Clark 1993 and 1997.

16. This was established in 1968, but had little success.

17. This was converted into Law No. 6998 in the Legislative Assembly on 20 August 1985.

18. Law No. 7134/89.
19. The Chamber of Industry participated most intensely, but also CADEXCO, the Chamber of Commerce, the Chamber of Textiles, the National Chamber of Agriculture and Agroindustry, the Chamber of Foreign Houses and the umbrella organization, the Union of Chambers and Private Enterprise Associations (Unión de Cámaras y Asociaciones de la Empresa Privada (UCCAEP)).
20. Later the business community started the Industrial Modernization Programme with funding from USAID and support from the Chamber of Industries. This was the Chamber's first action in acceptance of and adjustment to the realities of the new policies. During an important period, this programme was the responsibility of a young economist, José Manuel Salazar, who later became the Minister of Foreign Trade with the unanimous approval of the private sector.
21. Acta No. 95, Comisión de Asunto Hacendarios, 2 March 1994.
22. Some examples are the Convention on the Defence of Archeological, Historical and Artistic Heritage of the American Nations, known as the San Salvador Convention (ratified by law No. 6360 of 21 September 1979, valid from 27 August 1980); the Convention for the Protection of Flora, Fauna and Natural Scenic Arts of the American Countries (ratified by law No. 3763 of 19 October 1966, valid from 12 April 1967); and the International Treaty for Tuna Fishing in the East Pacific (signed on 15 March 1983) (Assamblea Legislativa, 1997).
23. For instance, they do not specify punishments for environmental crimes.
24. INBIO has gained international reputation for its work on protecting the environment. It has been rewarded a series of international distinctions, and the roots of its success have been the object of a series of academic investigations.
25. The background for this agreement was ICE's plans for modernizing the hydroelectrical dam at Brasil de Santa Ana, for which it acquired financing and technical consultations from the Norwegian government and other hydroelectric companies. The Ministry of Environment and Energy found out about the ongoing process and saw it as an opportunity to acquire resources. The Norwegians made a US$2 m investment in the Virilla River Basin, the river at which base the dam is located. Meanwhile, the Ministry of Environment and Energy raised money by selling coal certificates (at US$10 per certificate) transferring the money to the Forest Financial Fund, an office in charge of administering funds targeted at reforestation. In this way a comprehensive plan for reforestation along the river Virilla became a reality: it was one of the components in the agreement made with the Norwegians. The government uses a system of incentives, partly financed by foreign contributions such as the one from the Norwegian government, to attract property owners to come forward and sign contracts. The Forest Financial Fund coordinates the various incentives to be used for the conservation and management of forests. An internationally certified company is said to have been hired to accredit the coal certificates. A representative from the company evaluates the projects and calculates the annual price per unit.
26. The alliance is supposed to work at two levels. First, through the Central American Sustainable Development Council which is made up of the Central American presidents. Their decisions and agreements are supposed

to be implemented by regional councils with the people's participation. Second, it operates through National Councils for Sustainable Development which consist of public sector officials and representatives for the public in each country.

27. For example, it was a local committee that reported pollution, destruction of forests and coral reefs, and violation of the law that regulates the marine/land zone on the Rajada Beach, caused by the tourist resorts of Papagayo and Aurora del Pacífico (Bull, 1996).

28. Among the examples are: Frank Tatembach from the Development of the Volcanic Central Mountain Range Foundation, and nephew of ambassador Cristian Tatembach, had a high position in MINAE. Carlos Valerio, Dean of the Department of Science at the University of Costa Rica, has represented MINAE on several occasions. The scholar Mario Boza from National Parks is the Vice-Minister of Natural Resources, Energy and Mines. Other scholars from the National University that became involved in environmental tasks include Jorge Cabrera Medaglia, Claudia Charpantier Esquivel, Olman Segura Bonilla, Roxana Salazar and Beatriz Villareal. Lenín Corrales and Raúl Solórzano have begun work for two NGOs, the United States Rain Forest Alliance and the Tropical Scientific Centre respectively.

29. An adviser to the Minister of Foreign Trade, Amparo Pacheco, assisted them by publishing a letter in *La Nación* in April 1998 entitled 'A Dangerous Blend: Trade and the Environment'. This was obviously a reply to Olman Segura's paper, one that had been widely distributed, arguing that it was important to link trade and the environment (Segura, 1998).

References

Newspapers and journals

La Gaceta (Official Journal of the Republic of Costa Rica), La Nación (independent newspaper) San José, Costa Rica, La República (independent newspaper) San José, Costa Rica, Reporte Político (independent weekly journal), Guatemala City, Guatemala.

Interviews

Brenes Rodríguez, Carlos, Oceanógrafo, Universidad Nacional.
Castro Salazar, René, Ministro del Ambiente y Energía.
Dengo, Jorge Manuel, Ex-Vice-Presidente de la República.
Echeverría, Carlos Francisco, Ex-Ministro de Cultura.
Llobet, Gabriela, Investigadora, Universidad de Costa Rica.
Madrigal, Rodrigo, Ex-Canciller.
Martinez, Luís, Diputado.
Mora, Marcela, Area de Conservación de Guanacaste.
Murillo, Carlos, Investigador, Economista, CINPE, UNA.
Pérez, Gabriela, Asesoría Jurídica, MINAE.
Pisk, Sandra, Defensora de los Habitantes.
Segura, Olman, Investigador, Economista, CINPE, UNA.

4
Weaving through Paradoxes: Democratization, Globalization and Environment Politics in South Korea

Chung-in Moon and Sunghack Lim

Introduction

South Korea has undergone a profound economic transformation over the past five decades. From a dirt poor country of per capita income of $89 in 1961, it has emerged as one of the most powerful economies in the world. Per capita income had risen to almost $10 000 by the year 2000. It now has the thirteenth largest economy in the world. Beneath the miraculous economic transformation lie the workings of the developmentalist coalition that has crafted the political and institutional foundation for rapid economic growth (Lee, 1992; Evans, 1995; Weiss and Hobson, 1995; Maxfield and Schneider, 1997; Moon, 1998). It is through the developmentalist coalition that the South Korean government had been able to implement the policies of 'growth first, distribution later' and 'growth first, environmental integrity later'. Such orientation might have been inevitable in order to overcome the vicious circle of poverty and underdevelopment, to mobilize resources, and to expedite the process of industrialization.

But the developmentalist paradigm that governed Korean society and the Korean economy since the mid-1960s, began to reveal new limits and contradictions. Worsening social and economic inequalities, a repressive political regime, and resource scarcity and environmental degradation – all of which were by-products of the developmentalist paradigm – severely undercut gains from rapid industrialization and economic growth. Facing formidable internal and external challenges and constraints, the developmentalist paradigm and underlying dominant political coalition were also subject to the law of diminishing returns. They could no longer serve as *deus ex machina*. Liberty, equality and environmental integrity have emerged as new social values that are as critical as growth and security. Two major trends have made an important contribution to precipitating the paradigm shift. While democratic transition in 1987 opened and expanded new space for popular political manoeuvering of these alternative values (Lee, SH, 1993; Kim, SH, 1996; Yoo, 1995), the grand process of globalization has also itself fostered such transition (Smith, 1998; Yearley, 1996). Of these transitions, the politics of democratic transition and distributive justice have drawn extensive scholarly and policy attention. But very little attention has been paid to the case of the rise of new environmental politics in South Korea.

Against this backdrop, this chapter is designed to explore the dynamics of environmental politics in the context of democratization and globalization. First, the chapter makes an overall assessment of development and environmental performance in South Korea. Second, the chapter elucidates the impacts of democratization on environmental politics through case studies of non-governmental organizations (NGO) activities. Third, the contribution looks at how new forces of globalization have affected the changing nature of environment politics and policies. Finally, we analyse the dynamic interplay of democratization, globalization and environmental politics in South Korea and derive several theoretical and comparative implications.

Development and environment in South Korea: an empirical overview

South Korea used to present a classical example of trade-off between development and environment. While being obsessed with hasty economic development, the country had virtually ignored the environmental consequences of this. The trajectory of economic development in South Korea illustrates the fallacy of the 'Faustian bargain' in an eloquent manner.

South Korea was traditionally an agrarian society. To cope with poverty and the underdevelopment associated with it, the South Korean government initiated an ambitious development strategy. Starting with an aggressive labour-intensive, export-led growth strategy, it rapidly moved into the heavy-chemical sectors. In particular, its transition to the heavy-chemical industrialization in 1973 is noteworthy. Disregarding inflationary consequences, the Park Chung Hee government undertook an ambitious heavy industrialization plan, not only to adjust to shifting comparative advantage, but to create forward and backward linkages to the defence industry. Along with the export-drive, the South Korean government attracted foreign direct investment by creating 'pollutant havens' in free-trade zones such as Masan, Changwon and Goomi (Jung, JS, 1997).

Consequently, the South Korean economy showed a phenomenal growth, maintaining an annual average growth rate of 10 per cent for the past four decades. Per capita income rose from $80 to $10 307 in 1997. Exports grew from $33 million in 1960 to $130 billion in 1996, and the structure of exports was radically shifted towards the manufacturing sector (Song, 1997, pp. 60–1; The Bank of Korea (http://www.bok.or.kr), *Economic Statistics Yearbook 1997*). Such rapid industrialization accompanied a concurrent galloping urbanization and an exponential growth in consumption. Given South Korea's small geographic size, relatively large population, and poor resource endowment, rapid industrialization, urbanization and a sharp surge in consumption, brought about an almost unbearable load on its eco-system as well as severe environmental degradation. Authoritarian rule, backed up by the developmentalist coalition, virtually deprived South Korea of any other viable alternatives but 'growth at the expense of environment'.

In fact, South Korea underwent serious environmental degradation throughout the 1970s and 1980s. Air pollution posed a new social problem. It was closely related to the pattern of energy consumption. Coal consumption doubled from 10 million tons in the mid-1960s to 20 million tons by the mid-1970s. Consumption of all sorts of petroleum increased by seven times during the same period – from 14 737 barrels in 1966 to 105 119 barrels in 1975 (National Statistics Office, http://www.nso.go.kr). A sharp rise in energy consumption resulted in severe air pollution. Emission of air pollutants increased by 2.7 times, from an annual average of 5.4 ton/km^2 in 1965 to 14.5 ton/ km^2 in 1974 (Jang, 1980). In addition, the widespread use of automobiles created new environmental problems such as smog, the emission of sulphur dioxide, nitrogen dioxide and carbon dioxide. Large metropolitan cities such as Seoul, Busan and Taegu became victims of air pollution. Water pollution also became serious. Construction of large industrial complexes along major rivers such as the Han, Nakdong, Geum and Yeongsan, severely damaged the quality of water with large-scale releases of industrial sewage. Heavy population density of these river basins further complicated the situation. Up-stream of these rivers – areas which are the sources of tap water for residents of metropolitan areas – could not satisfy the necessary standards of fresh drinking water.

Along with air and water pollution, disposal of solid wastes emerged as a major problem throughout the 1970s. While increased consumption led to a sharp rise in solid wastes, rapid industrialization entailed enormous amount of industrial wastes. Yet, South Korea lacked both the technology and facilities to process these wastes. Moreover, the collective action dilemma further prevented the government from finding suitable sites for disposal, aggravating the pollution problem (Moon and Oh, 1999).

What is really amazing is the reversal of trends since the mid-1980s. According to the 1998 OECD report of environmental indicators, South Korea has performed quite well in improving its environmental quality. The most remarkable improvement has been made in ensuring air quality. For example, emissions of carbon dioxide per capita in South Korea improved from 8.3 tons in 1995 to 7.8 tons in 1997,[1] lower than the OECD average of 10.9 tons. The United States (19.9 tons), Germany (10.8 tons) and Japan (9.2 tons) emitted more carbon dioxide than South Korea in the same year. Of major industrialized countries, only France (at 6.2 tons) was better than South Korea. South Korea has also performed better regarding emissions of sulphur dioxide, another important indicator of air quality. Its per capita emission of sulphur dioxide was 34 kg, which is lower than the OECD average (in 1997) of 40 kg. In the case of nitrogen dioxide, South Korea has shown an improving performance. The emission of NOx per capita was 26 kg, which is much lower than the OECD average of 40 kg.

The OECD report provides further interesting data on the improvement of water quality in South Korea. When measured in terms of demand of oxygen and amount of nitrates, the water quality of the Han River, the primary source of tap water for Seoul metropolitan city, was better than that of the Donau and the Rhine in Germany, the Mississippi in the United States and the Seine in France (OECD, 1998). South Korea also scored positively in the area of solid wastes. Disposal of solid wastes per capita in the South Korea's urban area was 390 kg in 1997, lower than the OECD average of 530 kg. The figure is far better than major OECD countries such as the United States (720 kg), France (560 kg), Great Britain (490 kg) and Japan (400 kg).[2]

As Table 4.1 demonstrates, data from the Fraser Institute in Vancouver give a more precise picture of environmental improvement in South Korea during the 1985–97 period (http://www.fraserinstitute.ca/publications/critical_issues/2000/env-indic/section_18.html). In four categories of environmental integrity (air quality, water quality, solid wastes and conservation of natural resources), South Korea has

Table 4.1 Environmental indicators: relative severity of environmental problems in South Korea (base year 1985 = 100)

	1985	1986	1987	1988	1989	1990	1991	1992	1993	1994	1995	1996	1997	Net change
Air quality	100	92	94	92	87	85	82	78	71	67	65	65	59	-41
Water quality	100	99	91	96	101	83	76	69	76	93	95	99	119	19
Solid waste	100	84	95	79	74	74	78	65	71	70	70	68	67	-33
Natural resources	100	100	101	106	110	114	124	109	101	101	96	113	119	19
Overall average	100	94	96	93	93	89	90	80	80	83	82	86	91	-9

Note: Annual values >100 represent an increase in environmental degradation; annual values <100 represent a decrease.
Source: The Fraser Institute (http://www.fraserinstitute.ca/publications/critical_issues/2000/env-indic/section_18.html).

shown a remarkable improvement in air quality and solid wastes. Using 1985 as the base year (benchmark index=100), the Fraser Institute calculated that South Korea has decreased its environmental degradation to 85 in 1990 and to 59 in 1997. Net change between 1985 and 1997 was –41. This is quite a significant improvement. Overall degradation in solid wastes has also been reversed, from 100 in 1985 to 74 in 1990 and to 67 in 1997. However, water quality and conservation of natural resources continue to remain major sources of degradation. Water quality has degraded from index value 100 in 1985 to 114 in 1990 and to 119 in 1997. The profile of conservation of natural resources has not improved either. This might be attributed to a sharp rise in water and energy consumption. The changing structure of lifestyles from traditional housing to apartment living, increased water consumption, precipitating an acute fresh water shortage. An exponential growth in ownership of private vehicles could be expected to have an effect on natural resources. For example, South Korea's daily oil consumption was the sixth largest in the world in 1999, and imports of crude oil accounted for 66 per cent of all energy imports in the same year (*Chosun Ilbo*, 23 July 2000).

Despite sagging performance in water quality and conservation of natural resources, South Korea has demonstrated a gradual improvement in terms of environmental integrity. As Table 4.1 reveals, since 1985, the overall average of environmental quality has improved over time. What accounts for such improvement? We argue that while a changing social paradigm has improved people's awareness of environmental issues, democratic changes, expansion of civil society and non-governmental organizations (NGOs), and increased political bargaining power by environmental NGOs, facilitated overall changes in South Korea's environmental policy.

Democratic changes and environmental politics

South Korea underwent a dramatic democratic transition in 1987 after 25 years of the iron-fist authoritarian rule of Park Chung-hee and Chun Doo-hwan.[3] The transition underscored profound changes in Korean society and politics, and these had far-reaching implications for environmental politics and policies.

First there was an overall realignment of the dominant social paradigm. To borrow Inglehart's (1989) terminology, South Korea underwent a major paradigm shift from the materialist to a post-materialist one. The developmental era in the 1960s and 1970s emphasized materialist values framed around growth, productivity, exports and national security. Throughout the 1980s, however, South Koreans began to show the pronounced effects of fatigue with these values. While the advent of the post-Cold War order undercut traditional emphasis on national security, relative material affluence, attained through two decades of successive economic growth, induced the public, especially the middle class, to defy old materialist values. Instead, new social issues such as economic justice, environmental conservation, women's rights, and the prohibition of corruption began to dominate public discourse[4]; this eventually emerged as major political issues, fuelling public discontentment with the Chun regime as well as fostering the democratic transition. It is through this overall change in social ambience that environmental issues were able to attract social and political attention.

Second, democratic opening not only precipitated the proliferation of civil society, but also contributed to NGOs' political activism. As Table 4.2 illustrates, prior to the 1980s, NGOs activities were virtually negligible. Of a total of 3643 existing NGOs, only 765 (22.5 per cent) were established prior to the 1980s. The large majority of Korean NGOs (2878 cases, 77.5 per cent) were established in the 1980s, especially after the democratic opening in 1987. The expansion and empowerment of NGOs fundamentally undercut the power and influence of the developmentalist coalition. In fact, it was on the wane not only because of diminishing state intervention in markets and ruptured relationships between the state and business, but also because of new political governance that undermined the organic ties between the two (Moon, 1998; Fields, 1997). Such changing political terrain opened a new space for intensified political manoeuvering by NGOs, facilitating social movements for environmental issues. The number of environmental NGOs is relatively small (259), compared with other NGOs, but their political activism has been most pronounced.[5]

Third, expansion of environmental NGOs and their political activism have made a significant contribution to fostering changes in environmental policy. As early as the 1980s, the number of environmental NGOs was less than seven. But the number has grown at a phenomenal rate since 1988 (Goo, DW, 1996, pp. 163–4). According to the Ministry of Environment (MOE), environmental NGOs are classified into three major categories: officially approved NGOs, non-official voluntary NGOs, and comprehensive NGOs (MOE, *Environment White*

Table 4.2   Establishment of NGOs over time in South Korea

	Number (cases)	Pre-1940s (%)	1950s	1960s	1970s	1980s	1990s	Total (%)
Civil society	908	4.9	1.7	5.4	7.6	18.4	62.0	100.0
Local community	192	–	–	–	7.7	27.4	52.8	100.0
Social service	686	1.6	4.1	6.4	7.7	27.4	52.8	100.0
Environment	259	0.4	–	0.8	2.7	8.5	87.6	100.0
Culture	563	5.3	2.5	7.6	10.5	23.8	50.3	100.0
Education/Academic	208	2.4	1.9	3.8	7.7	28.8	55.3	100.0
Religion	97	5.2	–	9.3	21.6	27.8	36.1	100.0
Labour/Agriculture	1997	3.6	4.1	10.7	9.6	25.4	46.7	100.0
Economy	473	2.7	2.7	15.6	15.2	22.2	41.4	100.0
International	42	2.4	4.8	21.4	21.4	19.0	31.0	100.0
Others	18	–	16.7	16.7	–	22.2	44.4	100.0
Total	3643	3.2	2.4	7.2	9.0	21.0	56.5	100.0

Source: Compiled from the Directory of Korean NGOs by the Citizens' Movement Communication Center (http://www.kngo.net/new/pds/pds-cmcc.htm).

Paper 1999, p. 169). The number of officially approved NGOs which are devoted solely to environmental activities with a high degree of professional competence and accountability, increased from 63 in 1992 to 119 in 1999. Non-official voluntary environmental organizations, which are geared toward social and political activism at the grass-roots level, have become most pronounced in terms of size and social impacts. Their number was 30 in 1992, but rose to 271 in 1999. Comprehensive NGOs refer to those NGOs which include environmental issues as a part of their catch-all agenda. Before the rise of specialized environmental NGOs, these comprehensive NGOs played an important role in attracting public attention to environmental causes (MOE, *Environment White Paper* 1998, 1999). Likewise, the quantitative expansion of environmental NGOs emerged as a new social and political deterrent to the dominance of the developmentalist coalition, leading to major changes in environmental policies and people's attitude towards development and environment.

Finally, the most significant impact of democratization on environmental politics was the qualitative change in environmental NGOs. They no longer remained as passive public interest groups. They have become larger in size, relatively rich in human and financial resources, and innovative in crafting new strategies and tactics of environmental movements. Table 4.3 presents a comparative overview of the evolutionary dynamics of environmental politics in South Korea.

The evolution of South Korea's environmental politics can be categorized as four major stages (Jung and Lee, 1994; Goo, 1996; Son, 1996; Lee, SJ, 1998). The first stage (1960–70s) is the Park Chung-hee period during which environment movements were extremely passive and relatively primitive, paying attention primarily to the compensation of victims. While the government was less attentive to environmental issues, being preoccupied with growth and exports, the public was also tolerant of environmental degradation. Moreover, the government tried to conceal environmental disasters and to repress all kinds of environment movements through authoritarian rule. Public tolerance, however, also resulted from the fact that public attention during this stage was paid mainly to the termination of authoritarian rule and the creation of a democratic opening. Thus, environmental movements were confined largely to self-help movements organized by the victims, who engaged in sporadic protests, but, overall, the impacts of these movements were minimal during this period.

The second stage (1980–87) involves an interesting convergence of democratic movements and environmental ones. During this period,

Table 4.3 A comparative overview of environmental movements in South Korea

	1st stage 1960s–70s	2nd stage 1980–87	3rd stage 1987–92		4th stage after 1992
		Onsan disease	Anmyeon Island	Nakdong River Phenol	Dong River Dam
Characteristics	Damage compensation	Damage compensation	NIMBY	Damage compensation	Environment conservation
Democratization (political system)	Pre (closed)	Pre (closed)	Post (open)	Post (open)	Post (open)
Main activists	Victims	Victims and environmental NGOs	Victims and environmental NGOs	Victims and environmental NGOs	Environmental, civil movement organization
Result	Minimum compensation	Relocation/compensation	No construction	Tolerable compensation	No construction
Goals	Damage compensation	Damage compensation	Damage prevention	Damage compensation and prevention	Damage prevention
Role of government	Tolerance of pollution	Damage compensation	Dual: preservation and development	Dual: preservation and development	Dual: preservation and development
Response of government	Concealment, suppression	Pacification	Reactive	Policy change	Policy change

Table 4.3 A comparative overview of environmental movements in South Korea   contd.

	1st stage 1960s–70s	2nd stage 1980–87	3rd stage 1987–92	4th stage after 1992
Policy change	Sanitation Law, Prevention of Pollution Law (1963), Environment Conservation Law (1977, comprehensive measure)	Environmental rights included in the Constitution (1980)	Environmental measures on specific pollution medium (1990)	Environmental measures on specific pollution medium (1990)
Organizational development of environmental administration[6]	From pollution section in 1967 to pollution bureau in 1973	1980: Environment Administration established	1990: Upgraded to the Environmental Agency	1994: Upgraded to the Ministry of Environment
International NGOs help	No	No	No	Yes

the political system was still an authoritarian one under the rule of Chun Doo-hwan, but environmental NGOs began to emerge. They considered environmental movements to be part of the democratic struggle to topple the Chun regime. Thus, by forming an alliance with victims of environmental accidents, these NGOs became more assertive in pushing for the government's policy towards change and securing compensation for the victims. In encountering this new challenge, the Chun government tried to pacify the situation in part through co-optation and in part through the de-coupling of political and environmental issues. Despite the government's repression, however, specialized environmental activist organizations came into existence, and public attention, including the mass media, became much more attentive to environmental issues during this period.

The episode of the Onsan disease incident, which was reminiscent of the Minimata Bay incident in Japan, is a case in point. As part of the heavy-chemical industrialization plan, the Park Chung-hee government created a special industrial complex in the Onsan area in the 1970s: a large number of refinery, non-metallic, chemical industry plants were concentrated here. Since the early 1980s, the Onsan coastal area fell prey to pollution as accumulated lag time effects of previous pollution affected the area. Emission of heavy metal waste water and industrial fumes began to pollute both the air and the coastal area. The fish catch was drastically reduced, while residents of the area began to show collective symptoms of neuralgia and skin disease: known as 'Onsan disease'. For two years between 1983 and 1985, more than 500 local residents were plagued by the disease. In 1985, the Korea Pollution Research Institute diagnosed it as *'itai-itai* disease', a bone and joint disease caused by cadmium poisoning, endemic to chemical industrial areas in Japan.[6]

Local residents appealed to the government for the relocation of polluting industries and proper compensation for the damage. Initial responses by the government were rather lukewarm, even negative. As the 'Onsan' disease attracted extensive media attention, however, environmental NGOs began to assist local residents in formulating strategies of protest, elucidating the causes of the disease, and even joining street protests with them. Facing this new development, the government took quick action to control the damage and to prevent its spill over to the political arena. It announced a plan to relocate local residents to safer areas, along with financial compensation. Such announcements severed ties between local residents and environmental NGOs. While the former was preoccupied with negotiating with the government over the acceptable level of financial compensation, the latter wished to prolong the struggle until the government cames up with structural remedies. Lack of unity between the two made the government a winner. They neither induced government's fundamental policy changes, nor secured a satisfactory compensation package. Nevertheless, alliance between local victims and environmental NGOs opened a new chapter in environmental politics in South Korea. [7]

The third stage (1987–92) represents the take-off period of South Korean environment movements. Two events had greatly reshaped the political terrain of environment movements during this period. While democratic transition in 1987 demolished political and institutional barriers to the activation of environment movements, the Rio Earth Summit enhanced public awareness of environmental issues. During this period, environmental politics underwent four major structural changes. First, was the proliferation of professional, competent and specialized environmental NGOs. The government could no longer monopolize or manipulate knowledge and information on environmental issues. In addition, these organizations were well organized and funded, enabling them to reach a wide range of civil society in appealing to environmental integrity. Second, was the changing attitude of victims of environmental hazards. In the past, they were preoccupied primarily with relocation and financial compensation. During this period, however, they began to show a greater degree of analytical aptness to environmental issues, and called for structural remedies and preventive measures on environmental hazards. Furthermore, they started to form an equal partnership with environmental NGOs. Third, defying the inertia of the developmentalist paradigm, mass media became much more attentive to environmental issues. Some media organizations began to lead public opinion by engaging in environmental campaigns by themselves. Finally, the government also became much more receptive to public pressure, partly because of the process of democratization opening, and partly because of much more sophisticated strategies by environmental NGOs (Goo, 1995; Gang, 1997; Jung, 1994).

Such structural changes enhanced the bargaining power of victims and environmental NGOs in dealing with the government. During this period, in fact, environmental NGOs and local citizens became quite successful in championing their causes over a wide range of issues involving nuclear waste disposal sites, waste incinerator sites, a night-soil incinerator issue and environmental degradation associated with the construction of golf courses. In this regard, two cases deserve special attention: one is public rejection of the Anmyeon Island nuclear waste disposal site construction and the other is the incident of the Nakdong River Phenol pollution (see Table 4.3, above).

In order to cope with chronic energy shortage, the South Korean government had pursued an assertive nuclear energy programme since the early 1970s. Consequently, nuclear waste disposal emerged as a new public policy problem. On 3 November 1990, the government's plan to build nuclear waste disposal facilities in the Anmyeon Island, located at the west coast of the Korean peninsula, was leaked to the mass media. As soon as the news broke, over 20 000 local residents staged violent street protests, and destroyed police stations and government buildings. Chaos set in, and the government were unable to control the situation. On 8 November, environmental NGOs under the leadership of the National Movement to Expel Nuclear Power Plant and college students joined local residents in opposing the government plan (*Choun Ilbo*, 9 November 1990). The situation grew worse. Throughout the protests, people not only called for transparency and for more democratic procedures in site selection, but also requested the government to reconsider its nuclear energy programme. Finally, the Roh Tae-woo government made a formal announcement that it was to scrap the plan and minister of science and technology who was in charge of the project was dismissed. Local residents and NGOs had won; the government lost the battle.

Obviously, this incident epitomized a newly emerging 'not-in-my-backyard (NIMBY)' syndrome. Nonetheless, it offered a new momentum in the history of environmental movements in South Korea. The triumph of local residents and NGOs over the Korean government critically undermined its ability to govern, producing bandwagon effects on other pending issues. Moreover, it was the first time preventive and proactive action had been taken. Most importantly, the success in Anmyeon Island strengthened organic ties between environmental NGOs and local residents. The Korean government, which was known for its strength and autonomy, fell prey to newly emerging environment movements and the collective egoism arising from locality.[8]

The incident of the Nakdong River phenol emission also presents a changing social and political ambience during this period. In March 1991, residents in Daegu city, the third largest city in Korea, encountered a distasteful smell from tap water. Water supply authorities traced the origin of the smell. It resulted from the synergy of chloroform and phenol. Chloroform was routinely used in purifying tap water; the problem, however, was phenol. It was discovered that the Doosan Electronic Company released over 30 tons of phenol liquid into the Nakdong River without purification. The phenol release victimized residents, farmers and fishermen along the Nakdong River, and the entire nation was outraged. Environmental NGOs and consumer groups instantly organized a Doosan phenol incident investigation team and staged a nation-wide boycott of products from the Doosan Group, which ranged from beer, milk and ginseng tea to electronic goods. Group sales were cut almost by a half in less than a month (*ChosunIlbo* 26 March 1991). Mounting public outrage encouraged both the Doosan Group and the government to come up with remedial measures. While the Doosan Group pledged to contribute 20 billion won as a fund for cleaning up the environment, along with an official apology from its chairman, the government also announced a comprehensive policy package to ensure clean water. The organizational power of environment NGOs and public response shown during the phenol incident was an eloquent witness to the changing face of the environmental movements in South Korea. Indeed, the phenol incident was a watershed in the history of environmental politics in South Korea, not only because of its magnitude, but also because of its educational impact on environmental hazards.[9]

The fourth stage (since 1992) can be characterized as the period of maturation. Since the Rio Earth Summit in 1992, environmental NGOs have proliferated. And they began to form national alliances by creating organizational networks between those NGOs in Seoul and local areas. Even more interesting is the formation of international alliances (Bramble and Porter, 1992, p. 314). While domestic environmental NGOs began to extend their interests in the global environmental agenda by going beyond national boundaries, international environmental NGOs also became interested in working with Korean counterparts. Along with this, the operational mode of South Korean NGOs has undergone structural changes; it has moved from protest and opposition to policy consultation with the government. This proactive change was closely tied to the increasing policy competence of NGOs and their shifting emphasis from damage control and compensation to preventive policy measures. South Korea's environmental politics has gradually evolved from the politics of confrontation to that of compromise through the exchange of ideas and knowledge, revealing a maturity comparable to advanced industrialized countries.[10]

As shown in Table 4.3, a recent movement against the construction of a multipurpose dam in the Dong River presents a hallmark of environmental politics. Seoul metropolitan city, with a population of more than 12 million, has suffered from a chronic fresh water shortage. As a way of resolving the water shortage as well as managing flood problems, in 1996, the Ministry of Construction and Transportation and the Korea Water Resources Corporation decided to construct a multipurpose dam in the Dong River. Its planned completion date was 2001. But the plan had problems from the beginning since it failed to satisfy the environmental impact assessments required by the Ministry of Environment (MOE). A coalition of environmental NGOs, various civic groups, and local residents formed National Citizens' Solidarity to Preserve the Dong River, and unfolded a nation-wide campaign to boycott the government plan for reasons of natural conservation. The mass media sided with the citizen movement, and the general public were also critical of the government plan. In addition, on 20 April 1999, international environmental NGOs such as Green Peace, the Sierra Club, Friends of the Earth, and the World Watch Institute issued a special resolution supporting the national campaign, 'Save the Dong River'.[11] The Kim Dae-jung government faced a serious dilemma between resolving the fresh water problem and protecting the properties of Seoul residents from flooding on the one hand and saving the Dong River on the other (*Chosun Ilbo*, 8 April 1999). Extensive public debates took place between government officials and NGO representatives. NGOs also sent their own technical expert teams to make impact assessments. After going through the process, president Kim Dae-jung announced the cancellation of the plan. Civil society had won over the government without even engaging in any violent demonstrations. Public opinion, knowledge, information and international pressure were all involved in making this happen.

In view of the above, democratic changes have brought about profound changes in South Korea's environmental politics. Vertical decision and command, exclusion of the popular sector, and unilateral imposition of government policies, which were defining characteristics of the developmentalist state, are no longer possible. A logic of persuasion, with knowledge and information, winning public minds, and mobilization of domestic and international pressures have emerged as new determinants of environmental politics in South Korea. Indeed, democratization has fostered the demise of the developmental coalition, while enhancing the power and influence of environmental NGOs.

Paradoxes of globalization and environmental politics in South Korea

Insomuch as democratization has influenced the dynamics of environmental politics, globalization has also affected its nature and direction. Globalization has several meanings (Prakash and Hart, 2000; S. Kim, 2000; Moon, 2000a, 2000b), but it can be operationalized in terms of three types. The first type is spontaneous globalization; this refers to a growing interdependence evolved through expanding market networks and revolution in transportation and communication. It is a kind of natural evolutionary dynamics resulting from progress in human history. The second type is governed globalization which denotes international efforts to foster or regulate the process of spontaneous globalization through multilateral coordination and cooperation. Governed globalization usually entails international regulatory regimes. The third and last type is managerial globalization which can be defined in terms of the government's conscious efforts to cope with opportunities and constraints emanating from the first two types of globalization. In other words, managerial globalization can be seen as state's strategic responses to external stimuli.

With regard to the environment, these three types of globalization produce a structure of paradoxes. While spontaneous globalization compels countries to loosen environmental regulations in order to attract more foreign capital so that they can enhance international competitiveness (Porter, 1999, p. 136)[12], governed globalization urges countries to comply with a set of norms, principles and rules regarding environmental regulations. State authorities have mandates to balance the two. Such balancing acts are usually shaped by the dynamic interplay of international and domestic forces. In the case of the environment, transnational alliances factor in too; while developmentalist coalitions comprised of national and international capital push for lowered environmental regulations in favour of creating pollutant havens, domestic and transnational environmental NGOs as well as international organizations become counter-balancing forces. In many cases, state choice of environmental policy is by and large a reflection of this coalitional politics.

South Korea is not an exception to this general observation. It went through a severe economic crisis in 1997, which was very much a product of spontaneous globalization (Moon, 2000a; Moon and Mo, forthcoming). In the process of overcoming the financial crisis, the South Korean government as well as firms were forced to compromise some of the environmental regulations. As a matter of fact, since the crisis, government spending on environmental improvement has decreased. The relative share of the Ministry of Environment (MOE) budget in total government expenditure declined from 1.51 per cent in 1997 to 1.3 per cent in 1998 and 1.36 per cent in 1999 (Kim, 2000; *Environment White Paper* 1998, 1999). Although the reduction has been minimal, the trend seems problematic. It is so precisely because both President Kim Dae-jung and his predecessor Kim Young-sam pledged to pay utmost policy attention to environmental issues during presidential election campaigns. Their pledges have not been honoured.

The private sector has been particularly vocal about loosening of environmental regulations. Immediately after the economic crisis, the Federation of Korean Industries, the umbrella organization representing the interests of big business, called for relaxation of rigid environmental regulations in order to correct economic structure based on high cost and low efficiency (*Donga Ilbo* 25 November 1997). MOE has responded favourably to the demands of the private sector by pledging to remove 193 regulations (30 per cent of total regulations) and to loosen 185 regulations (28.8 per cent). The MOE decision was motivated by the mandate of promoting economic recovery through the relaxation of environmental regulations (*Hangyerai Shinmun*, 15 December 1998). The primacy of economic recovery over environmental preservation is also well reflected in the investment behaviour of private firms. In 1996, a year before the economic crisis, 30 top leading manufacturing firms in the areas of petrochemicals, steel, cement, pharmaceuticals, electronics, computers, automobiles and telecommunications invested 1.66 trillion won in environmental facilities. But in 1998, they invested only 424 billion won in environment-related facilities, which accounted for only 25 per cent of the 1996 figure (Kim Takyun, 2000).

Likewise, economic disaster triggered by spontaneous globalization has compromised democratic and even global mandates of environmental protection to a great extent. Governed globalization, however, has emerged as the primary deterrent to this trend. The first source of international pressure is the World Trade Organization (WTO). Since the Stockholm declaration on the Human Environment in 1972, the GATT and later WTO began to pay attention to relationships between trade and environment. But it was only in the 1990s that serious work was initiated. In particular, the Rio Summit in 1992 played an instrumental part in the establishment of the Committee on Trade and Environment (CTE) within WTO, an institution which is designed to harmonize trade liberalization and environmental conservation. In

December 1996, the WTO ministerial meeting which was held in Singapore began to deliberate on ten major agenda items (see Appendix on p. 00); it failed, however, to produce major agreements. Depending on the issue areas, WTO members took conflicting positions. The third WTO ministerial meeting held in Seattle in November 1999 also failed to produce a major consensus on the agenda partly due to protests by environmental NGOs and partly due to conflicting interests among its members. Since WTO/CTE failed to produce enforceable codes of conduct on harmony between trade liberalization and environmental conservation, South Korea has not so far encountered any visible pressures. However, once the so-called Green Round is eventually launched, and it represents an increasing pressure, then the South Korean government might have to initiate serious structural changes.

In the case of South Korea, the OECD became a more credible source of international pressures for environmental conservation and integrity. South Korea joined the OECD in 1996. In order to be eligible for OECD membership, South Korea had to comply with 171 rules, of which 71 are related to environmental conservation. OECD rules on the environment are quite comprehensive. They cover a broad range of environmental issues such as chemical materials, solid waste disposal, environmental policy, environmental impact statement, air quality and water quality. And OECD codes of conduct on the environment are composed of decisions which oblige its members to comply with environmental recommendations and declaration. Out of 65 codes, South Korea agreed to accept 53 codes upon admission to the OECD and accepted the remaining 12 codes with observation (*Earth Environment Information*, vol. 13, November 1996). In tandem with the admission to OECD, South Korea overhauled the environment-related legal system which incorporated the polluter pays principle, utilization of economic instruments in environmental policy, prohibition on environmental countervailing duties and export rebates, and implementation of environmental impact assessments. According to an OECD evaluation, South Korea still lags behind its standards in the areas of air quality, water quality, management of solid wastes disposal, and transportation. But OECD has become a major driving force of changes in environmental policies in South Korea (Ministry of Foreign Affairs, 'Report on Earth Environment Conference', April 1997).

The final source of international pressures is various kinds of multilateral environmental agreements (MEAs). South Korea has joined 49 out of 210 international conventions on the environment. They include the UN Framework Convention on Climate Change, the

Vienna Convention for the Protection of the Ozone Layer and the Montreal Protocol on Substances that Delete the Ozone Layer, the Convention on International Trade in Endangered Species of Wild Fauna and Flora (CITES), the Convention on Biological Diversity, the Basel Convention on the Control of Transboundary Movements of Hazardous Wastes and Their Disposal, and the Convention on the Prevention of Marine Pollution by Dumping of Wastes and Other Matter (*Environment White Paper*, 1999, p. 581). These MEAs have influenced the South Korean government to enhance its environmental standards in one way or another. Of course, many of these conventions are rather weak in terms of enforcement. Recommendations rather than obligations characterize the governance structure of these conventions. Nevertheless, they have been effective in altering South Korea's compliance behaviour.

What has been problematic for South Korea is its changing status in the international economy. With the admission to OECD, South Korea can no longer enjoy the status of a developing country; as a developed country, therefore, it is expected to meet much higher environmental standards. For example, in accordance to the Kyoto declaration, 38 advanced industrial countries have agreed to reduce the emission of greenhouse gases by an average of 5.2 per cent during 2008–12 by using 1990 as the benchmark year. South Korea, as an OECD member, is also obliged to comply with this. However, meeting such a standard could be extremely expensive. If South Korea has to freeze emissions of greenhouse gases at the level of 1995, its economic losses are estimated as increasing from 1.3 per cent of GDP (about 15 trillion won) in 2020 to 3.6 per cent of GDP (about 62 trillion) in 2030 (Hong, 2000, http://www.mofat.go.kr/main/top.html). Being aware of such high costs, South Korea has been reluctant to comply with the decision. Apart from the case of greenhouse gases, South Korea ratified the Vienna convention and the Montreal protocol on the ozone layer in May 1992; this identified 95 types of substance, including CFCs and halon, that deplete the ozone layer and obligated South Korea to make a gradual reduction of their production and consumption. By 2040, South Korea is expected to make a complete ban on both production and consumption of these materials. Such regulations are also likely to constrain its economic activities.

In sum, globalization has brought about mixed impacts on development and environment in South Korea. While elements of spontaneous globalization have favoured development and international competitiveness, a set of norms, principles and rules defined by governed globalization have fostered the adoption of global environmental standards. The South Korean government has so far been sandwiched between the two. Although it has accommodated a large number of international conventions, their enforcement has by and large lagged behind because of the institutional and intellectual inertia that has been fallen it as a developing country. Unless the mismatch of domain between development and the environment is structurally resolved, South Korea is likely to go through an erratic period of policy behaviour in terms of enforcing global environmental standards.

Conclusion

In view of the above discussion, South Korea has undergone a dramatic change in the area of environmental politics. Defying the previous dominance of the developmentalist coalition, democratic opening and consolidation has not only expanded civil society, but also proliferated environmental NGOs. NGOs have in turn become the most significant political actor in terms of size, resources, expertise and political activism. Meanwhile, globalization has resulted in a paradoxical outcome where forces of both developmentalist and conservationist coalitions are complicatedly intertwined. The future terrain of environmental politics in South Korea is dependent on how the state can weave through these paradoxes and underlying dynamics of coalitional politics. In our opinion, however, resurgence of the developmentalist ethos is temporal, being associated with the acute economic crisis in 1997. As South Korea normalizes its economic scene, alliance between domestic and international NGOs, both of which are being inspired and supported by new emerging global environmental regimes, is likely to prevail over the developmental one in shaping environmental politics in South Korea.

This is a positive development. But several *caveats* are in order. First, South Korea is still in the twilight zone of two competing dominant social paradigms, the developmental versus the conservationist one. Its environmental politics might encounter difficulties unless it realigns the dominant social paradigm. The spread of post-materialist values has been confined mostly to intellectuals. New efforts should be made to spread the messages of post-materialist values to a wider segment of Korean society. Second, environmental NGOs in South Korea need to restructure and refocus their goals, strategies and tactics, action programmes, and organizational structure. Despite their remarkable contribution in the past, they have often been criticized for being organizations which engage in 'civil movements without grassroots'.[13] And they have also occasionally been accused of being detached from reality by becoming too militant and politicized rather than serving as reservoirs of policy ideas and alternatives. Their restructuring should be framed around inducing more grassroot involvement and generating more innovative policy ideas. Third, South Korean NGOs should be more active in forming alliances with transnational NGOs. Events-oriented alliances aimed at generating short-term demonstration effects cannot produce long-lasting impacts on environmental policy and politics. Emphasis should be given to exchanges of ideas and information on policy, organization and education. Finally, the Korean state should overcome the bureaucratic inertia anchored in the developmentalist template. It should be proactive rather than reactive in enforcing international environmental conventions. Otherwise real changes in environment policy cannot be anticipated.

Appendix. 4.1   Committee on Trade and Environment (CTE) Agenda

	Items	*Main issues*
Agenda 1	Trade rules, environmental agreements and disputes	The relationship between the rules of the multilateral trading system and the trade measures contained in multilateral environmental agreements (MEAs), and between their dispute settlement mechanisms
Agenda 2	Environmental protection and the trading system	The relationship between environmental policies relevant to trade and environmental measures with significant trade effects and the provisions of the multilateral trading system
		Trade-related environmental policies: subsidies
		The environmental review of trade agreements
Agenda 3	How taxes and other environmental requirements fit in	The relationship between the provisions of the multilateral trading system and: (a) charges and taxes for environmental purposes; and (b) requirements for environmental purposes relating to products, such as standards and technical regulations, packaging, labelling and recycling requirements.
Agenda 4	Transparency of environmental trade actions	The provisions of the multilateral trading system with respect to the transparency of trade measures used for environmental purposes
Agenda 5	The relationship between the rules of the multilateral trading system and the trade measures	The relationship between the rules of the multilateral trading system and the trade measures contained in multilateral environmental agreements (MEAs), and between their dispute settlement mechanisms
Agenda 6	Environment and trade liberalization	The effect of environmental measures on market access, especially in relation to developing countries, in particular to the least developed among them, and the environmental benefits of removing trade restrictions and distortions

Appendix. 4.1   Committee on Trade and Environment (CTE) Agenda   *contd.*

	Items	*Main issues*
Agenda 7	Domestically prohibited goods	The issue of exports of domestically prohibited goods (DPGs), in particular hazardous waste
Agenda 8	Intellectual property	The relevant provisions of the Agreement on Trade-Related Aspects of Intellectual Property Rights (TRIPS)
Agenda 9	Services	The work programme envisaged in the Decision on Trade in Services and the Environment
Agenda 10	The WTO and other organizations	Input to the relevant bodies in respect of appropriate arrangements for relations with intergovernmental and non-governmental organizations (NGOs)

Source: http://www.wto.org/english/tratop_e/envir_e/cte00_e.htm.

Notes

1. The Carbon Dioxide Information Analysis Center has estimated the emission rate in 1996 to be 9 metric tons per capita.
2. Statistical data are used here from the summary of OECD Environmental Indicators in 1998 provided by the Ministry of Environment in Korea (http://www.me.go.kr/html/98oecd.html).
3. See Lee MW (1990), Cotton (1989) and Lee SH (1993).
4. On new social issues, see Ports and Diani (1999) and Scott (1990, p. 19).
5. See Goo (247) and Gang (1997, p. 450).
6. See Yoon (1999) and Heo (1997) for details on the evolution of the Ministry of Environment from the powerless pollution section under the Ministry of Health and Society in 1967 to a powerful enforcement agency.
7. See Goo (264–5) and Gang (1997, p. 451).
8. There were many instances of NIMBY phenomena. They include Goonsan Dongyang's Chemical TDI Corporation in 1989; Boosan industrial waste landfill, Oosan, Yeongduk and Anmyeon Isalnd nuclear waste disposal facility in 1990; and Kimpo solid waste disposal facility in 1991 (Jung, 1994).
9. According to a survey by the Green Korea Uniteds (one of the most activist environmental NGOs in Korea), the Nakdong River phenol incident was ranked as the most serious environmental hazard in South Korea (www.greenkorea.org/news/release/0907.htm).
10. See Goo (1996) and Son (1996).
11. http://www.kfem.or/krem/donggang/course.htm
12. There is a contrasting view about pollutant havens. Pollution haven phenomena have not been found worldwide (Adams, 1997; Jones, 1997; UNCTD, 1999). Mani and Wheeler (1998: 244). A reading of this literature explains why: '(1) consumption/production ratios for dirty-sector products in the developing world have remained close to unity throughout the period; most of the dirty-sector development story is strictly domestic; (2) a significant part of the increase in dirty-sector production share in the developing regions seems due to a highly income-elastic demand for basic industrial products. With continued income growth, this elasticity probably has declined; (3) some portion of the international adjustment probably has been due to the energy price shock and the persistence of energy subsidies in many developing countries. These subsidies have been on the wane for a decade; (4) environmental regulation increases continuously with income and seems to have played a role in the shift from dirty to cleaner sectors'.
13. See Kim and Kim (1999).

5
Industry Interests, Institutional Inertia and Activism. Late Liberalization and the Environment in India

V.K. Natraj

Introduction

India's economic reforms have been in the news since the country formally adopted a Globalization-Liberalization (G-L) model in 1991. The formal ushering in of G-L followed the return to power of the federal government (centre) of the Congress party which was in opposition for just under two years. The general elections of 1996, when the Congress party lost, also put the reforms on the front pages with some expectation that the new government would cause a change in the economic scenario. As will be seen from our discussion, such expectations were soon belied. Indeed, it is arguable that they were hardly ever realistic in the first place.

This chapter examines the manner in which India has coped with the effects of the reforms. In particular it addresses itself to the following questions:

1. which are the factors responsible for the formal adoption of the reforms?
2. to what degree did exogenous forces compel the reforms on India?
3. do the reforms signify the end of the earlier framework which is often described as dirigiste?
4. has the opening up of the economy meant the subordination of policy to external forces such as the influence of IMF and the World Bank and those emanating from the emerging international order?

These objectives can be answered through an analysis at two related levels. At one level the factors within the country – 'internal' as it were – which exercise an important influence on policy require examination. This includes tracing the evolution of the G-L model since this chapter argues that it is not as cataclysmic an event as is normally supposed, although its contribution to a comprehensive restructuring of the economy is not denied. Secondly, the analysis necessarily has to dovetail the abovementioned objectives into developments at the global level – the 'external' actors. The focus of the discussion is on the interplay between these two sets of forces. The basic argument is that the G-L model is largely explicable in terms of the internal forces. The external ones do exercise an influence but, most importantly, they are available as a camouflage, a 'soft option' which enables policy-makers to evade difficult political choices.

The agents of change

Among the *dramatis personae* who have contributed to the present state of policy the following are identified as principal:

1. the Indian political system and the role of the state, particularly in relation to development;
2. increasing importance of the environmental movement and the emergence of alternative development paradigms (ADPs);
3. growth of Non-Governmental Organizations (NGOs);
4. an activist judiciary;
5. changes in the political milieu and union -state relations;
6. the role of the capitalist class and qualitative changes in its conduct;
7. global influences mainly but not confined to the Fund-Bank prescriptions.

A few additional observations have to be made. In regard to the role of the state, discussion extends to issues such as decentralization, participation and transparency, all of which are part of the good governance agenda.

Secondly, one observes congruence in many of the factors listed above, even though this may often be unintended. Thirdly, the impact of the global influences leads to an examination of the interface between the internal and external forces which have caused India to adopt the G-L model.

The Indian political system has shown a great deal of resilience in coping with crises and by the standards of developing countries has an impressive record. At the same time it has experienced major qualitative changes in the recent past. An important dimension of this relates to the changing equation between the federal centre and the states. Discernible change has taken place in the locus of power which has steadily shifted towards the states. In part this is the result of the virtual disappearance of one-party 'strong' governments at the centre. Predictably, this has caused state-level and regional parties to become relatively stronger. The beginning of the era of coalitional politics at the centre also implies a greater level of bipartisanship between the centre and the states. The second change germane to this chapter concerns the dismantling of controls which started to occur from the mid-1990s. This was accompanied by an admission from the ruling parties themselves that perhaps the state was ill-equipped to manage business enterprises and this scepticism extended even to the welfare sector. The similarity between this and the general disenchantment with the state is too obvious to require elaboration. In addition, there is the quality of leadership; in many instances leadership has passed into the hands of those who can boast underworld links and other unenviable credentials.

The elections held since 1996 offer abundant evidence of the centrifugal movement alluded to above. At the risk of some exaggeration, it is arguable that a steady blurring of the distinction between 'national' and 'regional' parties is taking place. It also looks as if this trend is there to stay in the foreseeable future. This has obvious implications for union-state relations and equally apparently for carrying out the economic reforms which are the immediate concern of this chapter.

Legitimacy of the state

The legitimate economic concerns of the state are a live issue owing to two main factors. One is the disaffection, indeed disenchantment, with politics and governance in general. This is a near-universal phenomenon and has struck sympathetic chords in India (das Gupta, 1997). The very institution of the state has contributed to its discredit through corruption and inefficiency. Secondly, even the initial moves towards a more liberalized (at least less controlled) economy had led predictably to the argument that the state ought to step aside from those activities which it was not equipped to perform. Managing industrial enterprises is one such example. The argument rapidly became extended to include even social services. Both Rajiv Gandhi and Narasimha Rao have expressed dissatisfaction with the managerial performance of government. These negative perceptions of government, combined with other developments, only served to strengthen them.

One of the winds of liberal change which started a global flow concerned the dilution of the state's role. As may be expected the Bretton

Woods Institutions spearheaded market orientation. Lending a helping hand, was the collapse of the world's first command economy in the Soviet Union which obliterated itself as a political entity. No single event shook the raison d'être for a planned economy as convulsively as this one. Coupled with the growing evidence against a powerful state there emerged, as Manor puts it, an uneasy vague feeling everywhere that centralized governance had failed (Manor, 1995).

It is no accident that this period also saw in India a strengthening of the resistance against a dirigiste regime and the revival of the movement in favour of decentralization through institutions of local government (in India, the Panchayat Raj Institutions). Both trends have been strongly articulated since the 1980s, a period which witnessed the birth of Rajiv Gandhi's New Economic Policy.

The environment and ADPs

Dissatisfaction with centralized governance and the consequent plea for a decentralized form found a kindred soul in those who questioned the legitimacy of the conventional model of development. And the latter was generally identified with three visible symbols: (1) state-initiation and sponsorship (often accompanied also by management); (2) mega-scale projects; and (3) the primacy of science and technology. The mega scale project, like the state with which it was made synonymous, presented evidence against itself through an effective combination of delays, escalating costs and work of poor quality. The anti-mega scale coalesced, almost by serendipity, with the environmental movement. In turn this coalesced with the criticism that the prevalent development model entailed high human costs such as translocation of entire populations away from their accustomed habitat. Major movements against the mega scale in India are seen in the opposition to the Narmada Sagar-Sardar Sarovar project (Madhya Pradesh and Gujarat), Tehri (Uttar Pradesh) and the earlier ones mobilizing the local population (especially women) against indiscriminate tree felling (Chipko in the Himalayas and Appiko in Karnataka).

Industrialization and large projects have a shared identity with technocentrism. The last decade has been marked by a rigorous questioning of the claims of science and technology to a hegemonic status (Salomon *et al.*, 1994; Nandy, 1980; Alvares, 1979). The perceived indifference of a technocentric model of development to its human costs has led its critics to argue for the 'small' and the 'local' and in so doing they combine, possibly without design, with decentralizers. Environmentalists too join the group. Persuaded as they are that it is the unbridled pursuit of economic growth that leads to environmental decay, they urge a more benign approach to development which is responsive to human (and local) sensitivity and need. Not all the protagonists of such an approach are conscious that 'in the absence of an ethical imperative, environmentalism has been reduced to a technological fix' and 'solutions are seen to lie once more in the hands of manager technocrats'. And 'the environmentalist label and the sustainability slogan have become deceptive jargons that are used as convenient cover for conducting business as usual' (Kothari, 1990). Few perhaps would actually heed these sage words.

The congruence of environmentalists, decentralizers and critics of technological hegemony has found its most complete blending in Alternative Development Paradigms (ADPs). Although each group on its own might contest it, their convergence has added some weight to the dilution of the state's role. Also not to be forgotten is that in India decentralization derives philosophic inspiration from Gandhi in whose scheme an all-powerful state had little room. Indeed, it is arguable that at heart he was anarchist. Worth noting too is that in India the fortunes of decentralization have fluctuated inversely with the hegemony of science and technology (Mathew, 1994).

The confluences discussed above would be incomplete without a reference to NGOs which in Indian terminology are called the voluntary sector. There are several Indian NGOs with impeccable records but in the last decade there has occurred a proliferation of these organizations. Quite a few of them are not really imbued with the true spirit of volunteerism. Rather, in the words of a prominent figure in the voluntary sector, 'if poverty was big business in the 1980's volunteerism is big business in the 1990's with every non-gazetted officer (ngo) starting an NGO' (Roy, 1996).

The fusion (a) of the absence of an ethical imperative in the sphere of environmentalism; and (b) of the spirit of volunteerism in the nongovernmental sector have caused scepticism to surface regarding both these movements. Environmental activism has more often than not culminated in Alternative Design Paradigms (ADPs). While serving a useful purpose by exposing the unconcern of existing paradigms (at times at least), for the dispossessed, ADPs attract the criticism, quite a legitimate one, that they do not focus on viable alternatives. They frequently present a utopian appearance and look at the environment-development nexus in a dichotomous and even antithetical perspective (Balasubramaniam, 1998).

NGOs for their part are criticised on two grounds. One is the archetypal left-wing critique which sees in NGOs a trojan horse. This view regards them as 'agents of imperialist and neo-colonial interests'. This is a sweeping criticism which virtually dismisses the need for further more detailed inquiry. The second line of criticism is more selective. The argument advanced here is that NGOs are sometimes set up by foreign companies who have lost out to competitors in a bid to enter the Indian market. For instance, if a company from country A loses to another from country B it funds a local NGO to launch a protest and in the present context the chosen platform is environmental safety. Such suspicions are hard to substantiate but at the same time they cannot be summarily rejected. It is not unlikely that some NGOs might unwittingly become instruments of insidious exploitation. A further problem for NGOs is that they are getting slowly 'corporatized'; going to work for NGOs is becoming a career (Roy, op. cit; see also *Sunday*, 1997).

One final point needs to be made about the voluntary sector. NGOs, in particular the newer ones which are springing up, appear to hold considerable attraction for a section of young people. Imbued with some idealism, disillusioned with politics, governance and political parties, emotionally critical of the conventional development ethos and not kindly disposed towards authority, this group of young people finds itself in a quandary. It does not have the willingness to take on the system as a whole; that requires enormous sacrifices which are beyond the capacity of most. Nevertheless, it is unwilling to see itself as a partner in a corrupt system. NGOs of the newer genre offer an attractive option. They enable young people to express their frustration without the compulsions of either rigid party discipline or the need to opt out of the system altogether.

It is at the very least possible, therefore, that the young people referred to above are being co-opted into a global network, although it is admittedly a different one from what the G-L model represents. One paradoxical inference which follows from this is that 'globalization through co-option' consists not only of groups who willingly embrace G-L but also of those who are sucked into it even while they tend to disapprove of the model. In a sense this offers some evidence of the internal-external interplay alluded to above.

Judicial activism

In the last two decades the judiciary has become a major player in the socio-political arena. Initially, its expansionist and to some extent conscience keeper role was confined to questions which were not overtly political. In addition, in the main, the judiciary refrained from policy pronouncements. In the 1990s it has become less inhibited. In India, one of its latest incursions has been into the wholly political issue of who should be regarded as the Chief Minister of Uttar Pradesh when two rivals simultaneously claimed the top post.

Judicial activism as such is not a new or sudden development. From the beginning of the 1980s there has been a liberalizing in the judiciary in terms of relaxing the rigidity of rules and procedure. In particular, Public Interest Litigation (PIL) has come into focus. The principle in PIL is that a person acting on behalf of the people and not as a private party has a right to be heard. It is not necessary for the person to prove what in legal terms is called *locus standi*. In addition, PIL requires that the petitioner should have no private interest in the cause he pleads. Further, PIL is premised on the proposition that public spirited individuals render a service by taking up causes of a public nature. Judicial readiness to recognize that 'procedure is the handmaid of justice' (AIR, 1982) meant an extension of the sweep of courts. In a number of cases such as AIR 1980, 1991 and 1982 (op. cit.), courts have demonstrated a willingness to come out in favour of intervening to set right public wrongs. In the process, governments, city corporations and several quasi-governmental authorities have been pulled up not only for illegal acts but non-performance and for unjustified profligacy.

Over a period of time this widening has begun to accommodate grievances which would once have been regarded as lying outside the pale of judicial intervention. For our purposes, though, what stands out is the spate of cases where the attention is on the environment. Both the Enron power project in Maharashtra and the Cogentrix project in coastal Karnataka are the subject of PIL (of these, more later). Another example relates to the ban imposed by the Supreme Court of India on shrimp farming within a specified area from the coast. All these instances have a direct bearing on the conduct of commercial and industrial activity. Many of them are responses to the G-L model.

The extension of judicial frontiers can be explained as a global trend in the direction of more transparent governance. While this may largely explain judicial activism of the kind witnessed in the decade of the 1980s in India, it falls short when applied to the contemporary context. An additional and significant factor is that the judiciary is perceived as the one institution which is not corrupted by the prevailing ethos. It has come to be seen as the last bastion with which an exploitative political order can be resisted. Recourse to courts offers several advantages. It is a less exacting method of drawing attention to a potential harm from public policy than political action. A public agitation against, say, the Cogentrix power plant in Karnataka will require enormous organization and a movement which, to be successful, will have to be sustained over long periods of time. There is also the likelihood of opposition from other interested parties. In contrast, given the present inclinations of the judiciary, courts offer a simpler course. There are lawyers who, motivated as much by zeal for justice as by the chance to be in the limelight, often take up these briefs at a reasonable fee. Although courts are notorious for their ponderous slowness in disposing of cases, they are quick in issuing interim orders and this is often a principal objective in PIL. If an order can be obtained from the court, temporarily suspending an activity, the petitioner gains quite a lot at least by virtue of having focused public attention on it.

For the judiciary too this new phase of litigation offers an advantage. Courts in India are bedevilled by mounting arrears of work and are at the receiving end of strong criticism on this count. In this context, judicial activism does provide courts with an instrument to deflect attention from their in-house problems. But this activist phase carries within itself certain dangers. When the judiciary extends its sphere of action to monitoring the conduct of politicians who are accused of nepotism and corruption – the favoured phrase in India is 'tainted' – and sets itself up as a unit of surveillance, the wrath of politicians is aroused. There have been more than muted arguments that the judiciary cannot become a 'super-executive' body. Secondly, PIL, when carried to excess, invites its own doom. The former Chief Justice of India, J.S. Verma, has warned that courts ought to take a more careful look at PIL and prevent it from being abused (*Times of India*, 30 April 1997).

It is arguable that in a qualified sense the judiciary is becoming an extension of civil society. Judicial activism is being vigorously used by the following groups:

- those genuinely interested in promoting public welfare;
- NGOs;
- environmental movements.

Globalization-Liberalization (G-L): its antecedents

G-L, as adopted in 1991, was not as sudden an event as is sometimes believed. Many scholars agree that its antecedents date back farther than 1991 (Kabra, 1996; Patnaik and Chandrashekar, 1995; Das 1994; Ghosh, 1994; Natraj, 1995). With respect to the commanding role of the state, ambivalence was evident even in the historically halcyon days of planning (Hanson, 1965). Analysing more recent history, Kabra

(1996) remarks: 'As is the wont, Indian plans rarely take any categorical stand and always interlace their positions with caveats and qualifications, there are some muted references to "our basic policies" which "have stood us in very good stead" but nonetheless in this turbulent world our policies must also deal with changing realities.'

Notwithstanding declarations of commitment to a mixed economy, a socialist pattern of society and control over the commanding heights of the economy, planning in India has been subjected to a lessening of political support – once its great strength since it never reduced planning to a mere technical exercise. The mid-1960s witnessed the ushering in of the Green Revolution. While its achievements speak for themselves and the strategy was compelled by endemic crises on the food front, it was selective and wholly technocentric and was not complemented by much-needed institutional reform (Dantwala, 1970, 1992) This overt endorsement of technocentrism not only pushed to the background agrarian reforms but also local government and participatory governance (Mathew, op. cit). It is arguable that technocentrism, when unaccompanied by institutional reforms, to an extent 'depoliticizes' planning and 'dilutes' the state. Another major development of the 1960s was the first massive devaluation of the Indian rupee. It failed, though, to promote exports, its principal objective, and led to recession.

The 1970s saw some prudent fiscal management which helped the country weather the 1973 oil price shock. But the government had to contend with the consequences of recession expressed through strikes and a mobilization against the state which culminated in the Emergency of 1975 and which led to the first ever defeat of Congress in 1977. But the successor Janata government was short-lived and Indira Gandhi swept the party back to power in 1980.

From this period onwards two major developments began to emerge. One was the emergence of a truly consumerist class in India. Juxtaposed with this is the 'narrow segment into whose hands additional purchasing power accrues' and 'whose growing consumption therefore provides the main source of growth in demand for industrial consumer goods' (Patnaik and Chandrashekar, op. cit). It is here that India differs significantly from China, as will be discussed later, mainly due to higher income inequalities in the former (Ghosh, op. cit; Mitra, 1997). This consumerist class found the domestic economy incapable of satisfying its increasing appetite and desire for emulating metropolitan lifestyles. It took recourse to avenues such as clandestine imports and has been urging the dismantling of controls.

A second, not unrelated, development was rising deficits whose source unfortunately was not rising investment but a fall in public savings. Added to this was governmental reluctance to boost direct tax revenues. One result was a loan from the IMF in 1982, defended on the grounds that this was a better option than seeking commercial credit at higher tranches.

The Rajiv Gandhi government lent support, overt as well as implied, to the trends discussed above, and a pro-liberalization political coalition, dominated by reform-minded government technocrats, especially from the Ministry of Finance, led the way. The long-term fiscal policy of finance minister V.P. Singh, as well as the New Economic Policy enunciated in 1985, are the forerunners of G-L. The NEP not only sanctified the dismantling of controls but laid the foundations for diluting the state's role. It is to be noted, however, that the second quinquenium of the 1980's did register very high rates of growth in industry. Critics of G-L, some of whom are cited above, chose to gloss over the fact that the 8.8 per cent growth rate (1985–90) took place precisely when the precursors of G-L were being put in place.

Endogenous and exogenous forces in the crisis preceding G-L

The decades of the 1980s and 1990s were also characterized by spiralling deficits and balance of payments problems. Regionalization of Indian politics in the 1970s and 1980s made the federal government increasingly unable to mediate between conflicting interests and competing demands. Competition for votes led to increasingly populist policies and uncontrolled payments of side payments to attract voters, either in the form of subsidies which appeared as such on the budget or in the form of under-pricing of public services and goods. In addition, there was a proliferation of public lending to private companies as part of the patronage policies pursued by political and administrative elites. The political situation translated into growing fiscal deficits, financed by public borrowing.

Around 1990, these domestic problems were aggravated by changes outside domestic control. The Gulf War led to a large repatriation of Indians working in the Middle East and a significant reduction of remittances; in addition, India lost important export markets due to the breakup of the Soviet Union. The fiscal deficit now went along with increased balance-of-payment problems (Martinussen, 2001; Nayyar, 1998).

This period saw the confluences and congruences described in the beginning of this chapter. The anti-mega scale, pro-environment movement, gained in strength. So too did the privatization wave which in part was helped by the poor performance of some Public Sector Enterprises (PSEs). This was specially true of those which affect consumers directly, such as power supply. In addition, not even firm adherents of intervention could support the Indian regime of controls which essentially resulted in rent-seeking from government. Staunch critics of G-L have unequivocally declared that they do not advocate a return to controls or, in Indian parlance, 'licence permit raj' (*Deccan Herald*, 9 March 1995). Given the overall climate, the excellent record of some PSEs was forgotten, as was the fact that they labour under a stifling lack of autonomy and some face an acute demand shortage due to the opening up of the economy (Kurien, 1996; Ghosh, op. cit).

These developments meshed in with the arrival of another actor on the scene, namely, Non-Resident Indians (NRIs) anxious to secure a foothold in the Indian economy. The prevailing environment helped them secure connections to politicians as well as the top echelons of the bureaucracy. It is to be remarked that the growth strategy of the late 1980s emphasized the 'trickling down process'. Slowly, inevitably, the dilution of the state's role has resulted in disinvestment of PSEs. It is another matter that this has netted in far less than has been anticipated, as the finance minister, Yashwant Sinha, admitted in his 1998 interim budget (*Economic Times*, 27 March 1998).

These developments raise the question of whether certain parts of the G-L model have been truly implemented. Insofar as PSEs are concerned, they continue to be as fettered as ever. Autonomy for them was urged years ago by the Economic Administration Reforms Commission, yet their position has hardly changed (V.V. Bhatt, 1994).

It appears too that the entire package of conditionalities has not been complied with. The fiscal deficit is still high and clearly this is not consistent with the Fund-Bank advice. The inference this suggests is that where a particular set of conditionalities requires political toughness it is quietly buried. The acid test seems to be what the government considers 'politically feasible'. It has to be recognized that the adjustment of G-L/SAP is a continuous process, since the reform package is not implemented in a one-shot manner. And even if it is, the effects are likely to be spread over a period of time. In addition, they are likely to be determined by how gradually the package is put into practice (or otherwise) and on how 'costs' of adjustment are imparted and the willingness and capacity of the regime to cushion the most vulnerable. Above all, it is not possible to predict what exactly the effects of implementing G-L will be partly because of the influence of external factors. Nevertheless, the Indian authorities were able to promote a considerable, albeit selective, degree of liberalism. One possible reason for this 'success', was that liberalizing reform was a way to avoid much needed tougher structural reform. For instance, privatization policies along with new measures to encourage foreign direct investments and other external resources provided an alternative to mobilizing domestic resources through taxation (Bhaduri and Nayyar, 1996, p. 26).

G-L and foreign investment

G-L in India can be assessed by examining the country's record with respect to foreign direct investment (FDI) and the effort to invite firms from overseas to help improve infrastructure. The cases which are described below are expected to highlight the following features of G-L:

1. how far is the invitation to overseas firms, particularly in the field of power, a camouflage for 'political' inability to adopt and implement tough 'economic' decisions?
2. to what extent has the state shown itself to be responsive to the environmental aspects which are at the centre of protest apart, of course, from the argument against entry of foreign capital, MNCs?

The official defence of the 1991 reform package is that the economy had then reached a highly vulnerable point. Foreign exchange reserves were enough to cover only two weeks' imports – the reserves amounted to only Rs.2600 crores (each worth 10 million rupees). There were large outflows of NRI (Non-Resident Indian) deposits. The rate of inflation was rising. So was the fiscal deficit. 'It looked as if we might, for the first time in our history, default on our external payments obligations. Had this happened, the country's economic and financial system would have faced an unprecedented disruption, leading to widespread unemployment, loss of output and emergence of a higher inflationary spiral' (Singh, 1992, p. 282). The above quotation, from one of the reform's architects, Manmohan Singh, puts the picture in perspective. To add to the travails he has listed, we may add negative industrial growth and loss of credit rating. There are others who agree with Singh that the package was justified (Patel, 1992); some suggest it was inevitable.

As against this there is a line of thought which argues that the reforms were a product of a non-resilient political system (Patnaik and

Chandrashekhar, op. cit; Das, op. cit). Ghosh (op. cit) concedes that by 1990–91 some form of structural adjustment had become necessary but is not convinced that India's choice of policies is appropriate. Opponents of the reforms are especially vehement that opening up the economy to foreign capital was and is unnecessary.

Turning to the question of FDI and entry of foreign firms into India, there is the additional point to be made that, in contrast to China, India has not attracted spectacular FDI flows. In 1995, annual FDI flows into China (including Hong Kong) during 1994–98 amounted to between US$35 and 45 billion whereas the comparable figure for India was between 2 and 4 billion (UN, 2000). The most debated investment concerns the invitation to foreign companies to set up power projects in India. The justification for this, in official eyes, lies in endemic power shortages which in turn cripple industrial growth. It is further argued that foreign capital is required in view of the domestic financial problems. In addition, the losses constantly incurred by state electricity boards is used as an argument for privatization. That there are crippling power shortages is beyond dispute, as are the consequences for industrial growth. What is debatable is whether foreign firms are the answer. In what follows we focus on two power projects which have been in the eye of controversy right from their early days – Enron's Dabhol project in Maharashtra and the Cogentrix power project in Karnataka.

Two case studies

The government of India's policy on FDI was formulated in March 1992. As part of a package of incentives to attract foreign investment into power generation it announced a guaranteed 16 per cent rate of return on such investment. It may be pointed out that state electricity boards are expected, by law, to earn 3 per cent per annum but most of them fail this test. Government Officials visited both the UK and the USA to negotiate with companies willing to move into India. Public tendering was not adopted since it would prove to be time-consuming. It was in the process of negotiating that the idea of the counter-guarantee took shape. One of the US firms to evince interest in the Indian market was Enron.

The Enron Project

Between May and December 1992, Enron decided it would set up a project in Dabhol off the Konkan coast in Maharashtra. A memorandum of understanding was signed with the Maharashtra State Electricity Board (MSEB). By April 1993 the Foreign Investment Promotion Board (FIPB) cleared the Enron project in principle and the Dabhol Power Corporation was registered as a unit. The project was to be completed in two phases. The Power Purchase Agreement (PPA), critically important in such negotiations, was signed in December 1993. The details were not made public. What is known is that MSEB agreed to buy power at Rs.2.40 per Kw and also guaranteed a plant load factor of 90 per cent. Enron entered into agreements with Bechtel, a construction giant, and General Electric, which specializes in turbines, and sold some of its equity stake to them. In its anxiety to see the project through, the government waived norms which stipulate competitive bidding for purchases and construction. This 'liberalized' approach prompted the main opposition political parties to demand transparency. However, the government signed the guarantee by December 1994. The Union Ministry of Environment and Forests granted conditional clearance. Despite protests from local residents against the polluting effects they feared from the project, the union government signed the counter-guarantee.

Throughout 1994 there were various forms of protest against the project. Predictably, it was the environmentalists who were in the forefront. At the political level, opposition parties, namely the Bharatiya Janata Party (BJP) and the Shiv Sena (SS), alleged that Enron had bribed its way into the project. It is at this stage that the court became involved but the judgment held that, contrary to what the petitioner alleged, 'the Enron proposal was deliberated at length for two and a half years, draft agreements were prepared from time to time and it was ultimately the eighth or ninth draft which was finalised. Nothing was done secretly. There was total transparency at every stage of negotiations. There was nothing to show that anybody was favoured for any specific reasons' (*Business India*, 10 July 1995). This is a landmark since lack of transparency and corrupt tactics figure at the later stages as major components in the controversy.

Enron's troubles did not disappear; indeed, they started to mount. The March 1995, elections to the state assembly saw Congress lose power and a BJP-SS government brought in. The first is commonly identified as a right-of-centre Hindu party which also claims to be Swadeshi ('for India') in economic matters. The latter is not so much a political party as a group devoted to 'regionalize' Mumbai (Bombay) by making strident demands that non-Maharashtrians should be shown their place.

The BJP-SS combine had campaigned against Enron during the elections. It had promised a full-scale review of the project. It alleged that the Congress Chief Minister, Sharad Pawar, had received kickbacks. Soon after forming the government, the new Chief Minister, Manohar Joshi, ordered a review of Dabhol. And the review was to be done under the stewardship of the Deputy Chief Minister, Gopinath Munde. Finding itself in a muddle, not of its making though, Enron attempted to establish contact with the BJP but this did not help the cause. For its part, the BJP line was to stress that cancellation of Enron would send a message that India regards her economic sovereignty with pride. It is interesting that the Congress government at the centre viewed the state government's decision with disapproval. The New Delhi perspective was that cancelling would not serve the national interest. The then minister of energy, N.K.P. Salve, said: 'Enron is not simply another power project, the credibility of our reforms depend on it' (Bartels and Pavier, 1997). It was perceived as a test, the passing of which would 'ameliorate India's image as a viable investment location' (ibid.). India needed to demonstrate that the country was stable and its policies predictable. But the Enron story, as it unfolded, yielded more surprises. After speaking loudly and clearly about the less-than-transparent manner in which Dabhol was cleared, the BJP-SS government suddenly declared that it was not going to cancel the project and was open to renegotiation. Within the BJP-SS itself, there were serious divisions. Hard-liners urged cancellation; others preferred renegotiation.

The review committee, headed by the Deputy Chief Minister, a known and trenchant critic of Enron, recommended scrapping of the project. The grounds were:

1. Enron had inflated costs by at least 25 per cent;
2. DPC (the Dabhol Power Corporation) would prove more expensive than other fast-track projects;
3. the World Bank had reservations about the project;
4. the MSEB would lose heavily.

Scrapping the project would entail consequences such as:

1. in the absence of proven charges of corruption, the government would have to pay DPC compensation amounting to Rs.1000–1500 crores;
2. on the positive side, it would compel government to be more cautious in future and might induce other projects to reduce costs;

3. a possible negative consequence might be loss of foreign investor confidence in India.

For its part, DPC pursued two lines simultaneously. One was to declare that it would sue the government. At the same time, Enron stated it was open for renegotiation. The most curious reaction was that of the Congress party. The prime minister, Narasimha Rao, stated that the role of the union government was confined only to the counter-guarantee. He instructed his colleagues not to involve themselves in this controversy. The BJP was also experiencing division in its ranks. More importantly, it had differences with the Shiv Sena which favoured renegotiation. The left-wing parties were discomfited because the BJP had successfully hijacked their 'economic sovereignty' platform. The Janata Dal, certainly in Karnataka, expressed itself in favour of FDI.

In spite of the review going against Enron, the government did a *volte face* and announced a renegotiated settlement. Its highlights were:

1. the capital cost was reduced by $365 million;
2. both phase I and phase II were combined.

However, some of the most controversial and much discussed features were left untouched. One of these relates to the guaranteed offtake of 90 per cent which, it was earlier argued, would place a heavy burden on the MSEB. In the renegotiated settlement this stands unchanged; in fact, the burden might even rise in view of the increase in the project's capacity from 2015 to 2184 MW.

Judicial activism was also seen in this episode. Several legal challenges were made against the Enron deal. In one such, PIL, the Centre for Indian Trade Unions (CITU, which is Marxist-led) was the petitioner. The Bombay High Court, after expressing strong reservations about the government's handling of the project on virtually every count, nonetheless upheld the clearance given after renegotiation. Another significant legal event was the affidavit filed by the government. To begin with, the government itself stated that the previous government as well as Enron was open to charges of corruption and misrepresentation. Strangely, after the project was renegotiated, the very same government filed another affidavit practically withdrawing the allegations on the grounds that the earlier statement was based on newspaper reports. Then came the decision of the Supreme Court in a review petition filed by the CITU.

The court has held that the work on the project may continue but that it would monitor the conduct of government in relation to the project. Enron has now become the subject of US investigations.

Cogentrix

The second case relates to a power project of the Mangalore Power Corporation to be built by Cogentrix, a US-based 'unlimited liability' company. The plant is to generate 1000 MW of power at an esti-mated cost of Rs.4300 crores. This case differs from Enron in some respects. The project was first initiated and the MOU signed between the Congress government in Karnataka and Cogentrix as far back as 1992. The PPA was signed in 1994. Shortly after this, Congress was voted out of power and the Janata Dal formed the government in December 1994. However, unlike the situation in Maharashtra, the successor government in Karnataka not only did not repudiate the agreement but supported it to the hilt. Perhaps this is to be explained with reference to the fact that the Janata Dal (JD) has never expressed itself staunchly against Congress-inspired economic reforms. Deve Gowda, earlier chief minister of Karnataka and later the country's Prime Minister, has on several occasions affirmed the basic soundness of the Rao–Singh model. In addition, some of the 'ideological' compulsions influencing the BJP have been absent in the JD (Bartels and Pavier, op. cit). In this important sense, our two cases differ. A second noticeable difference is that while there is opposition to Cogentrix too it is based more on environmental grounds than on alleged 'kickbacks'.

Since the MOU was signed in 1992, the project has confronted one crisis after another. The environmental opposition is led by the popular movement Dakshina Kannada Parisarasakthara Okkuta which contends that Cogentrix will lead to imminent acid rain due to the estimated daily discharge of 70 tonnes of sulphur dioxide. In addition, it will result in the generation of fly-ash – 650 tonnes per day – and will use and discharge nearly 80 000 cubic metres of water from the Arabian Sea, required for its closed-cycle cooling process. At a more general level, the Okkuta point to the fact that the coastal districts of Karnataka, Uttara and Dakshina Kannada, have been the site of many projects aimed at accelerating industrialization, with serious repercus-sions for the environment. Part of their ire stems from the fact that most of these projects afford little employment to local people. The Okkuta has gained support from the fishing community which is apprehensive that the activities of Cogentrix will adversely affect marine life.

Despite enjoying the support of two successive governments belonging to rival political parties, Cogentrix had not had a smooth sail. Deve Gowda, often called Cogentrix's 'foster father', has continuously supported it and as prime minister ensured that it was cleared by the Union Ministry of Environment. It is this personal intervention which prompted the 'Green crusader', Maneka Gandhi, to allege that environmental safety was ignored, the reason being kickbacks for the prime minister. Strangely, over a month after Cogentrix had been cleared by the union government, the prime minister told parliament that clearance was not yet given. This led an angered opposition to move a motion of breach of privilege against Deve Gowda which the Speaker rejected. Deve Gowda was perceived as an all-out supporter of the project. This was true and as stated earlier he is a supporter of liberalization too. Yet when he was confronted with opposition he chose to soft pedal the issue with half-truths. Once again we see here the limits of transparency and the necessity for the state to take shelter under camouflage (see Jenkins, op. cit).

Sustained opposition by the project's critics has achieved some result. In January 1996, Cogentrix dropped an important clause which protected it from liability for the environmental damage. The Cogentrix case had yet more consequences. The Secretary to the Department of Environment in the Government of Karnataka, resigned. He made statements against the project basing his argument on environmental grounds. The government retaliated by suspending him and finally he resigned.

The judiciary is involved too. Maneka Gandhi filed a public interest petition before the Supreme Court. The court, speaking through Justices Kuldip Singh and Sagir Ahmed, directed the National Environmental Engineering Research Institute (NEERI) to assess the project's environmental impact. After inquiry, NEERI reported that the project violated the coastal zone regulations formulated in 1991 by the Ministry of Environment and Forests. The Institute also pointed out that the same ministry accorded conditional clearance to the project without considering all the information required. A further point made was that the 'no objection certificate' granted by the Pollution Control Board was conditional upon a public hearing which was to have taken place in August 1996 but in fact had not. In addition, no detailed plan was prepared for the families which the project would displace.

Based upon this report, the Supreme Court heard further arguments and referred the case to the Karnataka High Court. The latter heard the matter on a regular basis from 24 March 1997. A dramatic turn occurred in April 1997 when Maneka Gandhi's counsel petitioned that the case should be posted before a new bench of judges. The Chief Justice, however, declined to interfere. The petition was subsequently dismissed. However, a former minister has approached the Supreme Court seeking an enquiry into kickbacks, which he alleges Deve Gowda has received. The Court has asked the Central Bureau of Investigation to enquire into the matter.

Cogentrix erred in not taking the local people into their confidence from the initial stages. It depended, as did Enron, on the government's apparatus. Matters were made worse by a patronizing attitude and suggestions that Indians could be 'bought'. The Cogentrix Chief reportedly spoke disparagingly of the Dakshina Kannada district, arguing that he or his company had donated money to the Students' Union of the Mangalore University, located in the district (*Deccan Herald*, 2 May 1997 and 6 May 1997).

Of late there appears to have been a change among the leaders of the opposition to Cogentrix. In February 1997, young people from the area surrounding the location of the project met the officials of the Mangalore Power Corporation. They affirmed support for the project and branded the activists of the Okkuta as 'outsiders' whose protests emanated from less-than-laudable impersonal motives. This change may have occurred partly due to the efforts at public contact that Cogentrix has started practising. One spokesman from a nearby village stated: 'We are not against Cogentrix. We only want to get better facilities in our villages and are bargaining for it. The so called NGOs and environmentalists are outsiders and are using us in improving their "business"' (*Taranga*, 14 February 1997). The argument is also advanced that the local opposition to the project reflects the fight for land rights (Assadi, 1996).

Lessons from Enron and Cogentrix

What do these two cases, with their similarities and differences, show? At the outset, they illustrate how in a reasonably transparent system, public protest, irrespective of its motivating force, can effectively utilize the judiciary as an instrument in its crusade. If it achieves nothing more, it can certainly prolong the gestation period. Sometimes, as both Enron and Cogentrix demonstrate, the companies concerned yield a little. The case studies also bring out the differences between political parties. The BJP, having committed itself to opposing economic reforms and affirming national economic sovereignty, had little choice but to threaten cancellation of Enron. It might have done so to retain support of that class of the educated middle class which feels threatened by liberalization. At the same time, it was pulled in another direction by its partner in government as well as by realities on the ground. The picture in the Cogentrix case was always different since the Janata Dal has never opposed liberalization (Bommai, 1995).

These facts apart, quite aside from the fact that Enron itself is under investigation, both cases serve to highlight the changing nature of the relationship between the union and the states. The Congress government between 1991 and 1996 reveals a curious, even paradoxical, record. It started as a minority government but defying all expectations it ran its full term. It was responsible for initiating and sustaining the most far-reaching restructuring of the economy that the country has witnessed so far. Yet it was qualitatively different from preceding Congress governments because the states were constantly asserting themselves. A dominant centre started to diminish from the early 1990s. To an extent, the willing acceptance of reforms by the states is becoming a necessity. This is gathering reinforcement from the fact that coalition governments are appearing at the centre (Ashok Mitra, 1997).

Was SAP inevitable?

The question that engages scholarly as much as political attention is whether the form of structural adjustment adopted by India was inevitable. It cannot be answered in this chapter, at least not fully. But the two cases analysed above provide enough information to at least consider this question in part.

It was stated earlier that the shortage of power is beyond dispute. So are its effects. Let us start by posing the question whether there is no solution other than the input of foreign capital. In practically every state in India, power generation and distribution is a state monopoly. Most State Electricity Boards (SEBs) function under heavy losses. These characteristic losses are used to justify privatization and the opening up of the sector to foreign investors because resources are in short supply. How valid is this argument?

SEBs are expected to earn a minimum return of 3 per cent on their investments. This they are clearly unable to do. It is argued that this is because of the subsidies they are forced to give. They are not allowed to charge economic rates for the power they supply to the rural sector and to domestic consumers. One estimate given by Ghosh (1996), quoting from a Planning Commission publication (1995), is that in 1995–96 (all India), 'the effective subsidy on agricultural consumers alone was Rs.11,17 crore' (Ghosh, 1996). It is true that owners and operators of irrigation pumpsets (IP sets) enjoy free electric power in Karnataka. This can be regarded as an item of cross-subsidy. The estimate of this cross-subsidy is Rs.6666 million per annum (Reddy and Sumitra, 1997) but less well known is the fact that this 'loss' is more than compensated by surpluses from other sources such as users of high tension and low tension power (industry) and all-electric homes. Reddy and Sumitra (ibid.) argue that the supposed losses to the Karnataka Electricity Board from subsidising IP sets are used as a justification, first of the losses which the Board is known for, as well as for privatization. They agree that even though this particular subsidy is 'not mainly responsible for KEB's financial problems' it 'is no justification at all for continuing with this exorbitant subsidy' (ibid.). The answer to the riddle of losses lies partly in transmission and distribution losses, theft of power and uneconomic pricing.

The reasons for this state of affairs are not particularly complex. The subsidy to agriculture – to big farmers in fact – serves two purposes. One, it keeps the politician–big farmer nexus well lubricated. Secondly, losses arising from other causes, including inefficient management and improper tariffs, can be ascribed to the subsidy on IP sets. Governments are only too well aware that this subsidy is a 'holy cow' in India and there is in the foreseeable future no prospect of it being withdrawn.

The data given are from Karnataka but they are also likely to be true for large parts of the country. What concerns us though is the appalling reality that governments, unwilling to raise resources where they not only can but should, appear to be veering round to a soft option, namely, privatize and invite foreign investors. In terms of technology, power generation should pose few problems to a country which has a space programme and nuclear reactors, not to speak of a reasonable capital goods industry base. Opening up the sector to FDI can be justified only in terms of lack of domestic resources. But as the Karnataka analysis shows, and the all-India data confirm, there are ways in which losses can be reduced and resources raised. Ghosh (1996) tries to demonstrate that with rational pricing (including removal of subsidies where they are unnecessary), and if SEBs could earn the statutory 3 per cent return on their investments, they would be able to raise around Rs.15,000 crore annually. The estimate may be wide of the mark but it makes us confront a disconcerting possibility, namely, that the resort to privatization and invitation to foreign participation is a soft option. Ghosh (ibid.) draws attention to a feature of Enron which is rarely mentioned. It is, that the local construction cost of the project was to come from the Industrial Development Bank of India (IDBI) , in other words, from domestic savings.

The contribution of politics as practised, indeed that of the state as it functions, is in no small measure responsible for the present ambience in which both have become terms of dubious repute. The analysis presented above also invokes suspicion, not about the state *per se* as an institution or about politics as a process, but about both in a certain context. Is it possible to posit the view that the state in India finds it easier to open up, liberalize, and seek foreign capital, all the while being aware of the consequences of doing so, than to pursue policies which would strengthen the country's innate capabilities? In answering this point we should avoid doctrinaire extremes of glorifying the pre-1991 period or the recent reforms. It is beyond question that the pre-1991 economic management required massive change. On the other hand, the claims of government regarding the beneficial effects of the reforms are open to question. As shown above, FDI inflows have not been spectacular. Growth rates are not consistent but what can be said here is that there has been a spurt, especially in industry. With respect to trade, most noticeable is the increase in agricultural exports. Equally so is the not very fast or consistent growth in manufactured goods. The rate of savings is nowhere as high as China's. Yet it cannot be denied that there has been a surge forward. On the whole, SAP presents a mixed picture and its future in terms of liberalization cannot be forecast with any accuracy, given the multiparty coalition presently in power. In addition, coalition governments appear to be becoming a sustained phenomenon.

Trade and the environment

We turn now to the possible effects of trade liberalization, in particular on the environment. The opening up of the Indian economy has meant an increase in particular types of agricultural exports. For instance, shrimp farming spread widely, raising fears of a degraded environment. The thrust on marine exports in general led to traditional fisherfolk agitating against mechanized trawlers which began affecting their catch. In the first case, it is the Supreme Court which has, at least for the moment, clamped a ban on offshore shrimp farming. The Government of India considered legislation which would undo this judgment but the Communist Party of India, the Marxist CPM, reportedly objected to this. And since the CPM supported the ruling coalition, its views carried weight. There is a fear that the entry of foreign companies into agro-related business will intensify a shift of land away from food crops, and that among food crops, there may be a tendency for coarse grains, pulses and oilseeds to experience a decline with superior cereals such as wheat and barley gaining. It is argued that these trends will entail environmental consequences (Utsa Patnaik, 1996). But this is still in the realm of conjecture. What should be questioned is the effort of the government in relation to the environment.

Protecting the environment is high on government's professed agenda. It has shown itself responsive, at least in the face of popular movements when these have reached high levels of intensity. But it has not really proved responsive consistently. In fact, there appears to be a feeling that environmentalists succeed in impeding progress. For example, the Supreme Court's directive on shrimp farming provoked the government of Karnataka to state that it would seek a review of the decision. Both environmentalists and growth-proponents tend to see the environment and development in antithetical terms. Further, the imperatives in a developing economy are not always realized by environmentalists. In all this, what secures attention is the mega projects which carry the threat of devastation on an equally large scale. But the insidious erosion of the quality of the environment, often caused by the pressing demands of poverty, do not get the focus they deserve (Balasubramaniam, op. cit.).

The strategy towards trade should necessarily be seen against the background of global developments. The ones that concern us are Trade-related Intellectual Property Rights (TRIPs) and the establishment of the WTO. When the Dunkel draft was under discussion there was a hope that India would act as the 'spokesman of the developing world'. And there were sighs of disappointment that it did not. In fact, the erstwhile Congress government (1991–96) went in for an amendment of the Indian Patents Act 1970, but was unable to see it through the Upper House of Parliament where it lacked a majority. The US in particular is insistent on the amendment since the Act prohibits product patenting. Also required under the new international dispensation is an amendment with respect to plant breeders' rights so as to enable the *sui generis* system of the patenting of seeds.

It is argued by some that India, in its anxiety to promote G-L and attract foreign investment, has been lax in protecting its domestic interest and that the draft Plant Varieties Bill 1993, which bases itself on the 1991 convention on Plant Breeders' Rights, goes further than what the TRIPs provision requires (Krishnaswamy, 1998). It is also pointed out that the Indian Patents Act balances incentive to the patentee with protection of the public interest through compulsory licensing. If a patentee does not utilize his patent commercially within three years of securing it, the Act provides for its compulsory licensing (ibid.).

Another contentious feature of TRIPs relates to product and process patenting. The extant Indian legislation allows processes to be patented only in the field of agricultural chemicals and pharmaceuticals. This is regarded by many as a salutary provision. However, as pointed out above, the developed world, led by the US, is clamouring for an amendment which will compel India to accept product patent applications. Although patents need not be granted until 2005, applications are to be accepted from now on. India, pleading special circumstances, has sought an extension of time to fulfil its obligations under GATT-WTO. At the moment, India is accepting applications for product patents through an administrative order. The US contends that such a procedure does not satisfy the conditions laid down in the TRIPs agreement which mandates an amended legislation (*Economic Times*, 16 March 1998).

As against this, it is argued that restricting patents to processes enables copying and does not adequately reward inventors. There is also the argument that India's attitude towards changes in patent law is coloured by unjustified fears and a high degree of protectionism. The finance minister's statement that the WTO's present system is anti-India has attracted criticism (ibid., 27 March 1998). There is some truth in this argument because the fear that all of India's biodiversity can be patented is unfounded. As the *Economic Times* points out in its leader: 'The finance minister compounds this theoretical misunderstanding with factual errors. He cites the patenting of haldi, neem and basmati rice in the US as proof of patent imperialism. Nobody can take out a patent on natural stuff like turmeric, margosa or basmati because human ingenuity did not invent them. Patents can only be taken where the author can prove his originality' (ibid.). Much of this apprehensive attitude stems from some empirical evidence, once again originating in the US Scientists in the US applied for a patent for the medicinal use of turmeric, a traditional property known in India for generations. India successfully challenged this patent.

The latest case concerns a patent given to Ricetec, a Texas-based firm which claims to have found a new method of breeding basmati rice. Traditionally, basmati is an appellation which is 'geographically indicated', like Champagne and Scotch, and applies only to a variety of rice grown in parts of India and Pakistan. India's challenge must rest, it is suggested, on the geographical indication clause of TRIPs found in Articles 22, 23 and 24. (*Economic and Political Weekly*, 28 February 1998). Suman Sahai, a well known anti-WTO crusader, poses the question as to how the Americans 'dare to purloin the basmati name' while they would not dare something similar with respect to Scotch or Champagne (ibid.).

India also became involved in a dispute with Turkey. The issue relates to India's complaint that Turkey is imposing illegal restrictions on textile and clothing imports from India. Turkey countered this by arguing that import restrictions are introduced in order to comply with its customs agreement with the European Union. The matter as it now stands has been referred to a dispute settlement panel of the WTO (*Economic Times*, op. cit).

That agreements pertaining to international trade such as TRIPs and TRIMs betray weighting in favour of the developed world, cannot be denied. There is enough evidence of 'overlordism' in this sphere. Yet what must baffle any discerning observer is the complacent Indian attitude to vital questions in this area. Two points are relevant in this context. The first is that India has not devised a comprehensive strategy to protect its interests. A piecemeal, case-by-case approach will hardly help since it is both laborious and expensive (Sahai, op. cit; Krishnaswamy, op. cit). Secondly, there is an alarming lack of information (or if there *is* information, inaction) on patents granted abroad, something which entails adverse consequences for India (*Economic and Political Weekly*, op. cit). The conclusion which even this brief analysis suggests is that it is on the ideological-political plane that India is found wanting. 'External pressure' is being sought to explain away action or the absence of it which is basically motivated by other, principally internal, considerations. What else can explain India remaining ignorant of the basmati patent application which Ricetec made as far back as 1994. Even more odd is that the association of basmati exporters also were unaware until the government of India challenged Ricetec's application in the UK. These belated reactions speak both about governmental and business responses to a major issue. For India's basmati exports to the US alone are of the order of 45 000 tonnes per year – that is, 10 per cent of the total basmati exports.

Conclusion

There are aspects of India's political system which evoke images of the third world syndrome whose chief ingredients are endless red-tapism, endemic delay in decision-making, corruption, and the hijacking of the state by politicians of dubious repute. All of these are true, in lesser or greater degree. Yet, as was argued earlier, the system also possesses quite a remarkable aptitude for crisis management and, if for nothing else, for sheer survival. On the other hand, the country's fundamental problems remain. Unemployment is one such, poverty another. In view of their persistence, a considerable volume of literature has been produced, probing the all-important question – whether, as a consequence of G-L, social sector spending (on social safety nets) has declined. Nagaraj (1997) reviews the literature and contends that while government expenditure as a proportion of GDP has indeed declined from 11 per cent during 1986–91 to 10.1 per cent during 1992–95, the spending on health, education, housing and social services has remained constant during the later period. Further, he argues that even expenditure on rural development, which declined over 1991–93, was restored after the economy's performance improved. But as he notes, the impact of G-L on employment is hardly discernible. For example, the National Sample Survey in 1997 noted that almost two-thirds of the workforce is still in agriculture (ibid.). It is also worth noting that the intersectoral shift in the workforce started slowing down during 1989–94 and, even more disturbing, is the decline in the secondary sector's share in employment.

Despite the differences within agriculture, and the incidence of landlessness, as well as urban-rural inequalities, India is *not* an example of the typical Arthur Lewisian dual economy. The modernization of agriculture and the influence of the big farm lobby make it an atypical dual economy. Furthermore, it is necessary to take into account the survival capacity of the political system along with the presence of a strong judiciary and a fairly vibrant civil society. To this may be added a strong if ponderous administration.

The real failure is in terms of reducing the incidence of poverty. In part this is to be explained with reference to the 'slippage' phenomenon because of which beneficiaries receive only a small share of the intended benefit. What must also cause disappointment is the fact that the spectre of unemployment looms as large as it did a few decades ago. Even in periods of high growth, the contribution in terms of employment has not reached impressive levels. For instance, 1983–88 witnessed the highest rates of growth but also the lowest rate of growth of employment (Ghosh, 1994).

The problem is compounded by the system's known proclivity for indulging the affluent sections, be they the consumerist class, the capitalists or the big farm lobby. For instance, the state has shown a marked disinclination to secure surpluses from the agricultural sector. Also evident is the generally generous response to the demands for remunerative prices, despite the fact that at least 50 per cent of rural households are net purchasers of food.

One potentially important instrument is the constitutional status conferred upon local government institutions (Panchayat Raj Institutions or PRIs). As time goes on, they possess the potential to render governance more transparent and if they coalesce meaningfully with civil society structure they can act as a healthy check on the less endearing aspects of the political system.

We now sum up the results of our inquiry. Our first objective was to identify the agents and factors responsible for India's adoption of SAP, internal as well as external. It can be seen that to a significant degree India's internal management of the economy made G-L almost a necessity. In saying this, it is not implied that India had no choice and that there was inevitability about the emergence of the new policies. On the contrary, the argument is that given the political constellation in India the present model was inevitable. Fiscal profligacy, populism, lack of will to pursue policies which would, through austere measures, raise domestic savings, a propensity to indulge the consumerist class, pampering the big farm lobby – all these culminated in the crisis of 1991. Even at that stage total capitulation to a G-L model was possibly avoidable but only if the state had been willing and able to transform itself. To suggest that, however, is to wish away the problem. This situation has to be juxtaposed with the global scene. In addition to the state showing itself in a poor light in India (and elsewhere too), the case for a dirigiste regime was diluted by the collapse of the Soviet Union and the disappearance of the socialist states. To this should be added the anxiety of the West to ensure free trade in order to escape from the recession that is affecting the more affluent economies. The disintegration of the USSR produced a 'deterioration in the confidence of advocates of planned socialism in terms of state regulation of the economy' (Bartels and Pavier, op. cit.) and 'this erosion of confidence' helped achieve results in the field of trade which were not looked for when the Uruguay Round commenced in 1986 (ibid.). India's inability or unwillingness (or both) to champion the third world position should be set against this backdrop. Further, we have seen clear evidence of influential sections in India advocating that the economy should be linked with the outside world.

Obviously all facets of the G-L model are not negative ones in their impact on India. A spurt in growth has occurred although it is not consistent. It is true that the position of the poor has not improved; indeed, it may have worsened. But it is necessary to remind ourselves that, notwithstanding official pronouncements, India's earlier record in reducing the incidence of poverty is hardly inspiring.

To a noticeable degree the interventionist state is exiting from India. But this has not led to a more transparent system, nor to a slackening in the bureaucratic stranglehold.

Among the principal actors today should be counted the environmental movement, NGOs and the judiciary. All three coalesce at certain points, the first two almost wholly. By their trenchant critique of the currently accepted perception of development, they serve an important purpose but they are on less sure footing when it comes to framing viable alternatives. There is the possibility that some NGOs and environmental activists may be unaware that they are being utilized by strong vested interests who have little common with them. The attraction which NGOs hold for sensitive young people carries with it the danger that this group may be blind to the positive results which can be gleaned from the existing system, notwithstanding its shortcomings. The judiciary, while effectively functioning as a vigilante and watchdog, is not always sensitive to the demands which exert a pull on the economy and polity in a poor country. Adoption of western standards, be it in relation to the environment, child labour or human rights, may be justifiable but is not always realistic. It is wise to remember that even donors are swayed by market considerations when it comes to insisting in situations where these conditionalities exist.

The final question concerns the future of G-L. This assumes significance in view of the new political coalition at the centre. The finance minister has gone on record stating that the reforms will continue, but he has also qualified this by describing himself as a 'pragmatic Swadeshi'. In the absence of any precision attaching to the latter term, it would not be wrong to treat this as political populism. The BJP, the largest party in parliament, has (as noted earlier) relegated so many of its basics to the backburner that it might well not push the Swadeshi line too far. The government has the task of keeping its alliance partners happy. And they span a wide spectrum and at least three of them are essentially strong regional parties. One of them, the Telugu Desam Party (Andhra Pradesh), has been an enthusiastic adherent of reforms. Over and above this the ruling coalition has to reckon with the powerful lobbies within the country who have a vested interest in G-L. Given the fact that it does not enjoy an impressive majority in parliament, it will have to thread its way warily. It is as well to remember that the United Front (1996–98) did little to reverse the G-L model. Even the Marxist parties, particularly the CPM, while inveighing against G-L, have not been particularly successful, except in patches, in arresting its movement. The rest of the political array is not in any fundamental sense opposed to G-L.

What we may be witnessing in India today is a process in which the economic phenomenon is decisively triumphing over the political (*Economic Times*, 1997). Whether such a disjunction is ever fully possible, and more importantly whether it is desirable, is itself a worthy object of inquiry.

Acknowledgements

The author acknowledges with pleasure the assistance of Dr. Kripa, A.P. for discussion and secondary material, Mr. C. Shankara Murthy for reading and commenting on the draft, Ms. Rekha Rao for compiling the data for the statistical overview and Mr. G.S. Ganesh Prasad for untiring help on all fronts.

6
Reforms as a Domestic and International Process. Liberalization and Industry in the Ivory Coast

Alice Sindzingre and Bernard Conte

Introduction

In view of the failure of the structural adjustment programmes implemented in Sub-Saharan Africa (SSA) in the early 1980s, academic research now concentrates on analysing aspects which are not purely macroeconomic and which take into account resistance to reform as well as its negative effects. This has led to a political economy approach to reform, backed by an international political economy approach to developing countries.[1] Its concepts give preference to the role of international organizations and external aid agencies, their interaction with local institutions and groups, and the concrete process of implementing reforms, particularly conditionalities and the reactions they provoke, depending on the specific trajectories of the states and societies.[2] The theories focusing on market failures have reinforced these analyses, stressing the importance of institutions as a means of reducing risk and uncertainty. Conditionalities often entail 'an exchange of policy changes for external financing'[3] and limited to repeated games between bilateral and multilateral aid agencies and developing states. These games are, however, asymmetrical, and in the 1990s there was a certain amount of criticism of the effectiveness and role of aid institutions – so-called 'aid fatigue' (Van der Walle and Johnston, 1996).

The 'Washington consensus', which has now become global, agrees on the benefits of trade liberalization (Dollar, 1992), and exerts strong pressure on developing countries, using as justification their integration into the world economy (Lawrence, 1996). However, liberalization and globalization are processes that generate asymmetries and tensions (Rodrik, 1997). From the mid-1980s, the majority of developing countries initiated trade liberalization reforms and outward-oriented policies: lowering of tariffs, transformation of quantitative restrictions into tariffs, real devaluation, elimination of exchange and tax control on exports (Dean *et al.*, 1994, p. 3). However, numerous problems may be caused by the design of reforms, especially with respect to coherence, sequencing or rhythm: for example, shock therapy versus. gradualism; real depreciation accompanying liberalization; the order of tax, financial, monetary and trade reforms (Edwards, 1984; Bhattacharya, 1997). These factors are essential for credibility vis-à-vis the private sector and the effectiveness of liberalization when competition is imperfect. A poorly designed liberalization can be worse than the absence of liberalization (Rodrik, 1992b). In SSA, the franc zone countries should be distinguished from those outside the zone (and of course with the completion of European monetary unification in 2002, the franc zone was converted to the euro zone), the latter having put the reform of the exchange market and real depreciation before liberalization. The postponement of liberalization by the then franc zone countries led to the devaluation of the CFA franc in 1994. Reforms in SSA are characterized by an initial situation of high tariffs; the use of quantitative restrictions and exemptions; frequent policy reversals; resistance from local industries competing with imports and the fall in tax revenues.[4]

This has led to credibility deficits which continue to be a major cause of the weak investment response in the SSA region. Nevertheless, a theoretical basis for multilateral agreements is to constitute a signal and to confer some credibility to states vis-à-vis international markets, because these agreements bind governments and act as external 'agencies of restraint' (Collier, 1991; Rodrik, 1996; Collier and Patillo, 2000). SSA countries are part of a multiplicity of international and bilateral arrangements and institutions. This creates problems of coherence, passive governments, or the saturation of weak local capacities – the need for technical assistance and, consequently, a perpetuation of the asymmetry of aid in terms of financing as well as information.

This chapter analyses the positions, negotiations and degrees of freedom, of the international and national players respectively, in their asymmetric relationship in the areas of trade liberalization, industry and environment, in the case of the Ivory Coast. The country has limited room for manoeuvre due to: (1) constraints following from multilateral arrangements; and (2) domestic constraints, interest groups and the structure of institutions, which transform locally the regulations proposed by outside agencies. Finally, these multiple arrangements may not necessarily be coherent, a state of affairs which the Ivory Coast was able either to optimize or endure. The first part of the chapter presents the economic and political model which preceded the reforms. The second part describes the adjustment programmes and the resistance of the Ivory Coast in its relations with the Bretton Woods institutions and its principal bilateral donor, France. The third part focuses on other arrangements involving the Ivory Coast, the case of liberalization reforms and their impact on trade, industry and investment.

The specificity of the Ivory Coast

The population of the Ivory Coast, estimated at 14.8 million inhabitants, is the result of numerous migratory flows,[5] and the country is one of the most cosmopolitan in SSA. President Felix Houphouët-Boigny, after achieving decolonization in 1960, was able to establish a stable regime which lasted from 1960 until he died at the end of 1993. A political characteristic was his ambiguous attitude towards independence and French colonizers whose presence continued as a result of a deliberate decision (Zolberg, 1964; Sindzingre, 1995).

Membership of the franc zone monetary union[6] is essential for understanding the advantages, but also the handicaps, characterizing the Ivory Coast. The franc zone (now the euro zone) comprises 15 countries,[7] divided into three monetary sub-zones: the West-African Economic and Monetary Union (UEMOA/WAEMU),[8] the Economic and Monetary Community of Central Africa (CEMAC/EMCCA)[9] and the Comores. The zone is administered by three principles: a fixed parity of its currency, the CFA franc, with the French franc;[10] a joint Central Bank (Central Bank of the West-African States, BCEAO; Bank of the Central African States, BEAC); and the Central Bank of the Comores); a guarantee of the free convertibility of the CFA franc assured by the 'operation account' opened at the French Treasury.[11] From the mid-1980s, the zone was hit by a financial and structural crisis, leading in 1994 to the first change of parity since 1948.

The economic 'model' which followed independence

During the period 1975–77, the Ivory Coast experienced a boom in primary commodities, and the terms of trade increased by 73 per cent. This is referred to as the Ivoirian 'miracle'. The state's weight in the economy increased in a spectacular way, following a 'state capitalism' model through public investment, a liberal policy of direct foreign investments, but with control over agricultural exports through the

Stabilization Fund (Caistab) and protection vis-à-vis foreign competition. Public investment increased by 250 per cent in real terms between 1975 and 1980, representing 21 per cent of the GDP in 1978 (70 per cent of total investment) (Schneider *et al.*, 1992, pp. 27–8). In 1980, state-owned enterprises accounted for 7.5 per cent of the GDP (Berthelemey and Bourguignon, 1996, p. 12). Most of the public revenue comes from import taxes, tariffs and VAT (25 per cent), with numerous exemptions (40 per cent of the total; ibid., p. 16). Cocoa – of which the Ivory Coast is the leading world producer – coffee, fruit and timber are the main exports (WTO, 1995, p. 18). The role of the state in the coffee and cocoa sectors, via policies of guaranteed prices to producers by the Stabilization Fund (Caistab), equivalent to an implicit tax,[12] created a 'plantation economy'. This relied on public intervention and foreign private initiative and on agricultural exports representing 80 per cent of total exports in 1980 (Berthélémy and Bourguignon, 1996, p. 7). The earnings generated by the export boom were 'confiscated' by the Caistab, owing to the important differential between international prices and planters' internal buying prices, permitting the state to increase its expenditures and to develop the public sector.

The Ivoirian model had regional, geopolitical and economic dimensions.[13] The foundation of the West-African Economic Community (CEAO) in 1974 confirmed the Ivory Coast's supremacy over French-speaking countries of the region. Its prosperity enabled it to win the historic bet made against the choice of neighbouring Ghana (which had an equivalent standard of living at the time of independence),[14] and turned the Ivory Coast into the heavyweight of the franc zone, a position it tried to optimize during subsequent crises and negotiations, particularly with donors. The Ivoirian model functioned well for some time, and from independence until 1980, growth multiplied by a factor of four in 20 years. Later, the advantage of the franc zone became a constraint, and when external conditions altered, the model turned out to be fragile.

The state, the institutions and the interest groups

This state-led strategy was equally effective at the political level. The private sector in the Ivory Coast is either French or derives from an accumulation based on the state, according to a system of attracting potential clients and political opponents. This has led to rationalities of those state officials who favoured neither the public service nor an autonomous bureaucracy.[15] Since the adjustment, donors have played a major role in the configuration of public services, something not devoid of adverse effects (so-called 'enclave' projects instigated by outside donors). The construction of institutions is an endogenous process, as clearly revealed by the weak success of the numerous projects for civil service reform emanating from the donors.[16] The public services developed a resistance, outbidding the incentives, as well as corruption. In spite of the regulations, the institutions are not autonomous, an example being the Central Bank, which is hampered by the demands of the government,[17] or the banking system responsible for political loans which has led to several bankruptcies. The interest groups at work within the state follow a clientelist system. The local 'planter bourgeoisie' (Gastellu and Affou Yapi, 1982; de Miras, 1982; Conte, 1984, pp. 372–6) relied on the exploitation of agricultural resources for exportation authorized by the political authorities, and political posts gave access to private accumulation, licit or illicit, through public resources. The debate continues on the existence of entrepreneurs versus. the 'rentiers' created by those in political power.[18] Social disparities are marked and redistribution is unequal. The food-producing north is less favoured than the areas producing agricultural exports. Incomes fell during the 1980s, with 37 per cent of the population falling below the poverty line in 1995 (World Bank, 1997a). Houphouët-Boigny nevertheless managed to reunite the centrifugal forces of a country with numerous ethnic groups, particularly those in the north, a distinct entrepreneurial group having historically accumulated wealth through Sahelian trade networks (Sindizingre, 1996b). The regional balance has been broken by his successor. For political purposes, he activated xenophobic attitudes (ideology of 'ivoirité') vis-à-vis the northern population, aimed solely at the elimination of a potential rival originating from the north. This is the context of the serious political instability and the series of coups which began at the end of 1999.

The role of France

A vital factor for the international integration of the Ivory Coast and its capacity to negotiate with its creditors was the support from France, at least until the end of the Cold War, followed by the devaluation of the CFA franc in 1994. France is itself fragmented into diverse interest groups which are not necessarily congruent (political, private, technocratic). The French still maintain interconnecting networks of political and economic influence as well as a military base. During the prosperous period, quite a number of expatriates occupied positions in the civil service, setting the standard of a model of consumption and imports.[19] Official French reports acknowledged the importance of their interests in the sub-region.[20] In the early 1980s, the number of French was estimated at 50 000 (Delgado and Zartman, 1984; Duruflé, 1988), a figure which has since decreased. The staff of the French Overseas Co-operation Service, which totalled 1260 expatriates in 1960, rose to a maximum of 3901 in 1979 before decreasing regularly. In the 1980s, foreigners held 80 per cent of the managerial posts and 50 per cent of the administrative posts in companies belonging to the modern sector (Berthélémy and Bourguignon, 1996, p. 13). In 1983, 69 per cent of the capital was public, 9 per cent private Ivoirian, and 22 per cent foreign.[21] Among the firms operating in 1991, 25 per cent were Ivoirian, 47 per cent French, 8.7 per cent Lebanese and 18 per cent owned by non-Ivoirian Africans.[22] The country's banks remained for a long time subsidiaries of French banks. The industrial sector is still distorted by this path dependence, with a concentrated and dualistic structure: in 1997, small- and medium-sized industries, where there are more nationals, accounted for 80 per cent of the total member of firms, but their contribution to the GDP was only 18 per cent (*Marchés Tropicaux et Méditerranéens*, 1997, p. 6).

The private industrial sector

At the time of independence in 1960, the Ivory Coast, which specialized in primary products,[23] inherited a limited industrial sector, the colonizers having operated more in the export trade.[24] The sector's autonomy relied on rents, including those for foreign investors (Marchat, 1997b, p. 3; Barbier, 1993, p. 144). In 1959, an extremely favourable investment code for French firms was promulgated within the framework of an industrial policy based on that of the French and the state, on import-substitution, and on a customs tariff favourable to it (WTO, 1995, Vol. 2). With this code, investors were encouraged to move from trade to industry. A new strategy emerged at the beginning of the 1970s, aimed at inciting import-substitution industries to overcome the narrowness of the market through exports (Mytelka, 1992). The links between foreign capital and industry led to the choice of capital-intensive techniques[25.] The 1959 Investment Code, replaced in 1984, granted high protection and tax exemptions to industry, in addition to monopoly position that allowed for administered prices and comfortable mark-ups.[26] With its system of 'priority agreements', this code induced distortions within a similar sector and favoured the big foreign colonial firms (Conte, 1984–85). This constituted an entry barrier for the local private sector (Hopkins, 1973; Austen, 1987). In 1978, the 'priority' sector represented 60 per cent of industry's turnover (Conte, 1984). The state attempted to promote the industrial sector (Bénié, 1991), but its rentier nature, that of the banking sector fructifying these rents, the public enterprises and the links with politicians moving into a new industrial career, caused them to go bankrupt. The industrial sector grew from 1974 to 1980. During the period 1980–91, the industrial sector represented 42 per cent of the added value and 48.6 per cent of the jobs (Marchat, 1997b, p. 3). Its decline began after 1984, owing to the Ivory Coast's loss of competitiveness following the appreciation of the French franc and the strong depreciation of the Nigerian currency, the naira, after the 1986 adjustment. This loss, aggravated by the public finance crisis and the enormous internal debt and public arrears,[27] led to devaluation in 1994.

The political liberalization in the 1990s

In the early 1990s, in the Ivory Coast as in many other SSA countries, the democratic movement was more strongly voiced (Bratton and Van de Walle, 1997), and after 30 years, the single party had to accept a multiparty system. However, in reality, it retained access to the country's resources until the first military coup at the end of 1999. The democratization process was a source both of conflicts and paradoxes, linked to the problem of the sequencing and timing of reforms. The government was tied down by a double constraint, and now had to take into account the public opinion of a civil society, and the desire to maintain privileged links with France. After the reign of Houphouët-Boigny, a technocrat, Alassane Ouattara, from the Bretton Woods institutions (BWI), as in other SSA countries, came to power. Engaged in the reforms by definition, his brief government was marked by the classical paradox of a technocrat becoming a politician: in his efforts to establish the political anchorage necessary to make the reforms acceptable, he lost his technocratic credibility (Williamson, 1994). The two standards of legitimacy are not always compatible when it is necessary to pass reforms, especially in the context of three decades of government by a single party. After the long regime of Houphouët-Boigny, Ouattara's successor, Henri Konan Bédié, had to consolidate a less well-established legitimacy. Public opinion did not forget that Houphouët-Boigny removed him from his post as Minister of Economy and Finances for embezzlement. After 1993, the year of Houphouët-Boigny's death, a firm style was chosen, contrasting with the previous consensual authoritarianism,[28] and obliged to rely on more limited and ethnicized groups. As with F. Houphouët-Boigny, H. Konan Bédié wanted to stay in power whatever the welfare of the country, and he promoted a dangerous policy which F. Houphouët-Boigny would have strongly disapproved of: an ideology of xenophobia against Ivoirians originating from the north, likening them to foreigners, in order to disqualify the political credibility of A. Ouattara. H. Konan Bédié was ambivalent with regard to reforms, especially because his principal political opponent, A. Ouattara, occupied the strategic post of director at the IMF. Conditionalities of the Bretton Woods institutions were easily suspected of being influenced by A. Ouattara's political agenda. In a context of political liberalization, the reforms were filtered through the prism of local and political power relationships. But at the end of 1999, xenophobia and harassment of Ouattara's partisans – coupled with a severe economic crisis, obvious bad governance and the significant slowdown of external assistance, especially from the Bretton Woods institutions – all these ingredients led to social unrest and a military coup. This coup was followed by a series of others, and a civil president, L. Gbagbo, an historical opponent, was elected at the end of 2000, after an extremely controversial electoral process. The climate of political uncertainty was maintained by his inertia vis-à-vis xenophobia and the latent social tensions caused by the political exclusion of A. Ouattara and the persistence of the economic crisis.

Negotiations on adjustment: national players, bilateral relations and the Bretton Woods institutions

Below is a brief historical account of the reforms and the resistance they provoked. The essential concepts are the credibility, timing and sequencing of the reforms.[29] The Ivoirian players were faced with a bilateral player and with two multilateral Bretton Woods institutions (BWI). Before the adjustment programmes, France's influence was dominant, then the power of the International Monetary Fund and the World Bank rose with the financial crisis of the 1980s and the changes in the external environment, mandated by creditors because of the aggravation of the Ivoirian indebtedness. The emergence of a third player, embodied by the BWI, destabilized and complicated the dialogue between the Ivory Coast and French interests.

The successive programmes since 1980 and their conditionalities

In 1979 and 1980, the balance of payments deteriorated, and the Ivory Coast signed an agreement with the Monetary Fund, followed by an adjustment loan from the World Bank in 1981.

'Incomplete adjustment', 1981–93

The first Extended Fund Facility was spread over the period 1981–83. A second loan covered the period 1984–86. These ended in failure (Chamley, 1991; Demerry, 1994). The first programme implemented a successful stabilization policy. The second made an attempt at trade liberalization in 1984, but, being more sensitive, it failed (Azam and Morrisson, 1994, p. 18). Coupled with the fall in prices of exported commodities (a 40 per cent fall in terms of trade between 1986 and 1990), the programmes resulted in reducing investment and accentuating the decline of demand (Pégatiénan, 1988). A third adjustment loan was granted in 1986 for the period 1987–91, but the decline in the GDP and tax revenues led the government to suspend its obligations. In 1987, the government stopped paying interest on its external debt. The BWI broke off their loans to the country during the period 1987–89. A standby agreement was finally agreed with the IMF in 1989, and the World Bank resumed its loans with six sectoral programmes started between 1989 and 1991 (Demerry, 1994). To finance the fiscal deficit, the country had massive recourse to direct external indebtedness, facilitated by its membership of the franc zone, then indirectly through state-owned enterprises which multiplied domestic arrears. The rules of the franc zone, theoretically limiting the possibilities of internal indebtedness, were bypassed through the manipulation of agricultural credits (Michailof, 1994). Public arrears vis-à-vis public and private firms and banks accumulated, and many companies therefore stopped paying their taxes, proportionally reducing tax revenues and aggravating the public deficit.[30] From 1980, the public debt increased in an unsustainable way, and in 1990, its outstanding debt was over 11 billion dollars, a level of debt per capita which was the highest in Africa.

The roles of the BWI were not always in line. The Fund, by mandate, focuses on monetary and financial indicators and recommends measures aimed at increasing tax collection and reducing the fiscal deficit. As a development bank, the World Bank focuses more on structural issues. With its competence in the two essential dimensions of fiscal deficit and indebtedness, the Fund had, *in short,* the leadership. The

Bank intended to create incentives and restore the competitiveness of the industrial sector, but the measures fluctuated and failed to meet their objectives. Conditionalities accumulated following the poor results and postponements by the government. Since many multilateral organizations were able to intervene in external trade, their roles became entangled. The result was unstable trade liberalization measures and protection levels, and fiscal incoherence[31]. These effects created great uncertainty among economic agents up until 1993. The phasing of the tariff reforms was inappropriate, and it accentuated the decline of the manufacturing sector (Azam and Morrisson, 1994; Marchat, 1997b; Sindzingre, 1991). All this caused a growing distrust amongst the Ivoirians towards BWI programmes (Pégatiénan and Ouayogode, 1997). Supported by France, which held on to the intangibility of the CFA franc-FF parity, the Ivory Coast rejected the devaluation recommended by the BWI, and chose 'real adjustment' instead. This led to inconsistent measures, of which the failure of the export premium introduced in 1984 is an example. This 'real' adjustment entailed a reduction in the fiscal deficit, liberalization of prices, credit control, import taxes and export subsidies, despite the risk of fraud, high administration costs and the generation of considerable distortions, and it failed.

The World Bank wanted to suppress rents (i.e. government favours) and distortions, while in terms of political economy, Houphouët-Boigny wanted to protect foreign firms. A new investment code was promulgated in 1984 (it was replaced in 1995). It nevertheless retained discretionary advantages for certain individual firms, and distortions relating to competition (Marchat, 1997b, p. 6), based on unclear eligibility criteria. The dominant and foreign-owned firms, often the least competitive, benefited more than others (Marchat, 1997a). In 1984–86, the incentive scheme was reformed in order to encourage exports. The tariff was modified in 1986 (Berthélémy and Bourguignon, 1996, p. 16). Tariff exemptions were to be abolished as a substitute for devaluation. But the keystone of this substitution, the export premium, was not paid until the end of 1986, thus cancelling out the logic of the measures, and it was discarded in 1988.[32] The country was very much dependent on import taxes.[33] At the end of the 1980s, the 1985 reforms were reversed and finally led to increased protection. In 1990, a new reform was tried out.[34] In 1991, export licences were abolished (Dean *et al.*, 1994, pp. 40–1). Fraud was responsible for the failure of tariff reinforcement, and even threatened certain industrial sectors.[35] During the period 1980–87, industry experienced a negative growth rate of -2.4 per cent.[36] At the end of the 1980s, then, the instability of the measures taken induced a climate of uncertainty and an increase in both fraud and informal activities. The practice of circumventing regulations was intensified and the activity found new justifications.

Bilateral and multilateral games

France, the Ivoirian government, and the multilateral agencies formed more of a 'three-cornered relationship' than a 'double-edged diplomacy' (Putnam, 1993; Pégatiénan and Ouayogode, 1997). The French frequently criticize the Bank and the Ivoirians, trained in the French way, do not trust market forces. The Ivory Coast remains important to France, and reciprocally, although the game is asymmetrical. After 1990, aid started to represent significant amounts to the Ivory Coast: 6.4 per cent of the GDP (4.1 per cent in 1989), 7.4 per cent in 1993, taking all donors into account.[37] French aid, a component of its foreign policy, is dominant. The Ivory Coast, one of the principal beneficiaries of French development aid, was its primary recipient in 1996, with $569 m, out of a total of $968 m of net aid flow (DAC/OECD, 1998).

However, the situation in the years preceding 1994 was unsustainable: domestic arrears and arrears owed to the World Bank. The Ivory Coast lost its international financial credibility. It was only supported by France, which bailed out fiscal deficits, and thus accelerated the already weak local credibility of the reforms, incurring increasingly vocal criticism within the BWI where France had for a long time negotiated the *status quo* for franc zone countries. In 1993, after many years of deficits, France no longer had the means to pay out increasingly higher sums which did not serve development purposes but were used to reimburse the multilateral donors.[38] The resumption of relations with the BWI and the change from private to public financing became urgent. A 'division of labour' emerged between the BWI (economic credibility, binding of governments by multilateral arrangements) and the ex-colonial power (political influence, privileged relations and networks), and French aid was tied to the adoption of a programme with the BWI. Thus reinforced, the conditionality was swapped between donors who suspended their disbursements if there was a delay in the signing of agreements with the BWI. The devaluation was also concomitant with the end of the Cold War, in which the stake represented by the SSA diminished, the latter remaining a playing field for private multinational firms ('the profitable Africa' of mining and extraction opportunities which represent the major part of foreign investments).

The game between several international, multilateral and bilateral actors persists, and French influence seeks to retain its hold, but within a modernized co-operation scheme. When imbalances appeared at the end of the 1980s, the BWI insisted on devaluation. Benefiting from a strong and convertible currency, the Ivoirian elite turned this down – with the support of certain French political networks – but also for economic reasons, since the performance of the franc zone had for a long time been better than that of countries outside the zone; [39] furthermore, direct foreign investments were facilitated by convertibility (especially for French investors). The concomitance of the death of Houphouët-Boigny at the end of 1993 and devaluation at the beginning of 1994 led to the local perception that France was abandoning its ally. Technocrats considered that if devaluation had been introduced earlier, it might have been possible to avoid the economic paralysis of 1993. The attitude of the BWI was also coloured by their internal political economy – which had certain reservations about French-Ivoirian rents – by stopping their financial flows to the Ivory Coast during the period preceding the devaluation. The BWI were ambivalent with regard to the Ivory Coast since France was an influential member of the BWI and was able to take a free ride with respect to the reforms; France therefore clouded the signals from the BWI and the reforms which could have destabilized its interests in its client countries. The BWI claimed the role of agents of modernization and of rent destruction, and the devaluation was a victory for their technocratic orientation (Sindzingre, 1996a). The Ivory Coast attempted to exploit these divergences between donors. Criticized by other West African countries of the franc zone, the devaluation was 'tailor-made' for the Ivory Coast, in terms of anticipated effects and accompanying financial flows. In this context, the conditionalities ran the risk of remaining ineffective, and the government did not internalize the reforms which remained the donors' reforms (Collier *et al.*, 1997c).

The 1994 devaluation of the CFA franc and its consequences

Membership of the franc zone conferred some advantages. The overvaluation remains a controversial issue,[40] linked to the structural adjustment and devaluations of Nigeria, and the competitiveness of competitor countries in Asia. The same measure was uniformly applied to countries with different economies, and the institutional framework of the franc zone and the guarantee of the French Treasury[41] were maintained, with only the parity level being modified. The concept of 'financing in exchange for reform' functioned entirely, and the 'accompanying measures' from the BWI and France were substantial, according to an implicit bargain whereby the BWI could resume their financing as soon as the required devaluation was completed. The total net official development assistance to the Ivory Coast changed from $765 m in 1993 to $1594 m in 1994, $1212 m in 1995, and $798 m in 1998 (DAC/OECD, 1998 and 2000), and constituted 20.8 per cent of the GDP in 1994, and 12.1 per cent in 1995.[42] The devaluation was carefully prepared by the French and BWI authorities for the Ivory Coast, and the rate of 50 per cent adjusted on the country's loss of competitiveness (Rosenberg, 1995, p. 15). The economy responded positively, favoured by high commodity prices and by the resumption of international financing (Calipel and Guillaumont-Jeanneney, 1996, p. 67). After two years of negative growth (1992 and 1993), the growth rate of real GDP was 2 per cent in 1994, 7 per cent in 1995, and began to decline in 1996.[43] Competitiveness improved, the agricultural sectors became profitable again, and industry recovered (Goreux, 1995). Inflation dropped from 32.5 per cent in 1994, to 7.7 per cent in 1995 and 3.5 per cent in 1996 (*Marchés Tropicaux et Méditerranéens*, 1997, p. 11).

After the devaluation of 1994 and its 'reward' ('accompanying measures'), multilateral donors resumed their financing and relieved pressure on the debt from creditors of the Paris Club and commercial banks (Brooks *et al.*, 1998): an ESAF agreement, the Enhanced Structural Adjustment Facility, was signed with the Fund from June 1994 to June 1997, which comprised sectoral programmes: (1) adjustment credit for the agricultural sector, the CASA, in 1995, targeted at the Caistab and the privatization of the cotton sector; and (2) sectoral adjustment credit for private sector development, the CAS-DSP, in 1996, aimed at liberalizing the economy, reinforcing competitiveness and reforming the legal and statutory framework.[44] The conditionalities of the following ESAF agreement (1997–2000) still remained the restructuring of the external debt, the liberalization of the Caistab and the cotton industry and privatization. However, in spite of devaluation and the resumption of flows from the BWI, the situation deteriorated during the negotiations with the BWI in 1997: the 1997–2000 ESAF agreement was not signed until the beginning of 1998, after months of negotiations.[45]

The improvement period did not last. Competitiveness eroded rapidly.[46] The debt continues to be a major problem and in 1997, debt service represented 11.3 per cent of the GDP and 25.6 per cent of the export earnings, and the debt outstanding represented about 17 billion dollars (*Marchés Tropicaux et Meditérranéens*, 1997, p. 8). The Ivory Coast successfully negotiated with multilateral institutions for the reduction of its debt under the HIPC regime[47] in 1997 – even though it did not fit into this category – thanks to the support from France, and external debt decreased from 144 per cent of GDP in 1997 to 98 per cent in 1999 (IMF, 2000, p. 88). This game of negotiation is anchored in time for it was in 1987 that the Ivory Coast defaulted, and the composition of the debt consisted of a series of major projects put up for sale as part of privatization. But above all, mismanagement and resistance to reform led to an interruption of the dialogue with the BWI; this interrupted their programmes at the end of 1998, and consequently led to a sharp slowdown of official development assistance, aggravated by embezzlement of ODA funds. This was intensified by the collapse of international cocoa prices after 1999 and social tensions in the agricultural sector, ethnic turmoil caused by the 'ivoirité' ideology and the subsequent overthrow of H. Konan Bédié at the end of 1999, followed by a series of military coups and the controversial elections of L. Gbagbo at the end of 2000.[48] Policy choices always remained shaped by priorities of the internal political economy, and the prescriptions of donors, in terms of economic reform as well as democratization, remained secondary. All the reforms were put on hold. The World Bank halted its disbursements in October 2000 due to arrears. This measure marginalizes a country vis-à-vis the international donors' community, and France tried to organize a bail out. GDP growth was less than 3 per cent in 1999. However, the paralysis of the economy, the drop of private investment due to political instability, and the threat of fiscal bankruptcy constrained the authorities to reopen the dialogue with BWI in 2001, something that had the strong support of France.

Resistance within the core of the state and reactions of the interest groups

The Ivory Coast played a 'double-edged diplomacy', a dual purpose game for domestic and international use, underlying the attitude towards the reforms, privatization and liberalization. Reforms entail negotiations with local players as well as international negotiations, both multilateral and bilateral, where the financial games and defections are more or less constrained or voluntary. The winning and losing groups of the various reforms are difficult to identify in view of the fact that numerous reforms were partly adopted, apart from the devaluation, or reversed (trade liberalization), or diverted from their objectives to improve competitiveness (privatization). Since 1980, the reforms were 'resold' several times, for instance, those relating to the Caistab and agricultural liberalization, in a permanent negotiation game with multilateral and bilateral institutions, indicating that they were not internalized. Thus, the signs of a commitment to reform by the government were nullified by possible policy reversals and hence a mitigated credibility for investors.

During the period of adjustment programmes, resistance was expressed towards the liberalization of the coffee and cocoa sector, and the reorganization of the Caistab, the heart of the state's interests and rents (i.e. excessive economic returns), the Ivory Coast being the leading world producer of cocoa. Ivoirian authorities have not really given up their control. The conflict between the country and the Bank was also a fundamental disagreement over agricultural pricing since the Ivory Coast feels that farmers should not be directly exposed to the world market and to speculation. For its part, an external player such as the World Bank emerged as an agent beneficially destroying rents with the Caistab reform. Resistance also derived from differences in economic concepts. The privatization of the cotton sector was a sensitive issue, an example of the French concept of integration by sector, which the Bank, according to the principle of freedom of the market, wanted to dismantle, in spite of results that were not always conclusive in other countries.[49] The opposition of France was both justified, given the good performance of the African cotton sectors and the unclear privatization conditions,[50] and also due to its own interests.

From an internal political economy point of view, the previous accumulation regime continued: extravagant expenses, lack of transparency and diversion of conditionalities. The unexpected expenses exceeded the 1997 budget by 40 per cent.[51] In 1996, making use of the economic growth and the privileged ties with certain foreign firms, the government launched a series of 'major works', a programme of public infrastructures combining prestige and utility (a bridge, an airport, etc). In 1997, the country increased the producer prices of cocoa without informing the donors, thus provoking their irritation, and they also refused to disclose the Caistab's sales figures. For their part, the donors constituted an intrusion in national sovereignty which inevitably provoked resistance. The BWI therefore delayed the ESAF agreement until 1998, causing the suspension of other aid programmes due to crossed conditionalities.[52] In the meantime, the general aid regime changed in the 1990s (a drop in official assistance; aid selectivity), but the Ivory Coast hoped to rely on the support of France. The state did not want to modify its lifestyle, and as in the case of other countries, was reluctant to upset one of its foundations, that is, the civil service. The number of civil servants did not decrease during the adjustment whereas their purchasing power fell (Schneider *et al.*, 1992, p. 49 et seq.). Resistance was also strong with regard to reforming the bank system and customs as well as, improving statistics which, here as everywhere else, were impenetrable. An example of the donors' coherence problem, the Ministry of Finance favoured the collection of short-term data quantifying the performance criteria of the BWI. Correlatively, the statistics system declined, despite being supported by considerable technical assistance from the donors, even though the production of reliable statistics was a significant conditionality of the BWI.

The uncertainty intrinsic to the reforms is not necessarily correlated to a desire to maintain the *status quo*, as the crisis did incite some groups to change (Fernandez and Rodrik, 1991). Formal private firms, including French ones, were devastated by the banks' illiquidity in 1993 and the paralysis of the economy resulting from the internal public debt, and were therefore in favour of devaluation and liberalization.[53] The groups affected by the loss of employment, public or private, did not start reacting until after the democratization process, the unions having previously all been members of the single party. The rentier groups formed by those in political power and the ties with France (the flight of capital was enormous before 1994) were opposed to devaluation while making substantial profits when their own capital was eventually repatriated. The case of the Ivory Coast is specific owing to the coextensive nature of the public and business spheres. The interest groups may be for or against liberalization, and depending on their size and whether they are import- or export-oriented, firms stand to gain or lose by it.[54] The reform of public services was accepted with difficulty, as indicated by the repeated censuses neutralized by corruption and clientelist behaviour. The battle against fraud, supported by the formal firms, did not have the backing of the informal operators, especially since the harassment of civil servants vis-à-vis small operators is not affected by these reforms. Trade liberalization appears to have been easier than that of the Caistab, or the monetary adjustment, and better accepted by industrial firms than the political elite. However, the question is complex as these different groups overlap. Even if corporatism exists, in this type of weakly institutionalized state, an individual belongs simultaneously to several interest groups, and the frontiers between them are blurred (Haggard and Webb, 1993). This weak degree of institutionalization affects public services as much as political circles. Finally, the poor, a voiceless group, did not benefit from the reforms. As is the case with other countries, the poor are not identical with the peasant class since coffee and cocoa farmers benefited from favourable prices, but here the poor refers more to food-producing farmers and the urban informal sector.

Numerous vested interests, sometimes linked to the state, showed resistance, or an acceptance or even a determination to revert to previous protective measures. Among several examples, this was the case in terms of the liberalization of the transport sector, which lasted for several years.[55] Another example is that of the forestry sector, and the forestry project of the World Bank, aimed at preserving the overexploited forest capital, which we met with opposition. Private firms refused to be subjected to the tax imposed by the project to finance the replanting of trees. In matters of environment, there may also have been some inconsistency between certain reforms: for instance, devaluation and environmental objectives. As devaluation improved the competitiveness of the timber sector, second grade timber was exploited more in order to obtain export allowances, resulting in accelerated deforestation. The government was not committed to this project,[56] which got bogged down, and even had to be restarted. The timber sector also tends to attract fraud and corruption (Ekanza, 1997). One final example is that of the liberalization of wheat flour, which brought back import taxes to 10 per cent and which was for a long time blocked by a single firm, an interest group in a monopoly position.

Privatization

As in other countries, the privatization process was subject to obstacles aimed at protecting the rents of interest groups. The Ivory Coast was a precursor in the area of privatization.[57] Prior to structural adjustment, the first attempts at privatization took place in 1980, corresponding with a balancing of the political powers and state-owned enterprises (Contamin and Fauré, 1990; Conte, 1984, pp. 335–9). In 1983, the World Bank estimated the number of public enterprises at 113 (Berg and Shirley, 1987, p. 26). With the crisis, pressure from the BWI in favour of privatization was intensified, and the privatization programme accelerated at the beginning of the 1990s.[58] The Abidjan Stock Exchange was conceived as a privatization instrument. Since the beginning of the programme, about 60 companies were listed for privatization, this time including 'strategic' public companies. From 1991 to 1996, 36 companies were privatized. In 1997, two heavyweights[59] were privatized, and between 1998 and 2000, 13 other enterprises were privatized, including a major bank.[60] The example of electricity privatization shows that the process favoured a higher profitability of the company (the distribution of water and electricity experienced a strong growth from 1992[61]). However, firms continued to consider the cost of electricity excessive (Plane, 1997, p. 863). The factor costs, considered to be an essential cause of the mediocre Ivoirian competitiveness, were not radically reduced by privatization, nor by devaluation and liberalization.

The interest groups attempted to keep part of the rents they had obtained by buying back companies through allied networks, profiting from privatization through the Stock Exchange in order to constitute 'hard cores', and associating with French firms likely to retrocede part of the rents – private monopolies replacing public ones. The transparency of the privatizations, which were slow under Houphouët-Boigny, gave rise to controversies in the last years of his regime.[62] The privatizations were often favourable to French firms who, supported by their privileged networks, collected the lion's share.[63] They were allocated to a limited number of large groups, either French, American or Canadian, in the new sectors of mining and petroleum, or linked to political power. Deep suspicions persist over the continuation of clientelist practices.[64] The rapid rise of new groups is an example of this, some of them having known difficulties with political instability and the disappearance of their political sponsors.[65] As in the past, control is carried out by groups close to the political power of the moment.[66] For example, the privatization of CITelcom triggered a return of French expatriates, something which was criticized by the public.[67] Privatization may reduce the volume of the rent and the number of beneficiaries defending their claims (the ratchet effect), contracting the political base. Under Bédié's regime, the few diversifications towards USA and Canada (petroleum and mines) might also have corresponded to a rise in the influence of public opinion in favour of increased accountability in terms of the government's decisions – not all can be conceded to the French.[68] The democratization process is in this instance a constraint, destabilizing the foundation of the previous authoritarian policies – an example of the difficult compatibility of economic and political liberalizations, of the constraints on governments' room for manoeuvre and their actual commitment to reforms.

These privatizations question the real change of paradigm – modernization or preservation of a system that has lasted over decades. The Ivory Coast would seem to be a captive in the local transformation process of international rules; a prisoner of the weakness of the local private sector and the alliances of political power with certain multinational firms which were able to overcome the entry barriers to the Ivoirian environment, themselves being under the constraint of wider geopolitical interests. The Ivory Coast has an ambivalent attitude towards privatization and the private sector, as well as foreign investors. It is economically modernist, but continues to emphasize an excessive dependency on commodity economies vis-à-vis 'international speculators', and wants to encourage local cocoa processing and the creation of added value. The government seeks to attract foreign investors, but threatens them with enormous fines when domestic political economy and electoral promises become more urgent priorities – as in the campaign against tax evasion in 2001. The authorities deplore the fact that the share of the French market share in the Ivoirian trade is declining, while affirming that 'Côte d'Ivoire does not belong to anyone'. American firms try to invest, but encounter the old habits of short-term profitable opportunities (*Marchés Tropicaux et Méditerranéens*, 1998, p. 23). The non-entrepreneurial paradigm persists among certain operators, as well as the inertia of the public services towards the new rules of globalization whereby developing countries now compete to attract foreign investments.

International integration: the other multilateral and regional agreements and their impact of liberalization

The different multilateral arrangements

Like numerous SSA states, the Ivory Coast belongs to many formal regional institutions. Yet these often lack efficienc; states hesitate to finance them and they serve more as rents for their staff.[69] A theoretical justification of these arrangements is their capacity to 'tie hands' (Rodrik, 1996) and to function as 'agencies of restraint' for governments lacking credibility. The question is whether programmes with the BWI, trade liberalization and agreements with the WTO are strong enough signals for a government not to reverse its policy.[70] Considering their rise in power in SSA, the BWI are the most important of these institutions and agreements. The Ivory Coast belongs to several regional financial multilateral institutions (ADB, BOAD), in addition to the Conseil de l'Entente, the Joint African and Mauritian Organization (OCAM), the West-African Economic and Monetary Union (UEMOA/WAEMU, 8 states), the ECOWAS (CEDEAO, 16 states), an arrangement that is supposed to establish a preferential circulation of goods and people. The latter functions with difficulty owing to a historical antagonism between the influences of French-speaking countries and Nigeria, the incompatibility between the objectives of free circulation and fiscal dependency on customs duties, as well as public services relying more heavily on the users' predation than on a sense of public duty and the application of governmental directives (Sindzingre, 2000b).

The Uruguay Round and the WTO

The Ivory Coast joined GATT in 1963, and is a member of the WTO. The effects of the Uruguay Round (UR) on the Ivory Coast were varied, owing to its status as a developing country and the fact that it benefited from concessions under the Lomé Convention as an ACP (African-Caribbean-Pacific) country, and under the General System of Preferences (GSP) of OECD countries. Effects are rather weak, and even negative, owing to the erosion of preferences on OECD markets and increased competition (Blackhurst *et al.*, 1995). These regional arrangements of industrialized countries discriminate, however, against the labour-intensive products of SSA (Amjadi *et al.*, 1996). The principal export products of SSA were not subjected to non-tariff barriers to the US and Europe – for instance, crude petroleum, gems, coffee and cocoa. Although the majority of the barriers placed by the OECD countries (the main recipients of products from SSA) were abolished, some were retained. In the textile sector, the liberalization of the MultiFiber Arrangement may in fact intensify competition in the sector, one that is of great importance to the Ivory coast, in the same way as the suppression of voluntary restraints in sectors such as footwear and ferrous metals did. Structural adjustment and national domestic policies may in this case take advantage of or attenuate the effects, particularly those which may or may not favour local producers (Amjadi and Yeats, 1995a). The effects are negative for countries which are net importers of food products, since their prices increase with reductions in subsidies (Harrold, 1995). This is the case for the Ivory Coast for certain products such as rice, even if this could provide an occasion to promote the local food-producing agriculture. Important stakes of the UR, such as subsidies for agricultural exports, do not affect SSA countries much, since they tend to tax these exports, even if the Ivory Coast has some subsidy policies. For manufactured products, the UR has maintained the highest tariffs on certain key products, such as textiles, leather and fish, which is negative for SSA, but has lowered them on, for instance, wood as well as chemical and mineral products. Since it

exports to OECD countries, including 30 per cent of its industrial
products (especially wood and fish), the situation of the Ivory Coast
is relatively unchanged (Harrold, 1995, p. 25), although the erosion
of preferences on fish exports have induced a loss (Davenport *et al.*,
1995, p. 45). SSA countries do not take full advantage of the oppor-
tunitics offered by the WTO, in terms of negotiation and the credibility of their liberalization through international arrangements
(Sorsa, 1997; Blackhurst *et al.*, 2000). The multilateralism of the
WTO is compatible with regional arrangements, the pertinent criterion being the degree of discrimination against non-members
(Hoekman and Sauvé, 1994). There were exemptions for countries
belonging to the Lomé Convention until its transformation into the
Cotonou Agreement in 2000 which admitted and put an end to the
ineffectiveness of the Lomé regime's period of special and differential treatment for poorest countries accepted by the WTO. However,
some areas of ACP exports, such as bananas – which have serious
implications for an exporting country like the Ivory Coast – have
been a long-lasting source of conflict.[71]

The environment

The Ivory Coast has signed the major international agreements relating
to the environment. As in other arrangements – for example, the
WAEMU (see below) or product agreements – it knows how to use this
arena to assure its leadership. For the Rio follow-up after 1992, it took
over the co-ordination of consultations within the African group, promoted a common African position,[72] and committed itself to the
implementation of Agenda 21. In spite of the inclusion of environmental considerations in the WTO, its links to trade liberalization may be
uncertain or conflicting (Stevens, 1993). The environmental rules may
appear, to the Ivory Coast and to other developing countries, as a
luxury or an expression of the interests of Northern countries
(Whalley, 1996), as reflected in the divergences emerging at the time of
the global summits. For the Ivory Coast, the interaction between the
environment and liberalization is based on the promotion of its
primary product exports and on their compatibility with the natural
heritage of its plants and soil. A strategic product like cocoa, subject to
cycles, an extensive economy of land clearing and a 'race to production', is not easily compatible with the environment: the 'forest rent' is
consumed to the advantage of the 'cocoa rent', given the lack of land
rent (Ruf, 1995 and 1997). The strengthening of exports and foreign

currency sources (a recommendation of the World Bank) presents a problem of policy coherence.

The Ivory Coast initiated a National Action Plan for the Environment in 1992 for the period 1996–2010, as well as an environment code in 1996 and an obligation to study the environmental impact on development projects. Deforestation, loss of biodiversity, industrial pollution and urban environment, water resources and coastal erosion, are explicit themes of concern. Deforestation has been massive (1 per cent annual deforesting between 1980 and 1990[73]). From being a key export sector, wood declined after 1984, and its exploitation and exportation are regulated. However, the sector remains important in terms of employment and is entirely controlled by foreign firms. It is subject to tensions between these firms, official environmental regulations and local rural communities. The latter tend to overexploit the biomass, even more so with a trade liberalization supported by weak institutions, and also constitute a political foundation for the regime.[74] The priorities, which are expressed by conditionalities in a permanent state of tension with the objective proclaimed by the donors of 'reform ownership' by the government, are thus in disagreement with those of some donors, while they have the support of others. This induces coherence problems or creates obstacles (for the Forestry Sector Project with the World Bank, for example). Most of the government's projects are financed by aid agencies,[75] the Bank, the EU, bilateral donors such as Germany, France or The Netherlands, which makes its intentions of autonomy and ownership somewhat ambiguous. Environmental issues may also constitute an example of divergences with the donors, when they come within a wider scope of negotiations. An example may be the disagreement over a strategic topic like the institutional framework, that is, the project to create an environmental agency over and above the ministries concerned. This project caused tensions within these ministries, but is in line with the approach of the BWI to bypass administrative levels not considered to be effective enough, this line not being very consistent with the proclaimed intention of 'reinforcing the state'. Besides the institutional and regulatory framework, the order of priorities is another example of divergence, particularly in the areas of reducing precarious urban districts, improving biodiversity and forestry, and the public investment programme.[76] This contributed to reciprocal relations of mistrust, already analysed with regard to adjustment programmes: the government tends to submit itself to donor conditions, even if these are inappropriate, as almost all expenses are financed by donors.

Relations with the European Union

The Ivory Coast benefits from the Lomé Convention (the Cotonou Agreement since 2000). Its preferential trade regime, concerning traditional commodities only, excludes temperate agricultural products protected by the Common Agricultural Policy (CAP) and manufactured products. But the Ivory Coast has an industrial sector and is an exporter of wood, textiles and fish. In addition, certain products such as bananas, sugar, rum, beef and veal, fell under special protocols guaranteeing access and also establishing non-tariff barriers, in particular quotas (Amjadi and Yeats, 1995a). These non-reciprocal trade preferences eroded with the lowering of tariffs vis-à-vis non-ACP countries, and moreover placed the ACP countries in an increasingly competitive situation (Oshikoya, 1996). The preferences concerning duty-free coffee imports in the EU, for instance, protected the Ivory Coast from its non-ACP competitors paying duties under the Generalised System of Preferences. The Ivory Coast benefits from an export quota of bananas to the EU, an important export product. The conflict over the ACP banana versus the 'dollar banana', supposed to be resolved in 2001, was yet another example of the erosion of preferences resulting from the lowering of tariffs on tropical products (Stevens, 1996). The Ivory Coast runs the risk of being a loser in the sectors of tropical products and manufactured products (Davenport *et al.*, 1995; Pagen and Davenport, 1994). Moreover, EU trade policies have been inconsistent with its own aid policies ('taking back with one hand what has been given by the other'), particularly those of the Common Agricultural Policy and its subsidized surpluses of cereals or bovine meat, which endangered food-producing farmers in West Africa, simultaneously helped by the European Development Fund (EDF), or the purchase of fishing rights by European firms which penalize local operators.[77] The preferences and positive discriminations of the Lomé Conventions have not been efficient.[78]

This failure explains the shift in orientation of the Cotonou Agreement, which aims at a better integration of ACP countries in global trade, the end of preferences and a progressive compatibility with WTO rules. Although European trade policies have contributed to confine ACP exports to a small number of traditional products, local anti-tradable products policies have not favoured diversification either.[79] In the case of the Lomé Convention, the Ivory Coast had the support of

France to protect its advantages, France for its part used the multilateralism of the EU in its foreign policy, owing to its preponderant importance. In terms of international political economy, more than a beneficial interdependence or consolidation of a dependency, the relationship of some ACP countries with the EU also denotes a tendency towards increasing isolation from the EU and the rest of the world.[80]

In terms of aid, most of it corresponded to transfers through Stabex, in compensation for fluctuations in export revenues from cocoa and coffee, from which the Ivory Coast benefited amply. Being a heavy instrument with poorly controlled funds, the delay in disbursements from Stabex was criticized for having pro-cyclical effects (Collier, Guillaumont *et al.*, 1997d), and it was suppressed by the Cotonou Agreement. The Ivory Coast has at its disposal a budget from the EDF for its National Indicative Programme (von Brokowski, 1997), in addition to other instruments, such as support for structural adjustment, food aid or project aid, and loans from the European Investment Bank.

Product agreements

The Ivory Coast is a member of product agreements, such as the ICCO for cocoa, the ICO for coffee, and the INRO for rubber, in which developed consumer countries come to the arrangements that correspond best to their interests.[81] These agreements were permanently exposed to dysfunction and free riding, and also to criticism from the Bretton Woods institutions, which are against government intervention in product markets, whether international or national. Total liberalization and direct benefit of producers from world prices without taxation by national stabilization funds were motives for the suppression of the Caistab. Product agreements progressively kept only the objectives of production of information and statistics for the markets. INRO was thus liquidated in 2000. The Ivory Coast, as a leading producer of cocoa, exploited the product agreement in which it is dominant, the ICCO. As part of the ICO, the Ivoirian government decided, in 1993, to introduce intervention mechanisms in the market and participated in a retention plan for coffee export – by 20 per cent of their production volume. This permitted the group of African, Asian and Latin-American producers to exert pressure on world coffee prices. This strategy having shown its limitations, the Ivory Coast, within the framework of the Inter-African Coffee Organisation, introduced an export quotas system.[82] The country also participated in the plan adopted by the ICCO to reduce overproduction of cocoa. It managed to ensure that its interests prevailed in international arenas, as shown by its campaign in 1997 against the directive project of the EU authorizing 5 per cent vegetable fat other than that of cocoa in chocolate, a move which will result in considerable losses and significant fall in the demand of beans from the EU. The Ivory Coast won temporarily by using lobbying like its opponents,[83] it lost eventually since the EU directive was finally accepted. Having a negotiation capacity in the ICCO at its disposal, it seeks to optimize the organization of exporters, and to draw lessons from the liberalization reforms in Nigeria and Cameroon. On the issue of European chocolate, the Ivory Coast plays against its neighbour, Burkina Faso, with which it is associated by multiple formal agreements and an economic and migratory complementarity. But as a producer of shea butter, Burkina gains with the authorization of products other than cocoa within the EU. However, the Ivory Coast also produces shea butter.

The West African Economic and Monetary Union (WAEMU)

The Ivory Coast is a member of the WAEMU, established in 1994 after the devaluation of the CFA franc following the disappearance of the former CEAO. As in the latter, it is the 'heavyweight' of the WAEMU, and the position remains ambiguous with respect to Nigeria. The signing of the WAEMU Treaty may typically constitute a credible arrangement, having at its disposal guarantees from a developed country, France, supported by a pre-existing monetary zone, and by coercive institutional procedures and multilateral surveillance inspired by the Maastricht Treaty. However, during the years of crisis, the rules of the franc zone did not appear to be credible. Fiscal discipline was bypassed just as it was with respect to the other countries of the ex-CEAO, the Ivory Coast played free rider with a much higher fiscal deficit.[84] The WAEMU incurs the same risks. In addition to generating uncertainty, the signals remain somewhat unclear with respect to the consequences of the transition from the French franc to the Euro, and its implications in terms of competitiveness, vulnerability and political economy: delegation of the management of the exchange rate to the European Central Bank, or preservation of the present budgetary arrangement managed by the French Treasury, and open to criticism since it reduces the credibility of the Central Bank (Hadjimichael and Galy, 1997; Claeys and Sindzingre, 2001).

The WAEMU is a project that covers customs union and harmonization of tariffs (Common External Tariff, CET) and legal and tax environment (OHADA[85] Treaty of 1996). The disparity between countries in the zone, the informal exploitation of their differentials, and the multiple levies on the circulation of goods and persons exerted by civil servants, are a handicap, and the ex-CEAO, which was supposed to be a preferential trade zone, tended to discriminate against intra-zone trade.[86] There is a geopolitical dimension underlying these agreements. The objective of the WAEMU is to suppress non-tariff barriers between member countries and to reduce entry duties for industrial products originating from the zone, but economic differentials and political divergence make this task difficult.[87] The CET project is sometimes perceived by operators as not being very realistic, the tax revenues largely depending on customs tariffs, and promoted from outside, namely, by France, in counterpoint with, amongst others, Nigeria, the most important member of the other regional arrangement, the ECOWAS. As was the case with devaluation, the positions of the countries are asymmetric, and they do not benefit equally, having heterogeneous exporting structures and industrial sectors, as well as different tariff levels.[88] The Ivory Coast is a beneficiary, having the best industrial and exporting sector in the subregion (*Marchés Tropicaux et Meditérranéens*, 1997, p. 1417). This does not apply to the landlocked countries without frontiers to the outside of the zone, nor to countries bordering Nigeria. An evaluation of real trade remains difficult, since the official intra-regional trade is notoriously undervalued.[89] In terms of interactions with more comprehensive multilateral arrangements, the WTO, having 'tolerated' the regional arrangements for political reasons, recognizes the south–south arrangements. As these are more complementary than substitutes to multilateralism, they often imply a higher degree of liberalization than the latter (Hoekman and Sauvé, 1994, p. 61–5), which is the case with WAEMU.

The liberalization process

After 1985, the liberalization process was reactivated during the years 1989–90, then after the devaluation. The important point is that it is difficult to distinguish specific liberalization effects from those following from devaluation.[90] Liberalization improves a firm's competitiveness, in the same way as devaluation. The two processes were concomitant, and liberalization is a gradual process which is still under way. Some sectors have gained, others less so, but the two effects are combined. The Ivory Coast appears to have presented an average GDP growth of 1.8 per cent in the period covering the three years preceding and the three years following liberalization.[91] The consensus is however not total with regard to the beneficial effects of liberalization, and the private sector may be unable to alleviate the decrease in public prerogatives if the reforms are not credible (Greenaway *et al.*, 1997). The link between the opening up of trade and growth, usually demonstrated through investment, is uncertain for a country like the Ivory Coast (Harrison, 1995), particularly with respect to the export of commodities (McKay *et al.*, 1997). The 1985 liberalization was too ambitious, causing policy instability and a credibility deficit. A debate exists on the sequencing: liberalization following devaluation, or vice versa. Besides, the Ivory Coast is an atypical country since it has favoured investment policies open to foreign countries since its independence. Likewise, the behaviour of firms does not give a particularly clear indication, and foreign private investments may be nothing more than companies seizing short-term opportunities. This dilemma was faced by a number of SSA countries in the 1990s: they seek to attract foreign investors but are constrained by a tax system depending on customs duties, with fierce competition between them due to globalization and liberalization under the BWI programmes, which can induce a fallacy of composition.

Liberalization was reinforced by new codes promulgated in 1995: the investment code, mining code, labour code and telecommunications code. The first one followed previous investment codes (1959 and 1984) which were already liberal. The foundation of CEPICI[92] in 1994 instituted a unique 'gateway' for investors, a standard recommendation of the World Bank already implemented in other African countries. With the 1995 investment code, a general regime and two dispensatory regimes were established. Exonerations of the previous code were suppressed but the new code also largely removes taxes. The liberalization of external trade, initiated with the sectoral competitiveness adjustment programme (PASCO, 1991), was gradually implemented. In the case of imports, it abolished non-tariff barriers in 1994 (except those concerning health, security and the environment), and simplified the rates.[93] The sectors of rice and transport – in particular maritime transport – were totally liberalized, as well as internal trade and prices (1992), and the trade regime of the customs code.[94] Until then, industrial firms were highly protected, especially the food industry and textiles (Mytelka, 1984). Launched in 1993, the tariff reform spread the rates from 5 to 35 per cent, and abolished most of the other import taxes (Marchat, 1997a). In matters of internal taxation laws, VAT was simplified to two rates (20 per cent and 11.11 per cent). Monopolies remained,[95] each corresponding to specific firms – private or in process of privatization – connected to national or international interests. All other sectors were liberalized.

Liberalization has not always implied price decreases, rice being a case in point.[96] There exist *de facto* oligopolies (Marchat, 1997a, p. 9), and the industrial sector is characterized by an imperfect competitive structure varying according to the branches. Certain markets, occupied more by formal, older, and foreign-owned firms, and favoured by the regulatory framework, are concentrated and oligopolistic, creating an imperfect competitive environment, while the competitive markets (furniture, clothes) are dominated by informal, African-owned firms. In 1995, the manufacturing sector was composed of 2.8 per cent of formal firms, representing 16 per cent of the GDP, while 0.6 per cent were semi-formal and 96.6 per cent informal. This dualism led to distinct liberalization effects, the former firms being exporters and less exposed to competition, the latter being oriented towards the domestic market and more exposed to competition (Marchat, 1997a and 1997b). During the liberalization process, this imperfect market character has tended to increase the prices, and alliances and cartel phenomena were established. A small economy such as that of the Ivory Coast is not very competitive, and it has few companies per sector. Liberalisation encountered resistance in the monopolistic sectors. An example of this is wheat flour, a monopoly of French interests; these interest mobilized their political supporters, the World Bank having the destruction of this rent in its line of sight. Here too, the political authorities had to make a trade-off between the financial flows of donors and the preservation of interest groups. Some sectors lost as a result of liberalization, for instance, that of new vehicles (French and Japanese) with the liberalisation of second-hand vehicle imports (April 1996) which at the time increased considerably.[97] Another example is the liberalization of the telecommunications sector which led to the setting up of new companies producing cellular telephones.[98]

The effects on external trade

Since devaluation, the Ivoirian economy has increased its participation in international trade: the volume index of exports increased by 8.5 per cent in 1994, and even by 22 per cent in 1996, and the volume index of imports also increased by 41 per cent in 1995, with a decrease in the following years (IMF, 2000). It is difficult here to dissociate the effects of the devaluation of the CFA franc and trade liberalization.[99] This increase came from the exports of primary products, helped by their high world prices, but prices of cocoa collapsed after 1999. The liberalization-devaluation duo preserves the primary specialization of the Ivory Coast (cocoa exports increased notably after devaluation[100]). This reminds us of the intrinsic weakness of exports since they are linked to the behaviour of international prices. Their diversification remains difficult. The Ivory Coast is trying to transform locally, to create added value, especially in the sectors of cocoa and wood. Liberalization and the change of parity did not modify the geographic orientation of exchanges, which are still concentrated on industrialized countries, essentially the EU (in 1999, 45 per cent of exports and 51 per cent of imports) (IMF, 2000, Tables 40 and 42). France has retained its position as a leading supplier, followed by the United States. The reorientation of exchanges with Africa has not occurred. However, sub-regional exchanges with the WAEMU have increased. Exchanges with Asia remain insignificant. The Ivory Coast is still very dependent on developed countries both for its exports and its imports.

The impact on investment

Investments increased, even if it is difficult to distinguish the effects of devaluation and liberalization. Investors are sensitive to risk, in spite of the definite advantages of membership of the franc zone and the absence of foreign currency rationing (Fielding, 1993), as well as the market size, the openness of the economy and the quality of infrastructures. The physical infrastructures are an advantage in the Ivory Coast, but that is less the case when it comes to institutional infrastructures. Economic policies are not completely credible, nor are the commitment announcements with regard to the rule of law, the judiciary or security of property rights. The uncertainty dwells on a policy reversal, as well as on liberalization if public finances are in difficult situation.[101] The same applies to the external tariff reform of the WAEMU and the objective of the free circulation of goods (already anticipated in the treaty founding the ECOWAS, but ineffective), but not very credible in the eyes of economic operators who are well informed on the previous 'informal' customs levies and rents extracted from the circulation of goods. The goal of the ESAF 1994–97 was to reform the private sector and the legal framework, while ESAF in 1997–2000 focused on the legal framework and modernization of public services. This shows, on the one hand, a repetition of the same objectives which have not yet been achieved, and on the other hand, an awareness on the government's part of the contradictions between its agenda for economic growth and internal policies, and the credibility deficit of the institutional frame-work. The 'agencies of restraint' and external conditionalities were the object of too much bargaining between several players to be credible (Collier and Gunning, 1997b). Even if the Ivory Coast explicitly wants to attract investors, they suspect that the clientelist paradigm is still dominant. Another negative factor is that of a private sector which is often based on seizing commercial opportunities. Some researchers have isolated an 'African dummy': foreign investors do not come even if the reforms have been correctly carried out (Bhattacharya *et al.*, 1997; Englebert, 2000). In addition, African economic agents prefer to invest outside SSA owing to the political and economic credibility deficits.[102]

In many countries, decades of adjustment failed to rise the level of investment, which was about 10 per cent of GDP in the Ivory Coast between 1990 and 1995, with an amelioration after 1994. The total investment rate rose from 7.8 per cent of GDP in 1993 to 18 per cent in 1998 (Bouton and Sumlinski, 2000, p. 30). The public investment rate remained stable, around the low figure of 4–5 per cent of GDP.[103] Private investment was made by investors already established in the Ivory Coast, and by the arrival of new investors in the mining and oil sectors, as well as in the food sector (services, mining and energy, and the food industry represented 71.5 per cent of the total investment of the industrial sector in 1994–95 and 57.2 per cent in 1995–96). The French occupy a predominant place, followed by the Lebanese and Ivoirians. Two periods may be singled out: after devaluation, the growth in investment was due to the return of flight capital, expressed by a boom in construction and the creation of companies, followed by a contraction. The mining and petroleum sectors are specific because of the windfall dimension of their profitability (fragile for the unique operated well). US or Canadian investments (petroleum, gas, mining) may be interpreted as a determination to diversify by the Ivoirian gov-ernment. The activities of the energy and mining sectors increased by 45 per cent from 1994 to 1996 (FNICI, 1997).

Competitiveness and liberalization are still handicapped by factor costs, especially wages – their level reflecting the Ivoirian consumption model – electricity and freight: transportation costs of exports leaving Abidjan[104] are considered by investors to be a major problem, even more negative than the barriers established by importing countries (Amjadi and Yeats, 1995b). These costs are also the result of the history of the state, and the multiple informal customs, port and other admin-istrative taxes and bribes. The latter undermined the rules and the determination of the ex-CEAO and the ECOWAS to liberalize, turning border-crossing into a 'permanent negotiation' (Naudet, 1996). In the Ivory Coast, as in other SSA countries, the principal handicap is over-high transaction costs, due to a deficit in infrastructure and credible institutions. From a political economy point of view, the rules remain cumbersome and many did not change over time, and the bureaucracy exploits them to its own advantage. The historical ambivalence vis-à-vis the attraction of investors and the private sector persists: if it is not foreign or controlled by the political power. The entrepreneurial nature of the private sector, which had adapted to this situation – more or less enforced by foreign countries or re-interpreted by the political power – remains questionable.

The industrial sector after two decades of reforms

The Ivoirian industrial sector remains the most important among those of the franc zone countries. After 1994, the manufacturing sector (except petroleum, mining, water and electricity) experienced strong growth. The production capacity utilization rate was on the rise, situated around 86 per cent in 1999.[105] Some sectors have benefited, others less so – textiles and clothing production almost doubled over the 1994–99 period as firms took advantage of their renewed competitiveness. Depending on their historical structures, import-intensive or based on exports, industries oriented toward the domestic market (grain milling or bottling) increased only slowly (IMF, 2000). They show the advantages and constraints, both internal and depending on the international environment, not only of liberalization, but also linked to their political economy. The Federation of Industries referred in 1997 to contrasting tendencies, following from several factors, not only of devaluation and/or liberalization, but also the nature of the product, the structure of the activity, the type of market and the international economic situation. Industrial production, after devaluation, thus increased by 31.2 per cent between 1993 and 1996, with a significant progress in exports. The index of industrial production was 98 in 1994, and 153 in 1999 (for 1984–85=base 100) (IMF, 2000, Table 15). The redistribution of income linked to export agriculture favoured the industries operating in the domestic market, as well as trade and services, and an exporting sector such as the food industry. Production increased in the mining sector because of the rise of the production of gas, but the profitability of a sector such as petroleum, which came to a standstill after its new take-off in 1995, depends on external economic situations which are not controlled by the Ivory

Coast, as in the case of mines, particularly gold mines, with a profitability affected by the fall in international prices in 1997. However, the recovery remains fragile, as shown by the immediate impact of the political tensions occurring since 1999.

An unexpected effect: informalization

As in other SSA countries, international integration and responses to the external environment and the reforms of the Ivory Coast cannot be analyzed exclusively through official activities but should include informal activities. These may be cross-border exchanges,[106] activities of private operators or organized public agents. The phenomenon of informalization is an old one and linked to the nature of the political regime since independence. It intensified, on the one hand, with the prosperity period when individuals were incited by the enrichment of high officials and, on the other, with the instabilities of the tax and customs measures of the adjustment period, and it was accelerated by the fall in the standard of living. Attempts at making the informal sector subject to tax (lump sum tax) had the effect of encouraging tax evasion even more, a reaction which became routine with the loss of credibility of the state. A conditionality of the BWI programmes, an import control company commissioned to increase customs revenues, did not succeed in creating a 'binding agreement', and is still incapable of reducing fraud. In terms of political economy, it privatizes functions considered to be a matter of sovereignty and encounters resistance. At the same time, it is not free of credibility problems itself, since these controlling companies depend on contractual agreements with the states, and they therefore avoid coming into direct confrontation with local interest groups. Some formal firms in the import-substitution sector (textiles, and so on) have been close to bankruptcy since the crisis owing to pressure created by fraudulent imports and unfair competition, which they consider to be their principal problem.[107]

An important point is that trade liberalization actually increased fraud. The 'rentierism' of importers manifested itself even more (Boone, 1994), when faced with customs and tax authorities used to personal enrichment and little interested in controlling fraudulent imports from countries of the sub-region or 'sales' from the rest of the world (American and European second-hand clothes, Asian counterfeits, and so on). Because fraud can push formal firms to bankruptcy, liberalization in fact allows new entrants after the long protection period. Given the political economy of the Ivory Coast, these may avoid paying customs duties (corruption) and are therefore more 'competitive' than formal firms. The 'administrative rigidities' persist, the legal framework continues to lack clarity, and the judicial system is still not very reliable. Yet, the protection of property rights is an essential condition imposed by investors (Collier and Gunning, 1997b).

Conclusion

A first conclusion is that liberalization measures may be rational in theory. However, they may produce negative effects since they require, like all reforms, the existence of a genuine state that is not reduced to the mere juxtaposition of microeconomic calculations based on rent-seeking and the taking advantage of defects in the rules which the civil service has neither the capacity nor the will to apply. The reforms imply an efficient and non-predatory tax and customs authority, and transparent rules, as opposed to a regime founded on withholding information,[108] as well as a coherent system of institutions and markets, especially an effective financial market. But firms were severely hit by the paralysis of the banking system existing before devaluation, which affected those who did not have insider information. Reforms constitute a holistic system, going beyond debates on gradualism versus shock therapy, and implying the existence of markets and institutions suitable for responding to market failures (Stiglitz, 1989). In their absence, whatever the international requirements, and even more so if they are multiple and not necessarily coherent, the domestic responses risk being counter-productive, and may only meet short-term internal political priorities.

More generally, the Ivoirian model showed advantages, in particular its good infrastructures, while its ties with the former colonial power, France, had certain positive effects (Sindzingre, 1996b). However, the liberalization did not really modify a model which remains fragile even after the recovery, in an economic and international political economy perspective. The style of the previous regime, the structure of interest groups and the subordinate position of the Ivory Coast vis-à-vis international arrangements continue. Institutional reforms stumble against the political dimension, and the credibility deficit vis-à-vis international markets is accentuated by globalization which has caused emerging countries to compete with each other in order to attract international capital. The economic structure remains captive to a primary exporting model and the comparative advantages of the country depend on international commodity prices. This specialization may, in the long run, turn out to be impoverishing, with an industrialization developed on low labour costs. This opens the way to new modifications in the exchange rate which could erode real wages and increase poverty. In addition, in the case of multilateral arrangements, although the Ivory Coast is active at the regional level, with the support of the former colonial power, it is still constrained by the influence of international organizations in the core of its decision-making capacity (Strange, 1996), by a global integration which allows little room for manoeuvre as a developing and severely indebted country, and by its institutional weakness and domestic interest groups. All these factors are unattractive to investors. Liberalization and devaluation have not modified the country's vulnerability to external shocks.

Notes

1. See Strange (1996); see also Evans (1995 and 1997).
2. See the World Development Report of 1997 on the rehabilitation of the role of the state in developing countries; see also Johnson (1994).
3. The expression was used by Kahler (1992). Amongst an enormous literature, see Haggard and Webb (1994), Mosley *et al.* (1991) on conditionality as a bargaining process.
4. Ng and Yeats (1996, p. 25) show that the average tariff level in SSA is four times higher than in OECD countries.
5. In 1995: World Bank, *World Development Report 1997*, Table 1.
6. Unique in SSA outside the rand zone (Hadjimichael and Galy, 1997, p. 7).
7. Guinea-Bissau joined the WAEMU on 5 March 1997 and the franc zone on 17 April 1997.
8. Benin, Burkina Faso, the Ivory Coast, Guinea-Bissau, Mali, Niger, Senegal and Togo.
9. Cameroon, Central African Republic, Congo, Gabon, Equatorial Guinea and Chad.
10. 100 CFA francs for 1 FF, the parity being the same for the West-African and Central African sub-zones, and 75 Comorian F for 1 FF.
11. Amongst the vast literature, see Godeau (1995).
12. See J. Pégatiénan, quoted in Azam (1993).
13. Particularly vis-à-vis Senegal for the regional leadership and Nigeria (episode of the Biafra war, weak Ivoirian participation in the ECOWAS, especially exchanges with the Anglophone countries); see Bach (1982, p. 93).
14. The famous bet made in 1957; see Woronoff (1972), Foster and Zolberg (1971).
15. Rodrik (1992a), according to a classical contrast with the East-Asian developmental state.
16. Adamolekun *et al.* (1997, Chapter 7, concerns the Ivory Coast).
17. The rules of the BCEAO limiting its credit – its 'statutory advances' – to the Treasury, were bypassed (Stasavage, 1997); the governor *de facto* is Ivoirian, and so on.
18. See Rapley (1993), who is convinced of the existence of an old class of private entrepreneurs, versus Gouffern (1982) on their predatory character, or Boone (1994) on their 'rentier' character; see also Widner (1993), and Woods (1994).

19. See Duruflé (1988) on the model induced by the expatriates, Pégatiénan and Ouayogode (1997) on the role of France.
20. Fuchs (1995, p. 23) emphasizes the positive gains for the French market shares in the imports and exports of the Ivory Coast (58 per cent and 33 per cent respectively), or Marchand (1996) the trade balance surplus and the creation of jobs in France.
21. Schneider *et al.* (1992, p. 21).
22. World Bank (1994, p. 8); see Sindzingre (1996b), Chevassu and Valette (1975), Conte (1984).
23. According to a model of 'économie de traite', that is, open colonial economy (Hopkins, 1973; Austen, 1987; Assidon, 1989).
24. Dubresson (1989) analyses in detail the history and the trajectories of the industrial companies.
25. See Mytelka (1984) on the case of the textile sector.
26. The tariff protection was relatively high: 22–42 per cent nominal amount required by foreign investors (Mytelka, 1984; Marchat, 1997a, p. 12 and 1997b, p. 5).
27. Debt equalling a third of the GDP before the devaluation (Sogodogo, 1997, p. 142).
28. Mundt (1997) describes the evolution of the political liberalization.
29. Amongst an extremely large literature on the concepts of credibility, see Rodrik (1989).
30. The fiscal deficit changed from 2.9 per cent of GDP in 1986 to 12.6 per cent in 1990 (Azam and Morrisson, 1994, p. 67).
31. This was the case of VAT (WTO, 1995, Vol. 1, p. 12).
32. Only the large 'veteran' exporting companies benefited from it (Newman *et al.*, 1990, p. 27).
33. In 1984, 31 per cent of the total taxes, Dean *et al.* (1994, Table 6.6).
34. In 1991, the tariffs were spread from 0 per cent to 151 per cent.
35. See also Riddell (1992, pp. 219–21) on the evolution of measures relating to the industrial sector, and Sindzingre (1996b).
36. See Schneider *et al.* (1992, p. 34). Between 1980 and 1985, –42.5 per cent of jobs were lost in state-owned companies (Schneider *et al.*, 1992, p. 51), –22 per cent between 1982 and 1988 for SME, (Rueda-Sabater and Stone, 1992, p. 10; Kouadio Bénié, 1991). Private investment fell from 1977 to 1988, from 16.6 per cent of the nominal GDP to 4.5 per cent (Rueda-Sabater and Stone, 1992, p. 4).
37. Source: World Bank, *African Development Indicators*, 1997b, Table 12–9.
38. The French net Official Development Assistance to the Ivory Coast was 1.7 billion FF in 1991, 2.36 billion in 1992, 3.3 billion in 1993 (*The Franc Zone, Annual Report 1993*, annex 4, p. 264).
39. See the arguments against the devaluation of Coquet and Daniel (1992), or the debate on the compared performances of the countries inside and outside the franc zone: Devarajan and de Melo (1987), Guillaumont *et al.* (1988), Deverajan and de Melo (1991). See van de Walle (1991) on the political economy of the franc zone.
40. On the devaluation, amongst others, see Bourguignon *et al.* (1995), Guillaumont and Guillaumont-Jeanneney (1997), Goreux (1995), Clément *et al.* (1996), Le Dem (1994), Villa (1994).

41. See the critics of Monga (1997).
42. Source: World Bank, *African Development Indicators*, 1997b, Table 12–9.
43. Source: World Bank, African Development Indicators, 1997b, Table 2–18.
44. *Marchés Tropicaux et Méditerranéens* (1997, p. 11).
45. The Ivory Coast thus anticipated 215 billion of external resources and could not mobilize more than 40 billion (*Marchés Tropicaux et Méditerranéens*, no. 2771, 2 January 1998, p. 22).
46. On general effects, see Edwards (1989); Conte (1995 and 1997, p. 6).
47. Heavily Indebted Poor Countries.
48. See Sindzingre (2000a); see also Berg *et al.* (2001).
49. Fertilizer sector in Nigeria, cocoa in Cameroon.
50. *La Tribune*, 4 March 1998.
51. *Marchés Tropicaux et Méditerranéens* (1997, p. 16). The president boasted to his electors about the 'shower of billions' that the Ivory Coast had received after devaluation.
52. This is also the case in other countries, for instance, Ghana in the cocoa sector.
53. See Heilman and Lucas (1997, p. 159), on the example of Tanzania and Nigeria.
54. See Steel and Webster (1992) on Ghana; see also Azam and Morrisson (1994).
55. World Bank, PIC-CI, Transport sector, Project Document 29-01-1997.
56. As emphasized by the Bank (PIC, Project Information Document 12-07-1995, second forestry sector project).
57. Water distribution was privatized 30 years ago by leasing to a French company.
58. This process of intensifying privatization since the beginning of the 1990s is common to all of the SSA (Bennell, 1996).
59. The telephone company and the sugar plants, CITelcom and Sodesucre.
60. BIAO; see International Monetary Fund (2000, p. 27).
61. Source: industrial production indexes, third quarter 1997.
62. 'Privatization of the privatization process', Bennell (1996, p. 17).
63. Bouygues administers water distribution, electricity, constructs the airport, the bridge, the wholesale market, etc. France Télécom bought back CITelcom after privatisation.
64. Even French speakers like the Canadians had difficulties in penetrating the market in the energy and pharmaceutical sectors (Pégatiénan and Ouayogode, 1997, p. 130).
65. For instance on Octide, see Verdier (1996), *Marchés Tropicaux et Méditerranéens*, 5 September 1997, no. 2704, p. 1951.
66. For instance, the attempt at buying CITelcom by a previous 'client' of Houphouët-Boigny was a failure.
67. *Le Monde*, 7 February 1998.
68. The privatization of CITelcom having been criticized by the opposition press.
69. Söderbaum (1996), for instance, lists the numerous African regional organizations.
70. As shown by Collier (1997) in the case of Uganda.
71. Until 2001 Thomas (1997) recalls the silence of the European Commission's Green Paper on the compatibility of the Lomé Convention with the WTO, and the inadequacy of WTO's approaches to the actual situation with regard to the regional arrangements.

72. 'Republic of Côte d'Ivoire', Synthesis note: Agenda-21 implementation, May 1997, p. 22.
73. Source: World Bank, *World Development Report 1997*, Table 10.
74. These rural communities, contrary to a current opinion, no longer develop the appropriate controls to preserve natural forest resources (Lopez, 1998, pp. 124–5).
75. 'Republic of Côte d'Ivoire', Synthesis of the works of the PNAE-CI, July 1996.
76. 'Republic of Côte d'Ivoire', PNAE-CI: *Position of the Ivoirian Party on the Aide-Mémoire of the Mission of Evaluation*, July 1997.
77. See Jadot and Rolland (1996) on the contradictions of European agricultural trade policies.
78. Davenport *et al.* (1995) emphasize that the 70 ACP countries of the period represented 3.9 per cent of imports from the EU after decades of preferential treatment. In 1991, French exports to all ACP countries equalled those towards its overseas *départements et territoires* (DOM-TOM) (4.8 billion ECU, Sapir 1993, p. 436).
79. See the debates in Ng and Yeats (1996); Amjadi *et al.* (1996); Collier, Guillaumont *et al.* (1997d, p. 296).
80. See Mahler (1994, p. 247) on the Lomé Convention and the isolation of some countries.
81. Mori (1996) on the opportunism of the developed countries towards the preservation of the Coffee Agreement.
82. *Le Courrier*, no. 166, 1997, pp. 44–5.
83. And the publication of a White Paper (*Marchés Tropicaux et Méditerranéens*, 17 October 1997, no. 2710, p. 2255).
84. In 1993, it represented 16.4 per cent of the GDP versus an average of 8.4 per cent for other countries (Rosenberg, 1995, p. 13).
85. Organisation for Harmonising Business Law in Africa.
86. The tariffs on the zone's products were sometimes higher than those applied to imports from other countries, and the preferential tariff, the regional co-operation tax, was not applied (Rosenberg, 1995, p. 11).
87. See the ambiguous speech by President Moussa Touré (*Marchés Tropicaux et Méditerranéens*, no. 2704, 5 September 1997, p. 1948).
88. Benin has for instance a more liberal external trade policy owing to its proximity to Nigeria and the intense re-exporting trade between the two countries, one being a member of the WAEMU and the ECOWAS, the other being the 'heavyweight' of the ECOWAS.
89. Herrera (1998) shows the importance of unofficial exchanges with Nigeria to the economies of the countries bordering the franc zone; see also Sindzingre (2000b).
90. Collier (1993, p. 506) even considers that a devaluation is the *sine qua non* of trade liberalization.
91. Papageorgiou *et al.* (1991), criticized by Greenaway *et al.* (1997).
92. Centre for Investments Promotion in Côte d'Ivoire.
93. In 1993 there were 39 different tax rates (Naudet, 1996, p. 4).
94. Before the devaluation, in 1993, the effective protection was 37 per cent in weighted tariff, the highest of the ex-WAMU (Rosenberg, 1995, Table 1).
95. In sectors such as sugar, electricity, water distribution, oil refining, urban sanitation, fixed point telephones, transports and cigarettes.

96. After the devaluation, minimum import prices ('mercuriales' values) were introduced (WTO, 1995, p. 54).
97. 13 600 second-hand vehicles between April and December 1996, that is, three times more than new vehicles over the entire year (*Marchés Tropicaux et Méditerranéens*, 28 March 1997, no. 2681, p. 676).
98. Some with French interests or close to political power.
99. *La zone Franc, Annual report 1996*, Banque de France, p. 174. Institut National de la Statistique, *External Trade Annual*, 1985–1992, p. 8.
100. International Monetary Fund (1998, Table 10). *La zone Franc, Annual report 1996*, Banque de France, p. 174; Institut National de la Statistique, *External Trade Annual*, 1985–1992, p. 11).
101. Out of ten examined SSA countries, Oyejide *et al.* (1997) list seven who have comprised at least one major policy reversal.
102. Collier and Gunning (1997a). In SSA, investment goes primarily to oil-producing countries, UNCTAD (1995).
103. Source: World Bank (1997b), *African Development Indicators*, Tables 2–8 to 2–10 and Table 5–10.
104. See Biggs *et al.* (1996, pp. 74–6). The average worker's salary is twice as high in the Ivory Coast than in Ghana.
105. Banque de France, *The Franc Zone, Annual Report 1999*, p. 229.
106. See Stary (1995) on the example of the informal exchanges with Ghana.
107. FNICI (1997), especially cheap Asian imports re-exported by Nigeria or Nigerian imports.
108. Secrecy remains at the core of the operation of political power. The rent-seeking system relies on the fact that nobody may know the law, except at high transaction costs and through submission to political clientelist connections.

7
Sunset or Sunrise? Regime Change and Institutional Adjustment in South Africa – a Critical Analysis

Peter Vale and Larry A. Swatuk

Introduction

All writing on South Africa begins with a compulsory genuflection. This contribution can be no exception. South Africa´s transition, at the end of a troubled century, was hailed as an example to the world – irrespective of the horrors of Bosnia and Rwanda, the example of South Africa suggests that people of difference can live together in harmony.

For all the celebration,[1] this must be an interim judgement. South Africa´s future is far from settled – many areas are caught in terrible violence and the country´s people are only now exploring a series of associations in which publics, programmes, procedures and politics will come to play their respective parts. The celebration therefore for the Rainbow Nation seems associated more with liberation from the unhappy past than with belief in a secure future.

This chapter, like other contributions, is concerned with past and future: what comes between these two moments is the here and now. South Africa´s 'here and now' is etched in the idea of change: this word is found in each and every one of the country's many political lexicons, including those that deal with 'trade', the 'environment', and with 'trade and the environment'. It is therefore not surprising that the institutions which govern these aspects of South Africa's post-apartheid life are subject to all the problems implicit in the ideas of change and continuity.

For all the talk (and the reality) of change, however, there is a compelling consistency in the new South Africa. In many ways, it looks like the old South Africa and, unfortunately, often seems to behave like it. As a result, for all its change, South Africa essentially remains the same. 'Modernization', as represented by 'rational "progressive" bureaucratic administration', links South Africa's past and future: a past in which 'environmental' concerns were somewhat peripheral to a bureaucracy which was both closed and obsessed with issues of security (Thornton, 1996). As will be shown, the problems created by continuity for creative policy-making in the area of trade and environment – bureaucracy, hierarchy, state-centricity – are entrenched and not easily overcome.

Notwithstanding the thread of continuity, the fact of political change has generated wrangles over both the direction and speed of reform and this is set within discourses concerned with wider international change. This situation is not uniquely South African. Rather, it is the geo-specific expression of a dominant theme in contemporary social science, namely, the paradox between globalization and fragmentation. This reads disconcertingly like some sort of closure which is why the chapter concludes by suggesting that the new South Africa is more sensitive to the discourses of the market and globalization than it is to the pressures of communities: as a result, it remains, like apartheid South Africa, a controlling state. At the same time, however, there is as much change as there is continuity: as will be shown, there is evidence that in the flux of the 'new South Africa' there remains space for progressive thinking, forces and alliances to emerge on issues of the environment.

Our discussion proceeds in four parts. First, we examine the notion of 'change', in particular the causes of apartheid's 'end'. We suggest that, far from 'ending', there are many elements of continuity, of the 'old' South Africa cohabiting with the new. We also suggest that many of these 'continuities' arise from the way in which the apartheid regime responded over time to pressures for change. In particular, a 'siege mentality' gave rise to hierarchical, militarized, centralized and highly bureaucratized state structures which persist beyond apartheid, thereby limiting scope for innovative policy formation and implementation.

Second, we examine the process of regime change in South Africa. While the sovereign state was seen as the prize to be held or won by both the ruling white minority and the marginalized and oppressed majority, this state-centric contest was being undermined by changes in the global economy. In spite of the apartheid backlog, the 'new dispensation' found itself hamstrung from the start by a hegemonic discourse that counselled freer markets and limited state intervention. In the final two sections, of this chapter we apply these understandings of continuity in institutional thinking and form and the hegemony of neo-liberal discourse to issues of the environment generally and to 'trade and the environment' specifically. In section three, we examine the environmental 'outcomes' of apartheid engineering. We highlight the apartheid state's conflation of environmental issues with militarized conceptions of state security. We also devote space to a discussion of the impact of the coterminant struggles for the global mind on environmental issues and for the sovereign state in South Africa, noting the symbiotic relationship between progressive forces for change on the left (the so-called 'reds') and for environmental conservation (the so-called 'greens').

Fourth, we look specifically at the issue of trade and the environment, highlighting government, business and industry, and popular responses to emerging ISO and other pressures. We conclude that while the continuities of the apartheid state combine with the change toward free market thinking to limit capacity for progressive policy making in South Africa, there is evidence of positive change. Progressive change is often limited and issue specific – for example, in the area of formulating new water law – but it often brings together a broad band of consensus-seeking stakeholders from state and civil society and presents the possibility for further, environmental justice-oriented 'knock-on' effects. While this marks a hopeful development, we counsel against the understandable desire to overstate the positive impact of such developments.

Locating 'change'

A narrow beginning can be made by setting down the accepted reasons (Guelke, 1996; Daniel, 1996) why apartheid ended. Without listing these, there is no appreciation of the discourses within the country's many polities, including those concerned with trade and the environment. To be sure, apartheid´s ending was not monocausal. However, to understand the unfolding argument, it is necessary to distil five specific accounts of its ending to demonstrate the limitations of received knowledge. Their sequencing suggests, however, the deepening importance of adjustments in ways of explaining the end of apartheid.

The first links apartheid´s ending with the collapse of the Berlin Wall and follows from a structuralist analysis of the Cold War. Through this frame, South Africa – even though its problem was racial – was no different to any other post-World War II conflict. After those momentous hours on Friedrichstrasse in November 1989, all previous positions were closed-off and, *mutatis mutandis*, the way was cleared for the emergence of the new South Africa.

A second explanation suggests that political and military stalemate in the region drove South Africa to change. This too is structuralist, but unlike the first which is impressionistic, it is supportable by empirical evidence. While the minority's military power promised to prevail – certainly in the short-run – its long-term prospects were poor. In crucial areas, changing technology had left South Africa´s military further and further behind; as a result, the capacity to sustain a war, even an African one, was faltering.[2] More seriously, the struggle – for South Africa – had come home. Increasingly it was fought on the dusty streets of the country's townships, rather than through the gun-turrets of those weapons which the minority, despite sanctions, was able to export.

Equally, here was no hope that the majority could prevail: the very idea of wars of national liberation, with their roots in the romance of the Cuban experience, had been overtaken by new forms of surveillance. Old allies – the Soviets more than anyone else – faced changing priorities. As the bipolar world ended, it was inevitable that peripheral conflicts would also draw to a close.

A third idea advances the importance of the Cold War as a thread, but specifically focuses on the Southern African region. As the 1980s ended, South Africa´s long-running war on its neighbours, known as destabilization, was counter productive to Western interests which were, certainly officially, intent on stabilizing the region through what was increasingly called structural adjustment, and in promoting a multilateral regional project known then as SADCC.[3] Moreover, it became clear that the issues around Namibia, contrary to the mythologies of the minority, were quite easy to resolve. The multiparty constitution under discussion for that country offered insights into what, with sufficient goodwill and sound timing, might happen within South Africa itself.

Benefiting from hindsight, a fourth explanation points to the advancing years of the imprisoned Nelson Mandela and his colleagues. Although the great 'unspoken' of formal South African politics, their continued imprisonment became perhaps the single most important mobilizing issue in international politics in the late-1980s.[4] The arguments made for their release and, concomitantly, against apartheid – both domestically and abroad – were far more persuasive than those which South Africa´s minority government could muster.

A fifth and final explanation identifies apartheid as a casualty of a dramatically evolving global economy. Clearly, sanctions served to blunt South Africa's international economic competitiveness. However, they paled in comparison to the combined effect of, among other things, debt, capital flight, global economic recession, and the move away from gold towards reliable currencies such as the Deutsche Mark as security in troubled times. In such circumstances, 'sovereignty for the few' was a luxury state-makers could no longer afford. To continue to pursue a form of space-specific sovereignty where colour alone determined who was inside and protected and who was outside and feared was to court economic as well as political marginalization.

These five explanations help both frame the 'givenness' of the past and embed the mythologies as to why it was that apartheid ended. In the unfolding of this chapter, the point is to locate not only the importance of change, but to suggest the limitations of these approaches. The framing of events – theory, if you like – has a powerful influence on how events are understood and explained. Appreciating this establishes a platform upon which to understand the impact of change on the future, but to move in this direction requires a parallel set of understandings.

Narrow readings, narrower understandings

Experience suggests that the obstacles to change often lie in the memory-trap of an immediate past. This seems to explain the apparent determination of South Africa's entrenched minority to hold on to power despite the changing international agenda. The concomitant international isolation which they experienced further deepened a sense of paranoia and had the effect of shrouding the country in a culture of secrecy and suspicion. With traditions of authoritarianism close to hand as well as effective state control of propaganda, the government ensured that South African society was locked within a security-inspired administrative cage which was controlled by 'securocrats'[5]: bureaucrats who were cued by a militaristic discourse which, in turn, fed a vulgar anti-Communism, known as the 'Total Onslaught'. South Africa's own strain of anti-Communism, according to its proponents, was a manifestation of the exceptional/exceptionalist circumstances which South Africa's minority faced. But in its daily life, it was, like all ideologies, increasingly common-sensical. By the 1980s, the 'total onslaught' had penetrated the 'very stuff of everyday life, familiar assumptions, mundane practices and beliefs' (Gibson, 1986, p. 11).

To achieve the policy goals nurtured by this interpretation of reality, South Africa's government became highly centralized. Elaborately constructed intergovernmental committees ensured that few aspects of public policy escaped the close scrutiny of (and control by) government. In this structure there was little space to develop a regular set of instruments which could offer policy directions that reached beyond a strong compulsion to control. Serious consideration of all aspects of the country's future life – from AIDS, to education, to the environment – were ruled out of court. Yet, within less than a decade, the South African 'miracle' had been achieved. Looking backwards, we may ask why this obduracy actually mattered so little?

Regime change in South Africa

The increasing international fluidity to which we have referred helps in the search for an answer but it simultaneously provides a point of new departure. The growth of the idea of transnationalism in international relations was not a sudden development. By 1945, it had become clear that states could no longer hold onto each and every international activity. Many activities were simply not bounded by the accepted requirements of state sovereignty. The fact of transnationalism has always been central in international relationships – the Catholic Church as opposed to the sovereign status of the Vatican was the quintessential example – but the problem, as is the case so often, was not recognition but naming.

The 'sovereign' state as protection racket and prize

During apartheid, the power of residual understandings protected South Africa. As a sovereign state, even during the worst excesses of apartheid, it was an accepted member of the international community. This idea was never seriously in doubt. What was increasingly contested however was the legitimacy of its governing structures. This explains why demands for change rested on the principle of democratic representation and why the tokenism which was presented by South Africa's *bantustans* (black Africans confined to the former homelands) and its constitutional reforms, were so roundly rejected. This questioning of the government's legitimacy was especially intense in the aftermath of the civil rights movement in the US, because the accepted practices of state sovereignty were increasingly subjected to an ascending understanding which equated racial discrimination with the idea of illegitimacy (Fowler and Bunck, 1996). To understand the effect of this development on South Africa, we must turn to examine the idea of sovereignty.

Ali Mazrui offers a helpful litmus test on what constitutes sovereignty: control over territory; supervision of the nation's natural resources; effective and rational revenue extraction; maintenance of adequate national infrastructure; capacity to render basic services; the maintenance of law and order (Mazrui, 1995). By all and every measure, South Africa's minority enjoyed these in abundance. Indeed, the state's understanding of its own sovereignty was constructed to service their needs (and strengthen their claims) in these areas. For the minority therefore, the apartheid state was a 'giving', developmental state.

By the mid-1980s, however, *their* claims upon, and their capacity to sustain *their* rights to, *their* state and its sovereignty were under siege. As a response to this embattlement, *their* state was prepared to shed various bits of its territory to artificially-created homelands – four of which would enjoy 'independence' from South Africa. While these sacrifices were regrettable, and even divisive in governing circles (Norval, 1996), the minority was never encouraged to change the understandings that *their* quintessential claims on South Africa's sovereignty were to be lived and, as more young white men were conscripted into the military, died for. Body bags from Angola were testimony to the fact that by the end of the 1980s, the apartheid state was a protection racket unable to provide protection.[6]

Those who contested South Africa's *status quo* were informed by the same understandings of sovereignty. Their hope was that South Africa, which was for them an aggressive, 'gobbling' state,[7] could become a giving state: that instead of deliberately under-developing the majority, it could be turned to developmental ends. For them, the 'sovereign state' was a prize to be won. These ideas found expression in The Freedom Charter of 1955 (Suttner and Cronin, 1986) which, as some would have it, is a socialist document in the tradition of the Communist Manifesto. But an equally correct reading of the document suggests that it was a product of its own times, firmly positioned within the stream of post-World War II Keynesian social reconstructionism.

States and markets

As an 'enabling concept' (Evans and Newnham, 1992), the idea of sovereignty exercises a strong controlling dimension over discourses in politics. It also evinces a number of meanings and interpretations. In one, commonly associated with states and used by South Africa's minority, it marks a coincidence of the spatial organization of the state with its political essence. At the same time, it is a line demarcating one state from another, and one race from another. Contrast this with the idea that sovereignty, far from being enclosing, can have a meaning beyond state or race: for example, it can reside in and infuse notions of human or planetary security (Patterson, 199x).

The new forces of international relations are less preoccupied with traditional spatially-located understandings of sovereignty, and more with the idea of global sovereignty. This is most clearly expressed in what is now the hegemonic, neo-liberal faith in the ordering capacity of the market. This faith is given form through the creation of more and less formal institutions whose task it is to facilitate and monitor such expansion: the World Trade Organisation, the International Monetary Fund, the World Bank, the Trilateral Commission, the World Economic Forum. Presently there is discussion concerning possibilities for transforming the UN Environmental Programme into a World Environmental Organisation specifically designed to complement the activities of the aforementioned institutions.

The power of the market

Recognizing this takes us a conceptual step forward, but to appreciate it, we must return to the idea that continuities, which made South Africa's change possible, were afforded by the painless transformation of institutions and their practice. This does not mean that shifting policy items or restructuring apartheid's military machine has been a seamless process. These have been fraught with complex debates, wide and pressing demands. This partially suggests why, as we have noted, South Africa's 'transformation' has been and remains extremely violent (Murray, 1996). However, given the 'blood-bath' predicted for the country, it has in relative terms been easy. In the opinion of many, this feature is explained by South Africa's rational response to the 'inevitability of the market' and the resulting link to the totalizing power of globalization.

The idea that the market had an important role to play in the solution of South Africa's problems was not altogether new. In the late-1960s and early-1970s, an intense debate on the future of the country focused on the relationship between capitalism and apartheid. At the centre of this exchange was the so-called O'Dowd thesis which held that 'apartheid would eventually be brought down by the simple functional logic of the market – as the contradiction between the free market and the racist limitations on this market grew, the former would replace the latter' (O'Meara, 1996, p. 424). In its raw form, this idea was viewed with some suspicion by old-style nationalist politicians who remained wedded to the national/social origins of their party.[8] By the early-1980s, however, an alliance of sorts had developed between the business community and the government. For instance, the two were united in the effort to 'reform' the country by the introduction of limited changes to the constitution.

Institutionalization took the idea of the market further, however. Sponsored by the business community, organizations such as the Free Market Foundation flooded both the public and policy discourse with the 'reasonableness' of the solutions which they were said to offer. Like similar developments elsewhere – for example, the founding of the Heritage Foundation in the US – the free-market message highlighted the naturalness of the market as a tool for understanding and managing political conflict. Its solutions were appealing when set against the obvious obduracy of the state to reform itself (not to mention its levels of taxation to maintain its security) and the violence which, according to state propaganda, the liberation movement were held to represent.

As early as 1977, white business began to lobby for a more creative strategy. Both petty bourgeois and monopoly capital began to highlight the economic costs of apartheid and argue in favour of 'reformed capitalism'. This included a powerful lobby which favoured abandoning several cornerstones of apartheid: restrictions on the mobility of African labour; job reservation laws; restrictions on black trade unions; continuing strong state intervention in key areas of the economy. According to the Urban Foundation:

> [O]nly by having this most responsible section of the urban black population on our side can the whites of South Africa be assured of containing on a long term basis the irresponsible and political ambitions of those blacks who are influenced against their own real interests from within and without our borders. (O'Meara, 1996, pp. 184–5)

In essence, employers' organizations were calling for a new 'hegemonic project'.

Yet, South African President P.W. Botha's response was anything but enlightened. When he challenged the international community to 'do your worst' in his classic 1985 'crossing the rubicon' speech, he was virtually abandoned by all of the most powerful business and political factions within the ruling elite. As if to highlight the emerging two-track nature of South African 'foreign' policy, shortly following Botha's speech, representatives of anglophone capital travelled to Lusaka for talks with the ANC. This was followed by 'the dramatic 1987 session with a range of Afrikaner intellectuals and opinion leaders in Dakar' (Saul, 1993). In August 1988, the Gencor-sponsored Consultative Business Movement was inaugurated and issued a challenge to South African business:

> To define the real nature of their own power, and to identify how they can best use this not inconsequential power to advance the society towards non-racial democracy. (O'Meara, 1996, p. 387).

As the 1980s ripened, the 'solutions' to be offered by the market became more attractive to elites and the ruling National Party appeared willing to jettison its traditional national/social baggage, almost in direct proportion to the ANC's continuing embrace of communism.

The new dispensation

P.W. Botha was formally replaced by F.W. de Klerk in February 1989. As the Mass Democratic Movement's defiance campaigns grew in strength, and as international pressure for change increased, it soon became clear to de Klerk that 'we had to release Mandela'. Between Mandela's release on 2 February 1990, and the ANC walk out of negotiations in April 1991, the NP – the National Party – took a hardline.

The result of such 'obstinacy', O'Meara states, 'was perhaps the most dangerous six months in South African history' (op. cit., p. 411). In April 1992, Chris Hani was assassinated; in May, negotiations collapsed. This was followed by 'Mandela's referendum', a 'Mass Action' campaign which brought the country to a standstill.[9] In June 1992, 43 ANC supporters were massacred in the Boiphatong squatter camp. This was followed in August by the killing of 50 ANC supporters by Ciskei soldiers near Bisho. It was at this point that all actors took a step back. In September, the ANC and NP signed the 'Minute of Understanding'.

From then on the most reiterated phrase leading towards the multiparty elections that were planned for April 1994 was 'transformation through negotiation'. Adam and Moodley explain: '[N]egotiations grant all major forces a stake in a historic compromise by which each party stands to gain more than it would lose by continuing the confrontation' (1993, p. 3). And, indeed, all major forces did gain a stake.

> The ANC obtained 62.7 per cent of the vote, reassuringly short of the two-thirds necessary to write the permanent constitution alone; the NP got 20.4 per cent, so six cabinet seats and a Deputy

Presidency; and the IFP gained 10.5 per cent of the national vote, and three seats in cabinet.[10]

Globalization and political change

Clearly, things were less miraculous than deal-driven.[11] Central to the exercise was a convergence around the 'rationality' of the market, on the one hand, and on the other the idea that, for all the challenge of globalization, the control dimensions offered by the idea of sovereignty were not really negotiable. In other words, globalization may be both dangerous and irresistable to a small, vulnerable economy like South Africa's; however, all political parties, not least the ANC, remained confident in the leadership's ability to effectively manage change via the exercise of state sovereignty. Post-apartheid 'development', then, was to be a governance issue.

It was a short step from here to acceptance of the idea which would come to be known as globalization – both as a means to interpret a world and, as now, an ideology. The path to this was smoothed by a rash of scenario-building which was in the late-1980s also sponsored by the business community. The inability to reconcile the sovereignty approach to the country's politics with the 'sovereignty' requirements of economic growth was a recurrent theme.[12] The message was as deceptively simple as the scenario-building method: the cost of maintaining the state's sovereignty for the privilege of a minority was economic growth. Traditional obsession with spatial sovereignty was not sustainable; at a moment which was later to be described by Fukayama as 'the end of history', Western economic and political liberalism would bring an end to conflict, not least in South Africa.

The ANC's early confidence was most clearly expressed in its Reconstruction and Development Programme (RDP). This boldly proclaimed itself as 'an integrated, coherent socio-economic policy framework ... [seeking] ... to mobilise all our people and our country's resources toward the final eradication of apartheid and the building of a democratic, non-racial, non-sexist future'.[13] However, the irresistibility of the 'neo-liberal project' was soon made obvious. Less than 18 months later, this ambitious, neo-Keynesian project was replaced by GEAR – the Growth, Employment and Redistribution strategy. GEAR aims, among other things, to cut government expenditure to within the Maastricht targets. It hopes to promote growth to 6 per cent per annum, thus setting the stage for international investment which in turn will require, among other things, a more malleable labour market.[14] Driven by the 'neutrality and rationality of the market', to do otherwise, the media insisted, was 'to reinvent the political wheel'.[15] The programme was endorsed by the highest voices in the land and carried forward by Thabo Mbeki, the man then designated by Nelson Mandela to be the country's next President. The financial media were scarcely able to contain their joy at this appointment in a party which, less than a decade earlier, was committed itself to rigorous socialist policies as the answer to South Africa's racial divide and the means to economic justice.[16]

However convergent the rhetoric around this strategy, the structural problems of the South African economy remain. Three of these are listed to illustrate the point. Although South Africa's is Africa's richest economy, it remains primarily an extractive enterprise. In a world in which productivity rates are crucial indicators, South Africa's productivity is low and its wages high. In addition, due to levels of emigration, the country's level of expertise is low and possibly falling.

The neo-liberal economic solutions which have been chosen for South Africa's future juggle the single idea of redistribution through growth in an economy which continues to display the symptoms of 'white wealth and black poverty' which marked the country's unhappy past. One way through this dilemma has been the promotion of a new black middle-class[17] under the belief that 'democratic nations thrive on an economically secure and politically involved bourgeoisie'.[18] This is to be achieved by the promotion of affirmative action as a major instrument of policy action, both within and without government, and has included the direct economic empowerment of blacks by the racial redistribution of stock-market wealth. Its outcomes are not clear, and, understandably, a multiplicity of possibilities follow.[19] These may well be the most crucial trade-offs in the country's history. Empowering a middle-class may be at the risk of delivery to those who are, once again, excluded from the economy. This exclusion may, in part, explain South Africa's spiralling crime wave which in turn touches on the prospects for foreign investment.[20]

The emergence of GEAR as the driving force behind the government economic policy does not give confidence to those concerned with a fairer, 'greener', environmentally-sustainable South African future. Nevertheless, at the political level, very little is settled, old alliances are in constant flux. At times the ANC government seems closer to business than it is to its formal allies in the South African Communist Party;[21] at other times not.[22] There remains space for innovative policy making. Implementation and enforcement, however, are different things altogether.

Apartheid and the environment

Environmental problems in South Africa are either the direct result of or have been exacerbated by apartheid ideology and state policy, in particular agricultural and industrial policies designed to preserve white privilege in the face of a hostile global community. Because apartheid distorted all aspects of South Africa's social relations of production, any discourse that seeks to articulate 'trade and environment' as a single issue is doomed to failure. For example, continuing subsidies for agriculture in the form of drought and flood relief contribute to the unwillingness of farmers to consider the environmental costs of over-stocking. Continued over-stocking in normal years, combined with government payouts for stock deaths in times of drought, simply perpetuates the cycle and contributes to widening problems such as soil erosion, bush encroachment and desertification. A brief overview of some of South Africa's environmental problems will confirm the apartheid-environment link further.

Several years ago UNICEF articulated the vicious circle of poverty, population and environmental degradation. Over the years various government policies have led to the forced removal of an estimated 3.5 million people to the so-called 'homelands'. As a result, roughly 42 per cent of South Africa's population of 41 million reside on 13 per cent of the land. Of this 13 per cent, only 15 per cent is arable. Overcrowding on marginal lands has exacerbated the environmental problems mentioned above, in particular desertification, soil erosion and the siltation of rivers, streams and dams. With the end of apartheid and the removal of legislation prohibiting rural-urban migration, South Africa is presently facing an urbanization crisis of immense proportions. An estimated 20 000 people flood into Gauteng province each month, the vast majority heading for the townships and squatter camps surrounding Johannesburg.

This region, formerly known as the PWV (Pretoria-Witwatersrand-Vereeniging), is the industrial heartland of South Africa. Forty per cent of South Africans live here even though it is a water poor part of the country. Higher demands for freshwater means increased abstraction rates. Increased abstraction rates reduce available flow. When combined with increased levels of effluents from municipalities, agriculture and industry, the developing reality is one of increasing contamination of a decreasing supply of water.

Industrial emissions, including the direct discharge of toxic waste into rivers and streams, combine with municipal waste creation to produce an estimated 460 million tonnes/year in South Africa. Of this amount, 2 million tonnes is regarded as hazardous. The gold mining industry alone accounts for half this total of hazardous waste. Coetzee and Koch dub South Africa's gold mines 'arsenic factories'. South Africa's nuclear power station, operated by the electricity parastatal (state enterprise), ESKOM, and located at Koeberg in the Western Cape, is estimated to produce roughly 400 tonnes of plutonium per year. According to Koch, plutonium is so toxic that one millionth of a gram can kill a human; only 2.5 kilograms are enough to kill the entire human population. ESKOM stores this waste offshore in an underwater spent-fuel tank. While this waste must be relocated and stored permanently within 20 years, there is as yet no agreement about a viable permanent site.[23]

South Africa's agricultural sector has long been dominated by approximately 50 000 white farmers who occupy 87 per cent of the land. Of this group, about 30 per cent are large, commercial producers who account for 80 per cent of total commercial output. The other 70 per cent of white farm owners are less productive, surviving on a combination of loans and subsidies (Wynberg, 1993). In contrast, an estimated 14 million black subsistence farmers 'work' the remaining 13 per cent of the land. In combination, this sector contributes to myriad environmental problems: from the inefficient use of water resources (irrigated agriculture consumes more than 50 per cent of all available water), to siltation, soil erosion (an estimated 400 million tonnes of top soil are lost each year), desertification (a 1991 study suggested that 55 per cent of South Africa's total surface area of 106 million hectares is threatened), and pollution (involving, among other things, the unregulated use of pesticides, herbicides and insecticides).

South Africa also contributes disproportionately to global warming. Whereas South Africa has 0.7 per cent of the global population, it accounts for more than 2.0 per cent of global carbon emissions. This carbon is produced from the inefficient use of coal in the powering of South African industry. According to a 1994 IDRC report, '[L]ocal tariffs for high-load industrial users are among the lowest in the world at 6 cents per kilowatt hour (kWh) compared with 22 cents in Japan and 30 cents in Germany' (IDRC, 1994, p. xx). At the same time,

ESKOM's debt in 1992 stood at 45 per cent of the country's public sector debt and 16 per cent of national foreign debt.

The availability of cheap and abundant coal resources has meant that South African businesses in part derive their international competitiveness from under-priced bulk purchases of electricity. The incentives to conserve or improve the efficiency of energy use are minimal (Eberhard and Trollip, 1992).

This policy developed in an era when minority-ruled South Africa faced international sanctions on an increasing scale. South Africa's decisions to develop oil from coal (SASOL), liquid petroleum from off-shore natural gas reserves (MOSSGAS), and nuclear power (from its Koeberg power facility) are all legacies of apartheid. SASOL, for one, uses massive amounts of coal (and water) to produce oil that could be purchased much more cheaply (and without producing any acid rain or other forms of air pollution) on the international market. 'These investments were made on grounds of national security, benefitted mainly the white minority, and have uncertain and doubtful economic and environmental impacts' (IDRC *et al.*, 1994, p. 54).

In addition, while South Africa's coal reserves are the richest in Africa, most high-grade coal is exported whereas locally-burned coal is high in ash and sulphur content so contributes not only to global warming but to acid rain and heightened incidences of respiratory ailments in people living in or near the Gauteng region.

Poverty and marginalization among blacks, massive over-consumption by a tiny minority of whites, the production of hundreds of tonnes of untreated waste, much of it toxic including temporarily stored nuclear waste, the indiscriminate wastage and contamination of scarce water resources, dirty and inefficient industries, soil degradation and desertification due to poor or unviable farming practices: these are just a partial accounting of the legacy of apartheid engineering whereby 'state survival' was equated with the maintenance of minority white privilege at the expense of all else. Clearly, in order to be so 'giving', the apartheid state 'gobbled' too much. Undoing the environmental damage will take generations. Nevertheless, a start is being made.

Early institutional expressions: conservation as exclusion

During apartheid, environmental issues were handled by a separate ministry of central government. While individual views differ, a consensus of opinion suggests that the legislation on the environment was, generally-speaking, sound. Like many areas of life in apartheid

South Africa, however, environmental issues – such as health in the workplace, waste disposal, the conservation of scarce water resources – were subordinated to survival of minority rule. Over time, Wynberg tells us, this has resulted

> in an administrative and legislative structure which is top-down in approach, fragmented, polarised and inefficient. Existing links between environment and development authorities are often inadequate, and institution-building outside government has been stunted. (Wynberg, 1993)

Where government was actively involved, one could be certain that the activity was framed within the context of 'state security'. For example, the apartheid state devoted significant resources to the maintenance of South Africa´s impressive suite of national parks. The priority attached to national parks followed from their physical location on (or near) the country's borders, especially the border with Mozambique, where the world-renowned Kruger National Park is located. Parks became 'buffer zones' between those inside the state and those without. The so-called 'big five' were as much intended as deterrents to ANC infiltration as means of earning foreign exchange from tourism.[24]

Contemporary security discourses meshed easily with historical understandings of 'environmentalism'. 'Conservation' in South Africa since the mid-nineteenth Century has served racially-exclusive needs. According to Koch, during the colonial period,

> [C]onservationist legislation was diametrically opposed to the holistic relationship between people and their environment that had generally characterised the culture of most indigenous African societies. Crop and livestock farming by local peoples were seen as 'unnatural' and ecologically unsound ... [S]ubsistence hunters became defined as 'poachers' – often by the very same settler population that had once relied on this form of economic activity for its survival. The emergence of paramilitary conservation authorities, funded by the state and devoted to the armed policing of protected areas under their control, was a logical outcome of this preservationist way of conceiving the relationship between man and nature. (Group for Environmental Monitoring, 1994)

That conservation often leads to conflict should not be surprising. This is because when we speak of 'environmental policy', we are really talking about the allocation and usage of often scarce natural resources. Environmental policy making throughout the world is a highly politicized and problematic endeavour; however, it is especially so in the Third World context. For environmental 'management' – that is, the operational outcome of policy formulation and implementation – has historically been the preserve of the colonial masters. To be sure, in the post-World War II period, this 'management' has paraded behind the label of 'development'. But, given the legacy of colonial and settler societies dispossessing indigenous people of their land and blocking access to natural resources, 'environmental management' in all its forms – for example, conservation and national parks creation, industrial and agricultural development, land tenure and zoning policies – is a term which leaves a bitter taste in the mouths of most people living in the Third World. The South African experience supports this general observation. For Johnson and Chenje, the history of environmental policy-making and management in the region 'is one of policing of natural resources and criminalising their illegal harvesting' (Johnson and Chenje, 1994). According to Moyo *et al.* '[t]o this day, in the minds of many African farmers, conservation has not shed unpopular associations with coercion and restriction' (Moyo *et al.*, 1994, p. 308).

This mind-set helped to entrench South Africa's understandings that environmental matters could not be considered outside the security frameworks associated with spatial understandings of sovereignty. To help defend 'sovereignty', the bureaucratic organisation within the National Parks Board remains more military than civilian.[25] Cock and Koch call this the 'authoritarian conservation perspective' (Cock and Koch, 1991, p. 1).

Business and the environment

The other corner of South African apartheid power, business, was happily remote from the debates on the environment. Given the exigencies of the 'siege economy', pollution and inefficient use of scarce resources were not only tolerated by government; they were subsidized. Nevertheless, business was more open-minded about the world and, more importantly for our purposes, perhaps, business had learned the hard lessons of international sanctions which had deeply touched them. Although international sanctions against South Africa for environmental reasons were not immediate, there was, as the 1980s deepened, a growing awareness that the regimes which governed international trade were changing and that if South African business was not vigilant about them, their international competitiveness could be affected.[26] The result was the establishment in 1989/90 of the Industrial Environmental Forum (IEF).[27] It signalled a pre-emptive strike by South African business – although its immediate direction was and remains unclear. We return to this issue below. The point to be made here, however, is to remember that South African business has long experience in opposing boycotts. This history of survival in the face of myriad threats is once again being utilized to the advantage of business and industry.

Between Brundtland and Rio

The five years between the 1987 publication of the Brundtland Commission report, *Our Common Future*, and the so-called 'earth summit' at Rio de Janeiro in 1992 were tumultuous ones for South Africa. That South Africa was being eased back into the 'international community', was apparent at Rio. While not officially represented at either UNCED or any of the preparatory meetings, the South African government was nevertheless invited to attend as an observer, a status accorded to both the ANC and the PAC. In addition, the South African government was asked to prepare a report on environmental conditions and developmental trends. This it duly completed, submitting a 250-page officially government-sponsored report entitled *Building the Foundation for Sustainable Development in South Africa*. According to Wynberg, Rio played host to a 'large contingent of South Africans': extra-parliamentary political groups, youth and religious groups, environment and development NGOs, journalists and industrialists attended UNCED and the Global Forum. The IEF made a presentation to the International Network for Environmental Management and business was represented by a South African businessman who held membership on the World Business Council for Sustainable Development (Wynberg, 1997).

The Rio Earth Summit signalled the last moment of South Africa's isolation from the UN system. The country's foreign policy quickly moved from bilateral isolationism towards engaged multilateralism – a role for which the apartheid-oriented Department of Foreign Affairs was ill-equipped. Saying this brings us closer to understanding the response – institutional or other – of the state to the wider debates which emerged from that and other UN summits: for the most part state institutions had been scrambling to catch up with long-established global trends. As a result, there has been little creative thinking regarding policy formation; on the contrary, it has been reactive and too often 'guided' by bureaucratic inertia.

There are exceptions to this perceived, dominant trend, however. As will be shown below, with regard to environmental issues, certain ministries have been more pro-active, creative and responsive to popular pressure than others. For the most part, these ministries are driven by powerful political personalities. At the same time, how business, industry and popular forces have responded to and interacted with each other on the 'environment' has depended on the specific issue area. For example, water has concentrated the minds of all South Africans and has led to some creative policy formation. Trade and the environment, however, has simply fallen into line with present global trends and is dominated by business and industry. Dialogue has been most diverse and divisive where these issues overlap: for example, where mines border on communities and share the source of freshwater; where chemical companies discharge toxic effluent into streams and rivers commonly fished by local communities.

Confronting apartheid's legacy: red/green alliances[28]

During the post-Brundtland, pre-Rio time period, consciousness of environmental issues appeared to reach a new pitch within the country. This was in part due to the participation of environmentalists from South Africa's vociferous NGO community in the broader deliberations which took place at Rio.[29] However, environmentalism during the apartheid era was primarily concerned with 'green' issues, not 'brown'; poverty and over-crowding in the homelands, for example, were regarded as 'social problems' not environmental ones.

What changed both the scope and impact of the environmental debate was the political confrontation which commenced after the collapse of CODESA in 1993. Issues of public policy were instantaneously drawn to the fore. Through this, a greater consciousness of the links between environmental and more broadly developmental issues developed: formerly fragmented elements within civil society found common cause in overcoming the linked human and environmental degradation of apartheid. The role of NGOs therefore must be seen within a political discourse which was aimed not only at immediate environmental issues, but at wider political change.

Environmental NGOs pressured the government on two fronts: on the long-term goal of 'environmental justice'; and on the more immediate goal of 'institutional reform'. The apartheid state and its supporters – for example, parastatals such as ESKOM and SASOL, and many sectors of business and industry, all of which were under siege for environmentally unfriendly practices – aimed to preserve the *status quo*, or to accede only to incremental change. In the confrontation which followed, not only environmental issues in South Africa were advanced in significant ways; new social movements emerged drawing together formerly antagonistic elements of South African society. For example, environmental NGOs in South Africa have generally drawn together individuals holding tight to those traditional notions of conservation highlighted above. Yet, on issues such as the Richard's Bay Minerals (RBM) proposed strip-mining of the dunes at St Lucia, or the mercury-recovery plant Thor Chemical's negligent behaviour toward both its physical environment and its employees, 'white' environmentalists often found themselves sharing common cause with rural or peri-urban employed or under-employed 'blacks'.[30] Hence the so-called emergence of red/green alliances. With the establishment of groups such as the Environmental Justice Networking Forum (ENJF), which is a loose coalition of trade unions, civic groups and CBOs, and activist, policy-oriented think tanks such as the Group for Environmental Monitoring, new understandings of 'conservation' and 'development' – for example, as 'sustainable utilization' – are emerging in South Africa.

Popular participation and the state

To be sure, populism can be a destructive and divisive force, particularly in its more spontaneous forms. At the same time, however, it is clear that popular participation was and remains an important factor both in heightening national consciousness toward environmental issues and in demonstrating the links between and the potential power of individuals, groups and communities concerned with overcoming the dirty legacy of apartheid engineering. The Draft Water Bill presented to the Legislature in March 1998 and former Deputy Minister of Environmental Affairs and Tourism, Bantu Holomisa's commissioning of CONNEP which resulted in the White Paper on the environment are testimonies in this regard.[31] The Water Bill itself is discussed below.

This is not an insignificant achievement, given levels of literacy, cultural diversity and the sheer size of the country. To emphasize the point: these indicators need to be contrasted with degrees of policy-focus within environmentally-sensitive countries such as Norway, The Netherlands or Sweden, which are small and homogeneous. Looking back, South Africa almost certainly benefited from the intense 'politicization' (to deliberately use a South Africanism) of the environmental issue during this moment of direct confrontation. It was, in the words of one observer, 'an enormously beneficial and relatively cheap national education programme'.[32] The effects of this process have been felt – certainly formally – at the highest level of the country's affairs: environmental rights are recognized in the Bill of Rights attached to South Africa's new constitution.[33] Using a notion from Critical Theory, we would insist that these achievements arose from an emancipatory moment in the country's history.

On the frontline once again: trade and the environment

Having outlined the basic context within which political discourse is set in South Africa, we now turn to look specifically at the issue of 'trade and the environment'. As should be clear by now, policy-making in South Africa is prisoner to several historical trends and their remembering: the divisiveness and structural violence of the struggle for the 'state'; the centralized, secretive and overbearing bureaucratic structures which emerged not only in defence of white privilege and in support of non-white oppression, but in support of the liberation struggle as well; an obsession with the 'state as prize' and hence a generalized acceptance and practised defence of sovereignty; and the overriding dominance of globalization and neo-liberal market expansion in the late-twentieth and early twenty-first century world.

These factors intertwine and impact differently upon different segments of South African society. Filtering trade and environment issues through this complex socio-historical prism, therefore, has understandably resulted in stakeholders taking widely varying positions. We examine the issue in terms of three factors: developing environmental infrastructure and state response; the position of business and industry, particularly with regard to the ISO 14000 series of (voluntary) guidelines; and leadership and political will.

Trade, environment and state response

South Africa's foundational document on trade and the environment was commissioned by South Africa's Department of Foreign Affairs in 1995. Entitled *International Trade and the Environment: a South African Perspective*, it was written by Craig Mckenzie and Simon Foster for the Development Bank of Southern Africa (DBSA) (Mckenzie and Foster, 1995).[34] The document sets the debate over trade and the environment not in terms of progressive policy analysis, which would advance the long-term objectives of environmentalist NGOs or lobbyists, but within the context of accepted global thinking as articulated by, among other groups, the World Trade Organization and the World Business Council on Sustainable Development. In other words, the DBSA, unsurprisingly, supports a neo-liberal, business friendly position. In this way it counsels state support for business and industry and reproduces the historical alliance which obtained during the apartheid era.

According to Mckenzie and Foster, it is clear that South African exporters will have to meet internationally-negotiated standards, even in the case of the purely voluntary ISO 14000 series. At present there is increasing pressure on South African export customers to purchase goods that are 'ISO 14001 certified'.[35] It is not this sort of 'free market', green-conscious consumer-driven pressure that worries South African policy makers. What is worrying to South African producers and policy-makers alike, however, is the possible development of internationally binding legislation which imposes 'new environmental measures affecting both current and potential new exports'.[36] For Mckenzie and Foster, where measures do emerge at the international level, it would not be in the country's interests to resist them, or to argue for special concessions. Clearly, the long-term success of a liberalized trade regime depends on the emergence over time of WTO-supported *minimum, uniform* environmental standards. South African interests, it is argued, are best served by engagement in negotiation on the form and content of these standards, not resistance. This perspective, in combination with the belief that country-specific legislation on the environment more often than not fronts protectionist trade regimes, is generally held throughout South African policy making and industry and (agri)business circles.

At the same time, Mckenzie and Foster argue, it would serve South Africa's short-term interests to lobby in support of temporary exemptions 'on the grounds of historic political and economic isolation which has led to both environmental and social backlogs for the new government'.[37]

A central preoccupation of the paper is with the link between the country's dependence on coal, and the 'under-investment of environmental technologies in many sectors'. Fear of international sanctions in the form of 'eco-labelling' has led the government to allocate funds to the Industrial Development Corporation so that the IDC may begin to 'finance the introduction or upgrading of ecologically safe plant and equipment'.[38] Clearly, '[p]olitical realities dictate that the provision of cheap electricity, housing and food will take precedence over environmental concerns in order to maintain a stable democracy'. For these reasons, Mckenzie and Foster urge the donor community to assist South Africa in meeting increasingly stringent environmental regulations in traditional export markets.

In a detailed discussion of options on eco-labelling, McKenzie and Foster recommend a position of 'wait and see'. They argue that South African companies should be conscious of the efficacy of lobbying in support of their products in lucrative Western markets and point to the need for freedom of information in the 'new South Africa'. While the country is 'obliged to agree', this openness will 'create problems for companies such as ESKOM (who admittedly have started to make public their pollution data); AECI, AEC, SASOL, MOSSGAS, Armscor (and associated industries), ISCOR (and associated industries) and several large mining concerns'. The latter industries, the paper notes, are characterized by a 'considerable amount of environmentally unfriendly plant' which is expensive to upgrade and may be non-cost effective as a result in some cases.

Taken overall, the McKenzie and Foster paper warns against succumbing to popular pressure in support of environmental legislation which would harm domestic producers and exporters. In effect, they are arguing – as former-US Secretary of State Henry Kissinger argued against democratizing foreign policy decisions concerning the prosecution of the war in Vietnam – that trade is too important to be left to the masses.[39] In defence of South Africa's 'national interest', 'trade and the environment' should be left to the care of credential experts and bureaucrats.

Shortly following its release, South Africa's Department of Foreign Affairs responded to and drew upon the DBSA document to issue a public document entitled *Introductory Notes and Policy Considerations Concerning the Issue of Trade and the Environment* (van der Lugt, 1996). This document – which was to help work toward the national position for the December 1996 WTO Meeting in Singapore – builds directly on the DBSA paper by arguing for international acceptance that South Africa is 'indisputably part of the developing world'. In this way, the DFA is arguing in support of the Third World's general position, articulated at the Rio Summit, that developing countries should not be subjected to the same strict environmental regulations as are OECD countries. In this way, South Africa might be able to buy time for and build global alliances in support of the gradual retooling of its 'dirty industries'.

Perhaps the most progressive internationally-oriented department of state in the new South Africa is the Department of Trade and Industry

(DTI). A former institutional 'backwater' concerned chiefly with advancing the sectional interests of South Africa's minority, it has emerged as a dynamic player in efforts to relocate South Africa in (to deliberately use the phrase in order to make a point about neo-liberalism) the new world order. As with the Departments of Water Affairs and Forestry (DWAF) and Environmental Affairs and Tourism (DEAT) (see below), a number of senior appointments have helped to change both the internal culture and the mission of the DTI. Their interest in the link between trade and the environment and their commitment to advancing South Africa's status as a 'responsible global player' is therefore obvious.

Given the apartheid bureaucratic hangover (which negatively impacts on all departments at all levels of government), the continuing loss of skilled human resources to early retirement and the private sector, and the short time that has passed since the beginning of majority rule, it is understandable that the DTI's record, particularly in environmental issues, is mixed. With regard to the Montreal Protocol, for instance, the DTI was both responsive and creative. By drawing into the process a wider range of players and responding to the debate in nuanced ways, the DTI created the impression that South Africa was committed to changing perspectives within the country, especially in legislation. But things have been very different on the ground. The DTI has found it difficult to escape the traps of state bureaucracy. A sampling of insider knowledge suggests that progressive voices in the leadership of the department, who are fully aware of the issues, are poorly served by bureaucrats at operational levels who have either found it difficult to escape old patterns of behaviour or are simply hostile to switching from a policy which privileges trade concerns over those of the environment.

Part of the problem, too, stems from the fact that trade and industry stands at the frontline of the GEAR versus RDP, neo-liberal versus more state-interventionist/socially-conscious debate. In terms of international policy, this was never more apparent than during South Africa's 1996 hosting of UNCTAD. South Africa's NGO community, supported by the Third World network, organized a vibrant parallel meeting which was highly critical of government policy. Interestingly, the issues dividing South Africa's NGO community from the GNU mirrored those which divided the world's NGOs and its state-makers at Rio. In terms of national policy, the DTI stands between those businesses and industries seeking lower tariff barriers, freer capital movements and export-led growth and those who have long benefited from the apartheid state's long list of subsidies and barriers to trade.

Given these facts, it is no surprise that the DTI finds it difficult to articulate clear goals or develop a policy on environmental issues. Currently, the development of a coherent environmental strategy for the department is out for public tender. While this might well open the space for greater public participation, it will probably simultaneously draw more technical expertise into the process. As always, the true test is not whether space is created for its writing; rather, it is whether the final product will facilitate an open and ongoing struggle for the victory of ideas and understandings.

It is misguided to believe that simply opening up towards other state departments will change this. Harmonization of policy between state departments, seen by some as a desirable goal, often increases the gap between citizen and state. This seems to be the immediate goal of the Advisory Committee on the Environment, which was recently established by the Department of Trade, whose task it is to draw all the bureaucratic players and experts closer toward each other. We return to this issue below.

Business and industry

In a pioneering study, Bethlehem surveyed businesses across twelve sectors[40] of the South African economy. She suggests that South African companies experience direct and indirect environmental pressures from myriad sources: consumers; standards, accreditation and environmental labels; domestic regulations; multilateral environmental agreements; campaigns against particular products or substances; and multinational company policies. 'The experience of most sectors is that environmental pressures are building up in export markets but that there are no experiences of actual trade restrictions or barriers to foreign markets'.[41]

Bethlehem also suggests that while all relevant sectors of the economy have been affected, effects themselves have been uneven. For instance, the chemical industry has been most affected, mostly by the provisions of the Basel and Bamako Conventions and the Montreal Protocol (CFCs). Other agreements such as the Convention on Climate Change, and the impending ISO 14000 series standards have the potential to affect a number of sectors, including electricity generation, aluminium, chemicals, coal, minerals, food processing, pulp and paper, and steel.[42]

As previously suggested, business and industrial practices in South Africa have been and continue to be environmentally degrading. Since 1989, the media have done exceptional work in exposing these practices: from the presence of PCBs and DDT in dolphins off the Natal coast to apartheid government negotiations for a second nuclear plant; from SAPPI and other petrochemical company spills in the Vaal River to head of the former Ciskei homeland, Oupa Gqoza's plan to import toxic waste. In response, business has been very active in 'cleaning up' their act. Recently, Tosas (a Total and SASOL-owned company) became the first South African company certified under ISO 14001 series standards. In 1994, and in line with public pressure, SASOL introduced a self-regulating system of industrial environmental management (IEM). Whereas SASOL I continues to produce toxic waste and other effluent, each of its newer plants (II and III) emit no waste at all.

Both SAPPI and Samancor are moving in the direction of adoption of ISO standards. Given the weakness of South African government environmental regulations and enforcement capacity, interested observers suggest that these developments are the direct result from ISO and more general popular pressures. At the same time, environment and natural resource management, pollution control and prevention are said to be moving up the government list.

On the level of policy, Bethlehem suggests perspectives which aim to streamline policy without closing off opportunities for public participation:

> There may be certain institutional arrangements within the private sector, and between the private sector, government and other organizations that foster more successful approaches to international environmental pressures. The first of these is a set of institutions within sectors which provide environmental information, services and research for companies in the sector as a whole. The fruit sector is a good example of how a central organization can assist individual producers by gathering information on environmental requirements in export markets and conducting research to assist producers in meeting these requirements. Similarly, companies in the steel sector have established an industry environmental committee to co-operate on developing an environmental strategy for the sector as a whole. There may be economies of scale which make it easier to gather information or conduct research jointly. In this way, positive elements of competition can be introduced into an otherwise competitive environment. ... It may also be helpful to establish some

joint structures between government and business on issues such as the Climate Change Convention. Joint committee may also be useful in looking at issues like investment in environmental abatement technologies or in establishing a set of environmental targets for a sector as a whole. Such structures may also facilitate improvements in the services offered by government departments by providing clear information to government on the kind of assistance required by exporters.

An interesting and important development in these directions involved the May 1998 Southern African Regional Conference on Cleaner Production. Organized by the IEF and jointly sponsored by DEAT, DTI, the Water Research Commission and Dansid, this meeting built on previous IEF meetings[43] but was much more inclusive than hitherto. The meeting brought together representatives from government, industry, trade unions, educational institutions, consultancies, NGOs, financial institutions and organized civil society. It was divided into sector-specific workshops – chemical, mining, manufacturing, agriculture and food processing – and focused on legal and policy instruments, the role of finance and funding agencies, information exchange and technology transfer in facilitating cleaner production. This meeting marks a hopeful beginning along the lines of DFA recommendations:

> Mechanisms and structures must be established for reporting back to South African exporters and for obtaining their inputs in the preparation of international positions. The cross-cutting nature of 'environment' makes it inevitable that various actors and governmental departments need to be involved. Core activities can be undertaken between three governmental departments: Trade and Industry (DTI), Environmental Affairs and Tourism (DEAT), and Foreign Affairs (DFA). Again it needs to be emphasised that in their endeavours these Departments should take care not to think in terms of 'trade expansion versus environmental protection' or 'economic growth versus environmental protection'. Re-establishing this unhelpful dichotomy will undermine the goals of sustainable development.[44]

Political will

Like all polities, South Africa's is caught within competing understandings and interpretations of reality; indeed, the very newness of the new South Africa makes a variety of stakeholders interested in, but often unable to articulate/advance/defend, their positions. The unevenness of this contest is compounded by a lack of technical know-how in a field in which, all too often, knowledge is power.

Bureaucratic theory – sufficient in some explanations of South Africa's transition – suggests that bureaucracies are only as effective as their capacity to process information and to interact with each other. Progressive theory, in contrast, suggests that '[s]ocial decisions ... are increasingly removed from the rational-critical discourse of citizens in the political public sphere, and made the province of negotiation (rather than discourse proper) among bureaucrats, credential experts and interest group elites' (Calhoun, 1996, p. 454). Clearly, the compulsion to administer – hence, control – in the new South Africa is as alive as it was in the old South Africa: were it not so, how would we account for the power of South Africa's deal-driven miracle? At the same time, 'transformation' requires its champions if dysfunctional continuities are ever to be overcome.

Two hopeful signs in this direction are the emergence of progressive policy positions, pushed by powerful political personalities in the Ministries of Water Affairs and Forestry and Environmental Affairs and Tourism: Minister Kader Asmal in the case of the former; Minister Pallo Jordan and Deputy Minister Peter Mokaba in the case of the latter. Unlike trade and industry, which is increasingly dominated by neo-liberal discourse, both DEAT and DWAF have more intellectual space within which to articulate more progressive and inclusive approaches to sustainable environmental management. And unlike trade and industry, which lends itself to troublesome trends towards elite/expert policy domination and worker/owner confrontation, DEAT and DWAF have been able to focus on issues, admittedly equally contentious, of interest to the broadest of all possible publics: in the case of DEAT, environment and natural resource management, and pollution control and prevention; in the case of DWAF, water resource use. While neither department is directly affected by WTO, ISO and other international institutional positions on trade and the environment, actions taken within each department have the capacity to strengthen South Africa's trading position therein: by facilitating environmental justice in terms of healthier living environments and more equitable access to essential resources such as potable water; by encouraging industry toward resource conservation and cleaner and fairer means of production.

There is no better symbol of apartheid than the unequal access to scarce water resources. Coetzee and Cooper estimate that average per capita consumption in the late 1980s in the former Ciskei homeland was

9 litres/person; in the Eastern Cape townships it was 19 litres/person; and in the average white suburb, 200–350 litres/person. The World Health Organization suggests a basic minimum of 50 litres/person. In addition to unequal access is the waste and pollution characteristic of apartheid agriculture and industry. According to Coetzee and Cooper, 'South Africa, in common with other industrialising Third World countries, is trying desperately to develop in accordance with First World patterns' but uses legislation and administrative controls over industry that follow Third World patterns' (Coetzee and Cooper, 1991, p. 130). Whereas laws governing environmental management have long been on the books, for the most part they have gone unenforced. While there is some public pressure toward adoption of Environmental Impact Assessments (EIAs), business and industry continue to practice self-regulation.[45] Following a spate of mine and landfill closings due to poor environmental management, and rejecting 'self-regulation' as a viable concept, Asmal's and Jordan's departments have decided to have a joint look into waste and pollution control. The unstated but regularly practiced right to pollute with impunity because an industry earns foreign exchange and employs people is no longer thought to be sufficient in South Africa's case.

The DWAF have taken serious steps toward correcting this situation by rewriting South Africa's 1956 Water Act. The Draft Water Bill came before the legislature in 1997 and became law in 1998. According to one observer, 'without [Asmal's] political will the process would never have started.'[46] While a review of South Africa's water laws has been in the pipeline for more than 10 years, until Asmal became minister there was 'no political and little departmental support' for change.

Historically, the Water Act provided for both riparian and private rights. Riparian rights permit landowners to divert a portion of the normal and surplus flow of water passing through their property to private use. Private water is defined as 'rainfall, soil and ground water occurring on or underneath private land and streams which rise and flow over a single piece of private land'.[47] In effect, this meant that 65 per cent of all South Africa's water was in private hands. Given that South Africa is a water poor country forecasted to enter a condition of 'absolute water scarcity' by the year 2020, and given present trends in population growth and settlement, this condition is no longer tolerable.

The new legislation replaces 'ownership' with 'time-based administrative authorizations'. In addition to the issue of permits for water use, there will be well-defined limits to abstractions, taking into consideration, for example, the needs of the ecological system and downstream users' rights to sufficient supplies of clean, fresh water. According to a spokesperson at DWAF, the response of established agricultural and industrial users has ranged from 'sullenly accepting to enthusiastically averse'. Whereas vested interests who have long profited from established if unsustainable patterns of allocation are sure to challenge the constitutionality of the new law, the Constitutional Court also provides the right of citizens to sue 'horizontally', that is, to file law suits against private parties. So the Constitutional Court is sure to be the site of impending national 'water wars'. Clearly, with an issue as important as water, Asmal has gained great confidence from interested and affected parties at all levels of the state and beyond: from the World Bank, the EU and SADC, to CBOs and township civic organizations. On a more positive note, DWAF, DTI and other departments have taken pains to highlight the way in which the environment will provide new opportunities for employment and profit-making. For example, the new water bill will give rise to the need for millions of dollars in infrastructure investment: water delivery systems, sanitation, housing, solid waste treatment and disposal and transportation are all potential growth areas under the new water law.

Conclusion: South Africa's new world

Given all that has gone before, and the congratulations over its transition, it would be surprising if there were no wider lessons to be learnt in, and from, the South Africa experience. The clues to effective and democratic change lie in deepening levels of popular awareness. It is clear, certainly at the popular level, that South Africans are increasingly aware of the deepening importance of environmental issues, notwithstanding that the financial and popular media[48] address these only within the context of controls offered by the market.

This chapter offers lessons about the wider processes of institutional change in ways different from the celebration which is commonly associated with South Africa's 'miracle'. By carefully deconstructing the South African case, we have tried to show that it was never possible that change in South Africa could be both incremental and progressive. For one thing, the mood of the times was and remains against an ever-expanding, progressive agenda; the discourse of politics – so essential in helping to dislodge apartheid from the state – has moved towards that represented by the market and globalization. Their powers are to be seen in almost every sphere of the 'new' South Africa where political players have been forced to adapt platform positions to the 'realities' of the self-styled new world order. This is most clearly demonstrated in the general acceptance of neo-liberal dogma concerning trade and the environment. Even South Africa's Communist Party – notwithstanding public protest – seems to accept the necessity of neo-liberal economic outcomes. If regimes which link the environment and trade are within the framing of this 'new realism', then it seems as if South African institutions will be more responsive to their implementation. If this conclusion is abrupt, it needs perhaps to be set within a mood of further questioning. The more progressive and hopeful cases of DEAT and DWAF must be seen in this regard.

South Africa has moved from a militarized white view of the world to a view in which the interests of those who have been traditionally silenced are formally incorporated in democratic society. How these interests are to be served by neo-liberalism – trade and the environment included – especially in a context where the majority of South Africa's people are unemployed, remains uncertain. A struggle must follow because the issue clearly goes beyond the simple binary proposition that economic growth and trade should enjoy precedence over the environment now and forever.

The country's sense of its own sovereignty has, if anything, been deepened by the celebratory accolades which are attached to the idea of a Rainbow Nation. Here lies is the conundrum which runs through the chapter: liberal political discourse which has been so integral both to regime change and to changing South Africa's regime, is saddled with many illusions. A central and as yet largely uncontested one in South Africa is the idea that there can be only a single uniquely authoritative discourse about public affairs; that politics revolves around a single unitary state which sets a unilinear political agenda.

If activist academics are to insist on the importance of trade and the environment in the building of the new South Africa, they will have to understand how unsettling this exercise can become. Without locating these discourses in emancipatory frameworks, achieving new understandings on the issue will be difficult. Notwithstanding the applause which South Africa has elicited for its undoubted achievement, there can be no rest in the search for its place in a democratic twenty-first century.

Notes

1. A classic example of this celebration is Lyman, 1996.
2. The controversy over the Battle of Cuito-Cuanavale is most often used to advance this argument. On this see Willie Breytenbach. 'Cuito Cuanavale Revisited', *African Insight*, vol. 27, no. 1 (1997), 54–62.

3. Southern African Development Co-ordination Conference, now called the Southern African Development Community (SADC).
4. See 'Harmony over Mandela', *The Financial Mail* (Johannesburg), 24 June 1988.
5. Of the 23 permanent SSC members in 1988, at least 13 could be said to have been 'securocrats', including: the Minister of Defence; the Chief of the SADF and its four services (army, airforce, navy and medical corps); the head of Military Intelligence; the Director of the National Intelligence Service; the Minister of Law and Order; the Commissioner of Police; the head of the Security Police; the Director of Security Legislation; and the Secretary-General of the Office of the State President.
6. In Jindy Pettman's words, 'States are organized on the basis of a capacity for violence. This is the welfare state, claiming a huge proportion of state budgets for "defence", and often acting to undermine interstate security. Here states function as protection rackets, and often themselves directly endanger those they claim to protect. All too easily security becomes military security, security of the state or its current government'. See Pettman, 1996.
7. There are many statistical surveys to prove the underdevelopment of South Africa's majority by the state. But few accounts can be more moving and persuasive than that provided by Charles van Onselen in his acclaimed biography of the South African share-cropper, Kas Maine. See van Onselen, 1996.
8. Aletta Norval records a 1991 speech by Professor Jan Lombard, the then President of the Free Market Foundation: '[W]e all know that the crucial battle for the minds of the South African people has begun in earnest. ... In the leading cultural institution of the Afrikaner people, the *Federasie van Afrikanse Kultuurvereningings*, the idea of the free market economy as a political philosophy was thoroughly thrashed out as a principal theme of the annual congress less than a year ago ... the *battle lines will be drawn between the political philosophy of the free market economy, on the one hand, and the political philosophy of social collectivism on the other*' (emphasis added; see Norval, op. cit., p. 225).
9. According to Saul (1993, p. 174): 3 and 4 August 1992 'saw the biggest stayaway in South African history – an estimated four million workers – while on Wednesday over 70,000 ANC supporters demonstrated outside the Union Buildings in Pretoria. Indeed, it is not fanciful to see this period of mass action as a a kind of "second referendum", underscoring for those who wished to see that the vast majority of the black population were staunch in their democratic demands – and that the ANC continued to stand as the chief political vehicle of such demands'.
10. See Good, 1997a, p. 36. See also Good, 1997b and Southall, 1996.
11. One of the most pertinent observers of South Africa, Frederik Van Zyl Slabbert, in an Address to the Pretoria Press Club in August 1995, called South Africa a 'deal-driven' society.
12. There is an entirely separate paper to be written about the role, impact and influence of scenario-building in South Africa. For a preliminary view, see Beare and Bell, 1997.
13. African National Congress (1994), *The Reconstruction and Development Programme. A policy framework* (Johannesburg: African National Congress), p. 1.

14. On this see Hein Marias, 'The RDP: is there Life after Gear', *Development Update*, Vol. 1, no. 1 (June 1997), 1–19.
15. See *The Cape Times*, 5 August 1997, p. 4.
16. For a fairly typical example, see 'Trimming Socialism to Cut Cloth for Fiscal Measurements', *Business Report* (Cape Town), 17 February 1997.
17. A quick comparative framework suggested that South Africa's strategy might not be unlike Malaysia's: a point supported by the growing interest of Malaysia in South Africa. See *Africa Confidential* (London), 3 January 1977, pp. 5–6. For further background, see Muda, 1996.
18. 'Ex-activists contemplate what it means to become filthy rich', *Sunday Independent*, 3 August 1997.
19. These were interestingly caught on the letter's page of *Newsweek* (Europe), 24 February 1997. One letter angrily complained that not enough was being done for blacks; a second insisted that crime was responsible for South Africa's economic woes; and the third, from the public affairs officer of the country's richest corporation, complained that their efforts at empowerment had been ignored in the original *Newsweek* story.
20. On this there is an increasing literature; on the impact internationally, there seems no better example than the glaring headline in the *International Herald Tribune* (The Hague) 15–16 February 1997: 'Rape Shadows South Africa. Children Are Victims of Nation's Collapse into Crime'.
21. It is impossible to resist quoting Peter Mokaba, Deputy Minister of Environmental Affairs and Tourism, who urged that black business people 'not be shy to say they wanted to become "filthy rich"', *Cape Times*, 24 February 1997.
22. See, for example, 'The battle to control the soul of the ANC', *Sunday Tribune* (London), 30 March 1997.
23. Eddie Koch, 'Koeberg's two faces. Our nuclear programme is either safer than Sandy Bay ... or a menace for fifty thousand years', *Mail and Guardian*, 15–21 September 1989.
24. Tourists come to South Africa, it is argued, first and foremost for the flora and fauna. Tourism is very big business, bringing in an average 1.7 million visitors per year in the pre–1994 period, directly employing 300 000 people (that is, 1 out of every 14 'actively employed' South Africans), and generating 2.5 billion rand in foreign exchange per year.
25. South Africa's national parks followed the great modernization tradition of parks across the globe – the idea started in the United States and spread to Africa through the UK.
26. Telephone interview with Karin Ireton, Assistant Director of the Industrial Environmental Forum of Southern Africa, 16 January 1997.
27. Some background to this organization is given in Hobbs and Ireton (1996).
28. The term 'red/green' is taken from a chapter heading in Cock and Koch (eds) *Going Green.*
29. Hallowes (ed.) (1993) presents a record of the thinking on these issues by South African and other NGOs.
30. On both St Lucia and Thor Chemicals, see Swatuk, 1996. On the continuing propensity of environmentalism to draw in white, middle-class activists, see Muller, 1997.

31. CONNEP is the Conference on New National Environmental Policy. It was convened in August 1995 and attended by more than 500 delegates from state and civil society. The resulting discussion document, a draft green paper entitled *Towards a New Environmental Policy for South Africa*, was workshopped around the country in the run-up to the writing of the white paper on the environment. Holomisa, who has now left the ANC to form his own political party, is widely regarded as one of South Africa's more charismatic, populist leaders, particularly in the Eastern Cape.

32. Telephone interview with Karin Ireton, Assistant Director of the Industrial Environment Forum of Southern Africa, 16 January 1997.

33. In Section 24 of the Constitution it states:

    Everyone has the right:

    (a) to an environment that is not harmful to their health or well-being; and
    (b) to have the environment protected, for the benefit of present and future generations, through reasonable legislative and other measures that:
    1. prevent pollution and ecological degradation;
    2. promote conservation; and
    3. secure ecologically sustainable development and use of natural resources while promoting justifiable social and economic development.

34. A summary of this document can be found in 'Greening Trade. The Future of Environmental Trade Restrictions', *Trade Monitor*, vol. 10 (September 1995), 1–3.

35. The International Organization for Standardization's ISO 14000 series seeks to specify criteria by which products and materials may be deemed environmentally friendly. ISO 14001 focuses on 'specification' and is nearing finalization; ISO 14004 focuses on guidelines; others in the series focus on auditing, labelling, performance evaluation and lifecycle assessment. In South Africa, ISO standards are monitored through the South African Bureau of Standards (SABS).

36. Unless otherwise specified, all quotations in this section are from Mckenzie and Foster, 1995.

37. Ibid., p. 3.

38. *Business Day*, 17 October 1997.

39. An interesting conception if the object of liberalized trade is the creation of mass consumerism.

40. These sectors are aluminum, coal, chemicals, electricity generation, minerals processing, fruit, packaging, pulp and paper, steel, soaps and detergents, textiles, and timber. See Bethlehem, 1996.

41. Ibid., p. 57.

42. Ibid., p. 55.

43. In 1991, the IEF organized SAICEM I, the Southern African Industrial Conference on Environmental Management, which was attended by representatives from business and industry throughout the SADC region. In addition, the International Chamber of Commerce attended to facilitate discussion around the Business Charter on Sustainable Development. SAICEM has since developed into an annual event.

44. See Van der Lugt, op. cit., p. 15.

45. To Fuggle, '[t]here is no enforcement of the conditions EIAs impose on developers and all the checks and balances to protect the environment can

be virtually ignored. They are not worth the paper they are printed on' (As quoted in the *Cape Times*, 6 February 1998).

46. The following quotations come from a private source at the Department of Water Affairs and Forestry in Pretoria.

47. See Eddie Koch, 'Parting farmers and their water', *Mail and Guardian*, 29 November–5 December 1997.

48. A few exceptions are 'Overcoming technical barriers to trade' and 'Industry under international pressure on environmental front', *The Star* (Johannesburg), 13 December 1996.

8
Summary and Conclusions: Adjusting Trade Liberalization and Environmental Protection Demands in an Era of Globalization[1]

Helge Hveem and Kristen Nordhaug

Introduction

The story told in this book is one about public policy adjustment to environmental and economic change. The phenomenon analysed and partly explained is the *outcome* of such adjustment activity at the national level.

The results show a dynamic and also differentiated picture of the way political agents and institutions respond to political processes. Above all, practically without exception, the analysis demonstrates how outcomes are shaped by the interplay between the international and the national level. It is also a story about a world of complex policy outcomes, not one where public policy simply converges on one single policy track with respect to economic liberalization. The six cases investigated also display different patterns of response to the demand for environmental protection measures. Part of the explanation is that the sources of response differ. On the other hand there *are* certainly tendencies of convergence towards the liberal economic model in all of the cases. But we do not find a clear confirmation of the 'hyperglobalization' thesis in the cases surveyed; nor do they offer solid support for its antithesis – that of the globalization sceptics. Rather, the findings support the more pluralistic or neutral perspective with respect to the evolution of the globalization processes and their effect.[2] This latter perspective highlights continued divergence between national experiences, but at the same time admits the strength of convergence forces. The reasons for these results will now be summarized.

All of the cases reveal that the impact of pressure from the international level and the spread of prescriptions, recommendations and agreed rules for the conduct of national economic policies issued by foreign and international agents has been considerable. But the impact of such exogenous forces also varies from case to case and partly also, over the period surveyed – from the early 1980s to the end of the 1990s. If or when it occurs, policy change is often partly a result of domestic demands, partly the outcome of joint domestic-international agency. What some of the case studies show above all is that the pressure from abroad, either as the spreading of the ideas contained in the liberal economic model or as pressure being exerted through bargaining over debt handling and the SAPs (or both), is not effective *unless* it is also supported by domestic agents. It is at its most effective if or when it becomes legitimized by domestic political institutions. In this respect it obviously matters whether the political system is relatively democratic or authoritarian, but some degree of legitimation appears to be important even in the latter case.

In several cases, however, the real sources of policy change and adjustment are not foreign agents but domestic interest groups, notably environmentalist movements and organizations. Furthermore, these interest groups act in favour of their own policy goals rather independently of foreign agents. Thus the study shows that the emphasis on international level explanations of change in developing country polities, notably neo-realist or structuralist (*dependencia*) theories, are in general exaggerated. At the same time, most of the case studies offer support of the neo-Gramscian perspective that emphasizes the role of ideas and ideology such as those of global economic and political liberalism of the Anglo-Saxon variety in particular.

Cognitive factors and the way agents construct social reality have a clear effect both on behaviour and outcomes. It is possible to have a strategy of sustainable development whereby economic policy is reconciled with environmental concerns, and many decision-makers have perceived it thus after the Brundtland Commission report (WCSD, 1987). But a number of agents perceive the relationship between economic agency in investments and trade on the one hand and environmental protection on the other as a conflictual one and behave accordingly. Although the two policy arenas need not necessarily collide (Runge, 1994), there is nevertheless a widespread perception that 'environmental conditionality' is at odds with the liberalizing practice if not the theory. Decision-makers and regulators thus appear to find themselves confronted with a variety of potentially or *de facto* conflicting demands (Hesselberg and Hveem, 1998). In all the six cases, except that of the Ivory Coast which appears as the least affected by political environmentalism among the six, evidence is presented that illustrates both these tendencies.

Recapitulating the analytical approach

What is to be explained here is (to repeat) the policy (change) that results through policy-making processes in the countries investigated.

The study did not have a strict causal explanation in mind, whereby at the end of the analysis certain hypotheses are verified or falsified in a definitive sense. Rather, the aim has been to offer a plausibility test of the various types of causal explanation offered and to delimit the scope of relevance of the respective explanations. Evaluation of causality in a particular single case has been left to the individual author. As we take on the task of formulating comparisons, it should be said that the study's results are presented as fairly general observations about the impact of certain classes of factors on outcomes. The potential for generalizing the results to support or modify existing theory is briefly discussed at the end of this chapter. Before the results are presented, a brief recapitulation of the theoretical basis and the way it guides the present exercise should be made.

In the Introduction, two broad theoretical issues were introduced and discussed. The first was the *level of analysis* issue. Three approaches were presented: one which focused on international level causes of outcomes; another which highlighted domestic level causes; and a third which emphasized interaction among factors at both these levels. In the literature, the debate between international and domestic level theories has long dominated; this was particularly the case when *dependencia* and modernization theories presented a clear dichotomy on the level of analysis issue. If there ever was a good reason for making such a dichotomy, that is no longer the case. A certain emphasis has therefore been put on the third among these – the interactive analysis approach – as a particularly useful and yet underutilized approach.

The second issue was the *type of polity* issue. It raises the question whether or to what extent the type of political system characterizing the country examined determines the policy outcomes which are the object of investigation. Even on this issue, a typology consisting of three types of polity was suggested: the liberal market system; the capitalist state or state autonomy system; and the embedded autonomy system. All of these types may be democratic polities in some sense, the first and last ones probably most of all. The first of them favours the competitive market as a decision-making institution whereas the two last emphasize the power and capacity of state institutions and the elaboration and strength of state-society relations respectively.

Here again, theorizing options are several and varied. Type of polity is obviously a major element in an approach to the level of analysis problem that privileges domestic level explanations. Conversely, under a perspective that favours international level explanations, the role of the domestic political system is that of a channel that transmits exogenous influence into becoming national policy outcomes. The role of the state institutions and public policy arenas in this case is that of organizing the process of convergence of domestic agents, institutions and their practice towards the ideas and behaviour which dominate at the international level. The present project is not particularly informed by the structuralist perspective. However, both international market conditions and exogenous domination (hegemony) perspectives are reflected in the case studies, although in varying forms and degrees. There are international constraints to the freedom that national institutions and procedures enjoy in making policy – but, generally speaking, national institutions do still have some freedom of action.[3]

On the other hand, in an approach that locates the source of policy to the domestic level, the role of the national political system and its agents and institutions becomes not that of a facilitator, a passive channel, but that of an initiator. Under this class of more particularistic theories the 'statist' perspective emphasizes the entrepreneurial character of political leadership or bureaucracies, including the kind of leadership in terms of ideas and institutions that is known as the 'developmental state'. Although elements of that state form are found in some other cases as well – a point to which we return – in our sample there is only one case which qualifies under that sub-category – South Korea. However, as argued by Moon and Lim, the representation of South Korea as a 'statist developmental state' is now more history than reality. Under the transformation that took place in the 1990s, the South Korean polity turned from modern to post-modern ideas and the state became less corporatist and more democratic and thus more open to the influence of civil society.

One theory that emphasizes the role of civil society in a 'modernizing' tradition is the theory of 'social capital' (Putnam, 1993b; Evans *et al.*, 1998). It focuses on the strategies and role of non-state agency, economic and other. Some of its supporters have adopted it in an approach that argues that the more market based the economy becomes, the less influential (and relevant) becomes the state. The present project, however, is informed by a rather different view, one which *combines* state with societal approaches to emphasize that convergence towards a market economy does not exclude continued societal support for state strategies – for an active state. In fact, such support is vital for the legitimacy of state institutions, and it determines the shape and degree of co-ordination between state and societal agents. One concrete illustration of this perspective is Evans' modified state autonomy theory, referred to as 'embedded autonomy' (Evans, 1995).

At the same time, we believe that practically every nation-state entity must change under globalization. The issue is not whether or not to adjust, but how and when to do it. An exemption perhaps is the hegemonic state which, because it dominates the international system, can set the rules for others or attempt to monitor them without necessarily adjusting to these rules itself. The tendency for the US to retreat from multilateralism around the turn of the millennium is a case in point.

One particular issue to be addressed therefore is whether the embedded autonomy state is disappearing. In cases such as Argentina and Costa Rica, this type of state-society relationship has been found, at least to some degree and for some of the research period and in different versions: corporatist in Argentina, a quite developed 'spoils system' in Costa Rica. Have these embedded autonomy systems been seriously challenged and in fact dominated by the coming of the liberal market economy model? And how about democratic India in that respect?

These and several more questions belong within what may be referred to as an institutional perspective. Following up on the rather general observations made so far, one proposition that was formulated in the original project design is that the form and strength of *institutions* decide whether they modify or neutralize exogenous influence, either by filtering it, providing a shield against it, or opposing it.

These two broad theoretical perspectives, accounting for international and domestic (national) factors and agents respectively, both have substantial support in the literature. But there is a third way that holds a vast and still mostly untapped potential. The two may be *combined*: for instance, as when domestic institutions and actors not only interact with, but even co-operate and co-ordinate with, an exogenous agency. We have thus built on and transcended Putnam's double-edged diplomacy approach and its later application and modification in order to develop an approach that is less based on rationalist assumptions of decision-making and more open to a pluralistic theory-building.

There are several ways by which co-ordination across the international-national divide may take place. Co-ordination may also range from a rather hierarchical structure of influence on the one hand to a straight and balanced relationship of reciprocal influence on the other.

An interactive approach may be organized in several ways. The intention here has been to treat that interplay flexibly, with no preconceived categories. Two dimensions may, however, be said to have informed several of the case studies. The first of these is: (a) the distinction between a monopoly over, or at least substantial control of, foreign economic policy by state institutions and agents; and (b) a more complex policy-making where domestic coalitions, business ties and transnational coalitions play a central role. Greater complexity means that the two-level model is transformed into a multilevel model. The second of the dimensions represents the exogenous domination perspective and consists of two subcategories: one that emphasizes political bargaining between the parties, based on their respective interests in an outcome, and one that represents ideological or ideational sources of influence. There is no doubt that the very ideology of liberalization, giving priority to the establishment of a global market economy, *and* the idea of environmental protection, were strong motivating forces in the 1980s and 1990s. Their strength does not necessarily depend on these ideas being forced into the heads of decision-makers by arm-twisting techniques; it is rather that they are being spread and adopted voluntarily through imitation or as part of the learning processes.

Certain important implications follow from an interactive multilevel approach. This approach questions the idea that the state is being rolled back or that there is a zero-sum relationship between state and market in terms of power; it also questions a similar assumption about power shift under the globalization framework (Hirst and Thompson, 1996; Strange, 1996). Globalization means a shift in the relative importance of various state functions by which some are strengthened and others weakened. It is only under the unlikely event that globalization leads to a completely self-regulating market that it represents a zero-sum game between the state and the market. We still face interventionist states, as 'trading states' (Rosecranze, 1986) or 'competitive states' (Cerny, 1995). As Evans points out when offering a typology of four different state positions with respect to globalizing processes, withdrawal and involvement are not opposite alternatives. States may profit from globalization as much as lose from it; the crucial question is what kind of relationship there is between the two (Evans, 1995). One reason why the state may become strengthened from involvement in the process is that many private agents, for example, corporations operating in software, cinema and similar pirate-sensitive branches, need state support to protect their interests (Evans, 1997).

Secondly, the approach taken here makes a point about not privileging either a neo-realist or neo-institutionalist perspective; it rather supports the assumption that these perspectives may be combined (the so-called neo-neo-synthesis). But the study is also, and thirdly, making a contribution along what is referred to as non-utilitarian or post-structuralist theories, such as the social constructivist approach. According to the latter, the role of ideas and ideology in globalizing macroeconomic policies and markets is important, perhaps determinant. Several of the cases reported in this volume illustrate this.

The role of cognitive processes should also be considered in the context of supplementing theory with some post-structuralist contribution. As an example of the potential importance of cognitive processes, the state may, as we observed above, objectively retain its role and power in a globalizing environment. But *perceptions* of reality may be influenced by the public debate and by the constant communication of a different philosophy on state-market relations, one that not only preaches and predicts the roll-back of the state, but actually sees it as a *fait accompli*. State agents may thus act as if the prescription of neo-liberals were the reality – representing the case of a self-fulfilling prophecy. The radical shift from an interventionist to a neo-liberal paradigm that has taken place in a number of developing countries since the 1980s can be seen in this perspective.

From two-level to multilevel power play: a first attempt at causal explanations

Even though economic, ideational or institutional pressures for change of policy are strong, such change may still fail. Established policy-making routines represent a considerable degree of inertia. Bureaucratic procedure is hard to turn around. This is as true of international financial institutions (IFIs) as of national state institutions – and for that matter interest group behaviour. In the case of the state institutions, major policy changes will often not take place unless public institutions face *crisis* – either extremely strong political pressure or dramatic economic problems (or, indeed, normally both). In one reported study, which compared five countries during three different time periods, the latter assumption was the reason for the periodization chosen, the more explicit assumption being that policy is most likely to change during times of crisis (Gourevitch, 1986).

The following summary of the various case studies is organized so as to highlight the relevance of the interactive approach. The summary may thus be a little 'forced' in the sense that it collapses the six chosen cases into the three analytical categories, well aware that these cases are distinctly different in important ways. Differences within the categories ought therefore not to be overlooked when reading the summary that follows. By emphasizing the interactive perspective, we are also arguing that it is not always easy to establish whether a policy outcome (change) is caused by endogenous or exogenous actors and factors. It follows from the logic of globalization that the more it advances the more difficult this is. In addition, it appears easier in the case of environment protection decisions in those areas where the environment problem is one that is not clearly of an international character, such as is the case with climate policy. In the area of economic liberalization and above all with respect to integration of production and distribution entities across national borders under one organization, the transnational corporation, procedures and processes of influence appear less transparent and the relative weight of factors and actors less evident than in the case of freshwater pollution control or on-site control of air pollutants. The following observations on causality ought therefore to be read with caution.

Domestic politics prevailing over international influence in India and South Africa (prior to the 1990s)

In both these cases one finds the presence of a relatively 'strong' state, or a situation where state influence in the economy, as opposed to self-regulating market institutions, was relatively strong.[4] The rate and speed of change that took place should be evalutated against this background.

India: growing budget and balance of payment deficits were major problems in India during the 1980s. The Indian government had a long tradition of import substitution policy and of successfully withstanding international pressure for change. It reacted to the problems developing in the 1980s with a large-scale liberalization programme in 1991. In particular, policy on FDI was liberalized. The policy change did not, however, result in massive new inward FDI during the first part of the 1990s (Kumar, 1996), and the growth was still slow in the latter part of the 1990s.

In his case study, Natraj argues that external pressures for liberaliza-tion and improved environmental management in India were weak. The pressures for liberalization came from India's domestic polity; in part these started long before 1991, but materialized in terms of policy change only at that time. The reasons for this are largely of domestic origin and will be dealt with below.

South Africa: Vale and Swatuk argue that the South African apartheid regime cultivated a policy of resistance to all kinds of international demands, including international demands for environmental manage-ment. In the 1990s, however, there was a transition from isolationism to multilateralism in South Africa's official policy. In the economic field, although there are remnants of isolationism within both the business and political sector (for instance, the ANC), there has been a visible transition in the public discourse on ideas and ideology towards a liberal posture. The transition appears to have been caused more by deliberate imports and voluntary adoption of ideas than by foreign pressure. This is partly due to what the authors see as a void left after the demise of the apartheid regime and the subsequent need for the new leadership to fill the void with new policy content. In addition, as in the case of India, economic crisis has represented a source for change in South Africa.

In the 1990s the government policy on the environment has gradu-ally moved from a position of hostility to international environmental demands to acknowledging that these are problems which will have to be tackled. The government's main concern is South Africa's energy sector and its dependence on coal. There has been some, but compared to India less pressure from environmentalist groups and movements. The government seems to realize that after an initial 'honeymoon' with the international community, post-apartheid South Africa will be facing tough demands for environmental reforms, especially reforms of its energy sector. Thus, it is making what may be seen as an attempt at anticipatory adjustments to future economic problems.

US hegemonic influence in Costa Rica and (partly) in South Korea

In the cases of South Africa and India, international pressures and inducements for economic or environmental reforms were relatively weak, although South Africa has turned somewhat ideologically with the change of leadership in the ANC and while preparing for what it perceives as stronger future pressure from abroad.

In the cases of Costa Rica and South Korea, the initial pressure for economic liberalization – and in the case of Costa Rica a halt in her deforestation practice – came from the United States. In the case of environmental policy in South Korea, it came mostly as a response to domestic environmentalists' demands and then only after democratization was initiated in 1987. But South Korea's entry into the OECD strengthened the case for environmental protection. In addition, the interplay and respective timing of US geopolitical and economic interests differed widely in the two cases. The background against which the pressures took place also differed quite substantially. The state, having been quite influential in the economy until the 1980s, nevertheless was relatively less influential in state-market relations in Costa Rica than it was in the case of South Korea. In this respect, South Korea certainly is close to India.

Costa Rica: Bull and Lopez's case study shows that Costa Rica's turn to an export-oriented industrialization programme in 1983, and its ensuing decisions to join the GATT and to undertake structural adjustment programmes, were strongly influenced by its close and somewhat 'junior' relationship with the United States. Until the early 1980s, Costa Rica pursued a regional import substitution policy within the Central American Common Market based on protective barriers against the outside world. This arrangement favoured manufacturing industry in Costa Rica, which was the most industrialized country in the region, but its economic dynamics were limited by meagre regional markets. Thus, Costa Rica faced growing economic problems in the 1970s and 1980s, and, eventually, a debt crisis.

This 'crisis of regional import substitution' was an inducement to change to a new policy of diversifying exports and redirecting export to third markets. The change was encouraged by the US government as the Reagan administration launched the 'Initiative for the Caribbean Basin', strongly motivated by its Cold War efforts in the region and its attempts to isolate the socialist regimes of Cuba and Nicaragua. Central American and Caribbean products could enter US markets duty free, but signatory countries would have to apply for GATT membership. This would also serve as an inducement to US foreign investment in the region. Thus, the main external political pressure for liberalization came from the United States during a special period of strong US geopolitical interests in Central America. This initial bilateral pressure, which *inter alia* had US government agencies (notably USAID) initiate and support institution-building in Costa Rica, was reinforced by multilateral agencies as Costa Rica started its negotiations with GATT for membership. In addition, continuous debt problems forced the government to negotiate new structural adjustment agreements with the

Washington-based IFIs. Both the US-led reorganization and the initiation of negotiations with the IFIs had the support of significant segments of the private sector in Costa Rica.

South Korea: has a well publicized record of fast economic growth and a fairly equal income distribution, but a record also of periodical financial crisis. It represents 'the developmental state' in our sample. The country was badly affected by the Third World debt crisis in the 1980's and more recently by the regional Asian crisis in the autumn of 1997, but it apparently managed both crises relatively well. However, South Korea struggled with a number of problems in the 1990s, well before the 1997 crisis, especially a weakening of international competitiveness due to lack of restructuring and upgrading, and a negative trade balance which became apparent during its 1997 financial crisis.

South Korea resembles Costa Rica in some respects. It is strongly dependent on the United States for export markets. The United States has also had a strong geopolitical interest in its Cold-War alliance with South Korea, and, like Costa Rica, South Korea went through a major debt crisis in the early 1980s. But unlike the Costa Rican case, US geopolitical interests in South Korea have declined since the 1980s, at a time when South Korea's growing export surplus with the United States became a major irritant to US administrations. Thus, unlike Costa Rica, US administrations from the Reagan administration onwards applied the economic stick, rather than the carrot to pressure South Korea to change its economic strategy from a mercantilist to a liberal export orientation. The international political pressure for reform was fairly weak in the early 1980s, when the government undertook a structural adjustment austerity programme but maintained many of its previous mercantilist practices. The pressure intensified after the mid–1980s, as South Korea came under pressure to reduce its trade surplus with the United States through the removal of trade barriers and the revaluation of its currency. In the 1990s, South Korea was exposed to multilateral pressures from GATT/WTO and OECD as it applied for membership in these organizations. Finally, during the last (1997–) crisis, South Korea underwent a new structural adjustment programme with wide-ranging institutional reforms in return for a major emergency credit administered by the IMF accompanied by strong US pressure for liberalization of inbound foreign investment.

To turn to environmental policies, Costa Rica started relatively modestly and rather recently to respond to international, not least US environmentalists', concern over rain forest depreciation. Initiatives taken to preserve the rain forest were mostly motivated by domestic interests in promoting eco-tourism. During the 1990s, more involvement from societal agents was seen both on environment policies and in decision-making over trade and privatization policies (see below).

For South Korea, the major issue in the environment arena has for some time been whether its rapid industrialization and economic growth with distribution were conditioned on a serious mismanagement of the natural environment. What Moon and Lim refer to as the 'development coalition' implicitly held the view that such a precondition existed. Thus environmental degradation was a distinct trend in the case of the South Korean type of development (as in that of many other countries).

As the trend created its counter-trend, the source of the latter can be clearly found at the domestic level. After the democratic opening in 1987 there was a sudden burst of civil society activism and a rapid growth and proliferation of NGOs, including environmentalist NGOs. In several cases there was mobilization of community protest against what were perceived as environmental threats. At the same time, protest became organized. The NGO community of several thousand associations and organizations has become the most significant political actor in terms of number of participants, resources, expertise and political activism. The result has been a quite substantial improvement in environmental policy performance, such as CO_2 emissions and freshwater availability, both representing serious challenges.

While domestic mobilization of political demands for conservationist measures is the main cause for this change, part of the reason for it is the integration of South Korea into the world of developed countries as she became member of the OECD. Becoming a member of the 'club' means that the government has to take a set of international regimes more seriously. Globalization has thus resulted in a paradoxical intertwining of developmentalist and environmentalist coalitions in the course of relatively few years. After a short revival of the developmentalist credo as a response to the 1997 crisis, Moon and Lim expect that domestic environmentalist groups will ally with transnational NGOs under the inspiration of emerging global environmental regimes. This alliance should prevail over the developmental coalition in shaping future environmental policies in South Korea. This presents the state with the challenge of being able to weave through the paradoxes and underlying dynamics of coalitional politics. It has gone a long way to accommodate to international conventions, but the implementation of these is still lagging behind that of most other OECD countries because of South Korea's institutional and mental inertia as a developing country. If it is to overcome the paradox and the inertia, it will have to realign the two dominant paradigms – that of developmentalism and conservationism. For this to happen, environmental NGOs in South Korea need to restructure and refocus their goals, strategies and programmes of action and broaden their 'grassroots' base.

Divided hegemony and contradictory external policy recommendations in Argentina and the Ivory Coast (until around 1990)

The various actors that pressured for liberal economic reform appear to have been reasonably unified in the cases of Costa Rica and South Korea. On the other hand, the case studies from Argentina as well as the Ivory Coast demonstrate contradictory policy recommendations from multilateral agencies or hegemonic powers. These contradictions offered both countries a period of relative flexibility in the handling of exogenous demands.

Argentina: Diana Tussie's chapter on Argentina focuses on the trade policy reforms. The starting point is the debt crisis in the early 1980s triggered by rising international interest rates on loans which mainly went to finance unproductive investments and consumption. The crisis further escalated as the new democratic Alfonsín government (1984–89), during its first years in office, pursued an unsuccessful Keynesian counter-cyclical policy.

Initially, international pressures for trade reform were weak. The first structural adjustment agreement with the IMF was restricted to customary macroeconomic targets. From the mid–1980s onwards, the World Bank became involved in promoting trade reforms in close co-operation with the government, but apparently there was a conflict of view that resulted in lack of co-ordination between the World Bank and the IMF. In 1988, the World Bank granted a loan for trade reforms without approval from the IMF, which then withheld its own loan. This reform failed as a result of insufficient financial backing of the Argentine currency. There was a run on the currency and this resulted in the biggest banking and currency crisis of the post World War II period so far.[5] Hyperinflation was followed by a change of government. After this failure the two IFIs co-ordinated both their policy recommendations and policy implementation (see below).

The Ivory Coast: in 1979–80, the economy of the Ivory Coast was badly affected by declining terms of trade due to a fall in the prices of its main export products, along with growing interest rates on its debt.

In the late 1980s the country was again affected by a major decline in its terms of trade. It also faced an ecological crisis of deforestation as a result of long-lasting unsustainable forestry policy, including clearing of land for cocoa and coffee production.

The debt crisis was followed by pressure from the IMF and the World Bank for economic reforms. But this pressure was weakened by differences between the IMF and the World Bank over partly contradictory policy priorities of fiscal stabilization (IMF) and export diversification (World Bank). The two agencies' ability to impose conditionalities was also disturbed by the Ivory Coast's bilateral relations with France. France provided the country with large amounts of economic assistance, regardless of the country's non-compliance with demands from the IMF. Furthermore, the French supported a continued high value for the CFA franc, while the IMF wanted a devaluation. This situation ended in 1993/94. In 1993, the French government announced that its economic aid would be dependent on an agreement with the IMF and decided at the same time a major devaluation of the CFA ´franc-French ´franc exchange rate (implemented in 1994). Thus, in the same way as in Argentina, the government in the Ivory Coast has faced increasingly unified international inducements and pressures for economic reforms during most of the 1990s.

Different polities: country policy responses to exogenous demands

Our six countries were challenged by economic problems (market fluctuations) and international policy prescriptions, all of which had great implications for national economic prosperity, distributive issues and environmental performances. Their responses varied according to several factors referred to above – structural, institutional, circumstantial and societal – in ways that represent a fairly complex picture.

In terms of one background factor – level of economic and political-economic development – one would have expected relatively similar outcomes for the six cases. Although the variations in terms of GNP per capita between South Korea and the Ivory Coast are considerable, there are no truly 'weak' nation-states among them.[6] One would therefore expect a considerable degree of commonality of policies produced either by the pressure of systemic forces (but without necessarily representing asymmetric relationships of the dependency type) or through convergence of policy-making rationales.

The logical implication of the multilevel model is that to the extent broad national support of a policy outcome is achieved, and in addition a transnational alliance is organized in support of it, to the same extent can policy implementation also be expected. This cannot, however, always be taken for granted. Experiences with Structural Adjustment Programmes (SAPs) indicate that even in a relationship characterized by highly asymmetric power – the IMF versus a poor developing country – the latter may move the outcome a considerable distance from what the former would have wanted (Kahler, 1993). Even in cases where bilateral agreements are produced to supervise implementation, a process of 'involuntary defection' may occur and obstruct implementation. This happens because domestic interest groups mobilize, or because groups originally in favour change their mind in the process following international agreement and oppose implementation. Our analysis offers the following three categories of outcomes, as mentioned below.

Crisis and executive entrepreneurship in Argentina and South Korea

Executive entrepreneurs will frequently be hamstrung by their constituencies and various kind of vested interests, regardless of their own skills and of institutional autonomy. However, major crises may provide windows for pushing new policies; a crisis is a situation where the perception of standard operating procedures and customary practices is that they no longer work. In South Korea and Argentina, major crises gave political entrepreneurs the opportunity to ally with the IMF/World Bank and to reorganize domestic political alliances in support of liberal, even neo-liberal policies.

Argentina: In 1984, Raúl Alfonsín was elected president after the fall of the military junta. The Alfonsín government was a weak one, with a narrow middle-class constituency. During the hyperinflation of 1989, the Alfonsín government lost most of its political support and was forced to resign six months before its term was due to end.

Carlos Menem, from the Peronist party, formed a new government which forwarded a neo-liberal reform package. The policies were sustained by co-ordinated policy recommendations from the IMF, the World Bank and the Inter-American Development Bank. Fear of hyperinflation made workers and the wider public willing to swallow the bitter pill. Resistance in the Congress was overcome as Menem managed to get Congress acceptance to steer the new policies by means of decrees without prior Congressional authorization. With these measures, the prospects of reform depended on the balance of forces within the ruling Peronist party. The main constituency of the Peronist party was that of the working class. Menem's Peronist party maintained this working class constituency, while at the same time succeeded in enfeebling the powerful trade unions which represented a bulwark of resistance against economic liberalization. Menem also fashioned new ties with reform-oriented business groups. Thus the long tradition of corporatism Argentinian-style was broken.

The Menem government succeeded in stabilizing prices. Later, the 'honeymoon' was over and dissatisfaction mounted over the economic shock therapy with rising unemployment caused by reduction of public employment, bankruptcies as a result of growing import competition, and so on. The government responded by introducing compensatory policies to reinforce its alliances with business and labour. The landed oligarchy was given incentives to exploit new export openings, leading to environmentally detrimental effects on the land. Thus, in Argentina's agricultural sector, economic liberalization and environmental degradation appear to go hand in hand. The government's efforts to improve relations with industry, however, weakened its initial liberalization efforts as it introduced new forms of discretionary *ad hoc* trade protectionism, while the loyalty of the traditional working class constituency was strengthened by measures such as improved counter-unemployment measures and other social programmes which were supported by the IDB and the World Bank.

South Korea: as pointed out by Moon and Lim, considerable economic liberalization took place during the presidency of Kim Young Sam (1993–97). Indeed, it is hotly debated whether the liberalization of cross-border capital movement under Kim Young Sam went too far and triggered the 1997 financial crisis (Chang, 1998). In any case, some of the important economic reform attempts by the Kim Young Sam government failed as a result of its inability to muster political support and because of the 'unruliness' of labour and business. In December 1996, the government attempted to revise the Korean labour law in order to remove legal protection against the dismissal of workers. This attempt at reducing labour costs failed. There was strong opposition from organized labour which was inflamed by the government's procrastination of liberalization of labour unionization. Labour was supported by the political opposition which reacted to irregular legislative procedures in forwarding the revised labour code. Amid mass strikes and strong parliamentary opposition the government gave in and postponed its labour code revision.

The government also attempted in vain to reduce ownership concentration by big business groups. These groups continued to expand through cross-investment, cross-payment guarantees and cross-ownership, and their expansion was to a large extent financed by money borrowed abroad. Industrial restructuring failed. There were over-investment and thus surplus capacity in large industries such as automobiles and steel. These measures were exaggerated by the government's licensing of entry into these branches to political favourites, and its inability to decide on how it should handle delinquent firms. Thus, the unruliness of business along with so-called 'crony capitalism' relations between government and business impeded industrial restructuring and led to a swift expansion of South Korea's foreign debt.

The failure of the Kim Young Sam government's reform attempts can, then, be attributed to too close relations with big business as well as to its detachment from organized labour. If the state autonomy model was already on its way out, the potential for a transition to an 'embedded autonomy' situation appears to have been undermined. The financial crisis in autumn 1997 brought victory to opposition candidate Kim Dae Jung in the presidential elections. As South Korea faced a major financial crisis and strict conditionality demands from the IMF, Kim Dae Jung seized the opportunity to press for the reforms which had failed during his predecessor's term. IMF demands included labour reforms. With the backing of these demands from the so-called 'bad cop', Kim used his good relations with organized labour to initiate tripartite negotiations between government, business and labour on labour code revision. The end result was that the unions gave up the protection against layoffs in return for extended rights of organization and welfare provisions to the unemployed. This sacrifice from labour also allowed Kim, again with the backing of IMF demands, to pressure the large Korean business groups (the *chaebol*) to undertake reform to end their cross-investment patterns and trim down their size by selling out weak companies. This part of the reform package resulted, however, in only protracted and watered-down reforms from the *chaebol*.

Thus, in Argentina as well as South Korea, previous governments failed to muster support from labour and business. The growth of the environmentalist groups in South Korea had not resulted in the laying of a new power base for the political parties, whereas such groups were practically non-existent in Argentina. Major economic crisis led to changes of presidents in both countries. The new administrations took advantage of the crisis and of good relations with labour to promote reforms which previously had been resisted by labour. On the other hand, relations with business moved in opposite directions in the two cases. Kim Dae Jung 'cooled down' relations with business and enhanced his 'executive autonomy' by playing off labour and business against one another. Menem, on the other hand, 'warmed up' government-business relations to draw on business support for economic reform. More importantly, the results of the strategies pursued to handle the economic crises turned out finally to be radically different in the two countries – South Korea handling its crisis relatively successfully, while Argentina ended up in another crisis spiral which appears to be even worse than the one in the 1980s.

Transnational alliance-building in Costa Rica – and its gradual breakdown in the Ivory Coast

In two of the six cases, transnational alliances were quite decisive in shaping policy – Costa Rica and the Ivory Coast. But the effects of the alliance was rather different. In the former case it produced a gradual but relatively clear transition from import substitution policies to liberalization. In the latter, the transnational alliance upheld for a long time positions which partly contradicted the neo-liberal doctrine and the demands for broad liberalization.

Costa Rica: as discussed earlier, the Reagan administration's 'Initiative for the Caribbean Basin' allowed for duty-free access of goods to US markets in return for GATT membership. However, Bull and Lopez show that business was initially divided with regard to GATT membership as it would imply increasing competition in the Central American markets from external agents. As shown above, there were contacts between USAID and a constellation of technocrats and 'upcoming' capitalists who wanted a change to an export-oriented development strategy in Costa Rica. This transnational alliance may have had a decisive influence on the outcome. USAID strengthened its alliance partners by financing new government agencies and business associations in favour of GATT membership and a change of export strategy. In the next round the domestic alliance of technocrats and business in favour of a policy change managed to take control over the negotiations on Costa Rica's GATT membership, and to insulate themselves from domestic parliamentary influence.

Hence, the United States did not simply persuade Costa Rica to change its economic strategy from import substitution to export orientation. The US aid agency also actively boosted the power and resources of domestic proponents of a policy change. The strategy, however, was rather elitist, participants mostly confined to a few groups and institutions and the processes rather secretive. The social and political protests that followed at the end of the 1990s were both a confirmation that such elitism in the long run was impermissible in a country with such a relatively strong civil society and thus a proof that some policy platforms lacked legitimation. Mass social protest, peaking in the largest national strike for decades to protest against the privatization of Costa Rica's telecommunications body, may represent at least a temporary halt to further adjustment to globalization and the beginning of a period of more democratic decision-making. Before the anti-privatization rallies there had been a gradual process of building an alternative alliance around environmental protection concerns. We return to this briefly below.

The Ivory Coast: used to reflect transnational coalition-building quite remarkably as long as the French-Ivoirian 'special relationship' worked. This is a relationship based not only on close political ties, including French military presence, but also on a network of economic relations creating a commonality of interests between the local government – which has occupied a strong position in the economy ever since independence – and the French.

In the 1990s, elements of this relationship still remained, in for example some of the sectors where monopolistic or oligopolistic market arrangements have a long history and the 'rent' is divided between state authorities and foreign companies. Liberalization measures advocated by the IFIs were to a considerable extent directed against these 'special relationships'. Sindzingre and Conte show that the alliance withheld pressure for change quite successfully, not only during the period where geopolitical considerations that caused political friction between Washington and Paris were at work, but even later.

The alliance, once it eroded and started to lose its strength, gave way to a situation both more complex when it comes to alliance formations and potentially more vulnerable because of its internal incoherence. Structural change and economic conjunctures also make themselves particularly felt in the case of the Ivory Coast – an economy that is dependent both on manufacturing which meets heavy competition internationally and on raw materials extraction and exports in areas that are traditionally subject to highly fluctuating market conditions. But as these factors are largely beyond the control of the local agents, their capacity and in particular flexibility to initiate and carry through policy adjustments are crucial. One type of response which has its origin in the post-independence era – and which Sindzingre and Conte refer to as surprising – is the growth of an informal economy. It has to a considerable extent grown because public servants have seen the opportunity for rent-seeking being created by decolonization, periodic booms and gradual privatization. But it is also growing because of administrative clumsiness and unclear legal systems.

If the IFI package of reforms may be said to constitute a holistic and rational package (internally consistent among other things), the fact that the Ivory Coast's way towards political change represents an unsettled polity makes it difficult if not impossible to organize a smooth and efficient transition such as demanded by the IFIs. In addition, the 'Ivorian model' represented in several ways advantages (especially if compared to other countries in the region), in particular, good infrastructure and (until the end of the 1990s) fairly stable political institutions, something the national political-administrative leadership is aware of. However, these factors also represent stumbling-blocks to change. But since some change is perceived, even by the local polity to be necessary and hence implemented, the overall result has not been an internally coherent one. This treble pressure – the one of the IFIs, of international market fluctuations and competition, and the one due to domestic political and institutional defence of the *status quo* – results in a very complex situation. Added to this comes the personality factor at the level of individuals. It showed up in the interpersonal rivalries that erupted after the death of president Houphouët-Boigny in 1994. The situation may be said to have deteriorated to the point of breakdown in the form of a military *coup d'état* in 1999 that initiated a series of further coups and continued political instability.

Distribution policy and policy flexibility: India and South Africa

In the previous discussion, the point of view of the IFI's (the World Bank's and the IMF) was more or less taken for granted. The focus was on how economic liberalization can be implemented through political entrepreneurship without questioning the IFI-sponsored reforms. But such questioning was and is of course part of the discourse in several of the countries studied. Thus critical questions can at last be introduced: is economic liberalization really a panacea in forwarding flexibility? Or is an inability to make economic adjustment rather a result of socio-economic relations – as argued by several authors (Senghaas, 1982; Katzenstein, 1985; Evans, 1995)? The remaining two among our case studies indicate that a long history of unequal distribution of economic assets is highly detrimental to economic adjustment flexibility, and that economic liberalization is irrelevant, or even detrimental to these problems.

India: Natraj argues that the macroeconomic problems that were at the root of change in India in 1991, notably budget deficit and a deterioriating foreign account balance deficit, were largely 'internal', explained by endogenous factors. He sees them as the result of the dynamics of social and political power relations; public overspending, corruption, lack of will to undertake austerity policies which would raise domestic savings, and reluctance to abandon government favours that feed upper class consumption and the lobbies of large farm interests.

According to this analysis, India suffered from the effects of an unequal distribution of assets and political power relations, and from policies which reinforced these inequalities. But the policy response to India's economic problems, something that was discussed in public debate and gradually implemented, was economic liberalization. It included privatization of India's huge public enterprise sector, and removal of barriers to foreign investments and trade. As seen from this perspective, India's 1991 policy of liberalization was an inadequate response to its deep structural problems and one which avoided politically painful choices; namely, of undertaking redistributive policies and institutional reform.

It is consistent with such an analysis that the role played by state governments and not least by 'civil society' should be highlighted. Local state polities vary considerably with respect to how they cope with distribution as compared to giving priority to liberalization. Even more important, according to Natraj, is the role played by an independent judiciary and not least by local non-governmental organizations and social networks. His study is an embedded case study which focuses on two investment projects that are partly dependent on foreign capital and technology.[7] In both cases environmental issues were highlighted, and issues were developing in terms of bargaining – in one of the cases confrontation – between the political centres and local NGOs, with the judiciary as an active party intervening on both these issues.

India's long tradition of political democracy makes its state interventionist tradition – but maybe above all its NGOs or more generally its civil society – the strongest among the six country cases. This tradition, and also the mere size of the economy, makes the polity less vulnerable to exogenous pressure. There was no inevitability in India's change to a more liberal policy tradition, and there was little effect from exogenous agents' attempts to press for it. Rather, the change took place, as already shown, because of the necessity to reform the economy as a result of its growing tendency to stagnate. Contextual changes, notably the fall of dirigist regimes in the Soviet Union and elsewhere, helped speed up the process of a transformation of thinking in political circles, primarily in the Congress party. Business leaders (although not totally united) had argued for some time for a change – but mostly in vain. With the confluence of exogenous changes and a growing recognition that domestic economic stagnation was a result of bad management or an unmanagable economic system, policy also changed. Overnight, India reversed its resistance to Uruguay Round goals and stopped being the champion of sceptical Third World positions. She also opened up the economy to foreign direct investments. Towards the end of the 1990s, these started to become considerable, although they were markedly dwarfed by foreign direct investments in China and even in some of the East and South East Asian countries.

'To a noticeable degree the interventionist state is exiting from India', writes Natraj. But it is not becoming more transparent, nor less characterized by bureaucratic slowness. Nor is its political foundation at all internally consistent, one reason being that interparty rivalry continues and governments are formed on the basis of substantial bargaining of the 'horse-trading' type. The ruling coalition, which lost in the general election of 1999 but remained in power, is departing from its nationalist platform to become a pragmatic administrator of the changes so much wanted by powerful business lobbies in the country. The latter represent the best ally to the IFI programmes.

While the effect of the globalization and liberalization processes is not yet known, and, although it varies, its longer-term effects may be both positive and negative. The strength of the NGOs and the environmentalists, and the activism of an independent judiciary, are all potentially positive developments, but they are not without elements of populism and opportunism, the latter even covering India's relationship with foreign economic interests (something that is illustrated by the sponsoring that is taking place).

South Africa: while India is a long-established democracy, South Africa has a very particular and indeed different post-war history as an apartheid state and thus also an undemocratic state. Like India, South Africa is faced with great problems of social inequality which also threaten political stability. Vale and Swatuk argue that South Africa's economic and environmental problems are closely intertwined with the apartheid legacy of strong racially based social inequality in terms of distribution of income, education and land.

During the apartheid period, energy policies were oriented to promoting national self-sufficiency in order to offset the consequences of international embargoes. This led to polluting and to inefficient utilization of the country's coal resources. Apartheid was based on a low level of education within the black majority. Thus, South Africa is poorly equipped in terms of human capital for a more advanced form of economy, so that it may be forced to rely on its traditional export activities of agricultural goods, agricultural manufacturing and the mining industry. Industry still works on a tradition of neo-mercantilism, something which also is reflected in its current export profile (Betlehem and Goldblatt, 1996). The mining industry has very serious environmental consequences. The system of agricultural production is also based on an extremely unequal distribution of land, racially speaking. In addition, it has damaging environmental effects since it has been pursued with unsustainable uses of water resources and polluting farming practices at white farms. Hence, despite the enormous differences between South Africa and India, their economic and environmental problems appear to be strongly related to settled social and political orders based on unequal distribution.

The new post-apartheid ANC government seems to be incapable or unwilling to do much about this situation. After the regime transformation, dominant factions in the ANC swiftly changed from neo-Keynesianism to austerity-oriented development policies which played down issues of redistribution. There are attempts to promote a black middle-class in the hope that this will stabilize the political situation. If this strategy succeeds there may be more common ground for a 'rainbow' liberal consensus, but there is also the danger that this rainbow alliance will preserve South Africa's extreme inequalities. Although environmentalist groups are still relatively weak and unorganized, there is a growing awareness of the deepening importance of environmental issues in South African society. But it will not be able – even if it were to grow in strength – to make a real impact in a positive direction without this being closely linked to the distributive issue.

Conclusion

The six cases presented here all converge towards more liberal macroeconomic policies, including foreign economic and industrial policies – but to very different degrees and at different speed. There is change, but it is even less uniform across the cases with respect to adjusting to environmental protection as a policy priority. Whether this is imagined or real, economic globalization is widely held to be at odds with environmental protection, although the country studies also offer some illustrations of an emerging harmony. But attempts to move towards a sustainable development strategy that harmonizes industrial and trade policy on the one hand with environmental policy on the other, are still rare. A new coalition has been emerging in South Korea, and there are some signs of it in Costa Rica and South Africa. The general picture, however, remains that the two policy arenas are driven by different agents with differing goals and strategies. There appears still to be more competition than cooperation between the economic liberalization and the environmental protection agencies.

Convergence towards economic globalization varies considerably, both in terms of when it starts, what explains it, how fast it moves and how general it is. Costa Rica, to a certain extent also Argentina (at least until the 2001 crisis erupted), appear to have moved farther than the others, who reveal a very mixed category of 'latecomers' to globalization. South Africa, because of its international isolation under apartheid, is a special case; after apartheid and the success of the rainbow coalition the new leadership appears to have adopted economic liberalization as a new policy priority to fill an ideological vacuum. Whereas India appears to have shifted towards liberal policies only after being hit by economic crisis, South Korea started adjustment well before this happened. In the case of the Ivory Coast, coming late is to some extent explained by a particular exogenous factor – the fact that the country was shielded from pressure from neo-liberal hegemonic agents by its special relationship with France.

In all the cases examined, policy change may be partially explained by more challenging macroeconomic conditions, in India's case less dramatic than in Argentina's case where serious financial crisis and problems in coping with it appear to be endemic. In almost all cases ideational or ideological change: that is, an adoption of liberal and even neo-liberal economic doctrines, played a role. In Costa Rica it was part of a redefinition of public policy to accommodate the fact that long-awaited liberalization was wanted by an alliance of local business and hegemonic power. It is, however, in the case of South Africa that the ideational factor is claimed by the authors to be *relatively* the most important. In this case the shift was not preceded by strong pressure from exogenous forces such as was and is the case in Costa Rica and several of the other countries studied; it was a more discreet working of ideas. In addition, it is important to note that the ideational shift in South Africa coincides with the change of power to majority rule which makes the analysis of policy change in this country particularly complex. While bureaucratic inertia explains some of the failure of the country to adjust, it is also true to say that the broad and systemic political changes taking place in that country have opened up the opportunity for non-governmental agencies to play a greater role, not least in the field of environmental protection.

Both causes for change and the agents who carry it differ from one case to another, and so does the scope and timing of change. Some of the reasons for these differences, we suggest, may be found in differences in polity. Differences in political culture, formation of socio-political alliances, the form of state institutions and state-society relations all matter, as does the relationship between these agents and exogenous agents and institutions. These differences mean that the potential sources for change – either back to a state prior to the liberalizing period (if economic globalization stops and recedes, national manifestation of protest starts) or to a new type of policy mix – will also vary from one category to another.

As far as policy on environment *per se* is concerned, however, the kind of emerging *policy commonality* among the six that is visible in the case of investment and trade policies is not found. This may be at least partly explained by a general global factor: simply the fact that ideas of economic liberalization have had much more forceful backing, become globally spread for a much longer time, and thus been accepted more commonly, than is the case with environmental protection. But the difference between the status of the two issue-areas also probably reflects at least two more factors. First, that the saliency of and type and strength of coalitions behind environment policy in the countries differs and that the environmentalist position is the strongest where it has been able to gather support from political and/or business quarters at home and from transnational environmentalist coalitions. Secondly, the claim that the 'South' is *all* environmental policy hinterland is wrong. In other words: the 'South' is certainly no homogeneous category with respect to environmental policy, but reflects widely different trajectories of and stages of policy development.

In both India and Costa Rica, environmental policy advances do not depend on exogenous pressure, but emerge mainly from within. Policy is high on the political agenda due to an activist NGO and environmentalist community, but also due to initiatives by politicians and, in the case of India, an entrepreneurial independent judiciary. In the South African case, a more heterogeneous and a changing coalition of social forces have been mobilizing behind demands for environmental protection ever since apartheid. Popular and populist mobilization, some of it being part of the anti-apartheid struggle, has been seen in parallel with gradual business awareness of the need to adjust to changing international policy contexts in trade and industrial policy. Both have put increasing pressure on the orthodoxy of national sovereignty considerations and a conservative bureaucracy. Environmental policy has thus moved from being defined on national security grounds during the apartheid period to becoming a broader issue of social and industrial policy.

In the environment policy arena, the one country in the sample that grew fastest in the recent past, South Korea, appears also to have seen the most striking growth in environmental activism. Such activism is also strong in the case of India where policy entrepreneurship in this arena is more a matter of state and local effort than of federal government effort. There is also probably a causal relationship between the fact that the Ivory Coast is relatively less industrialized and hardly demonstrates any environmentalism, either public or civil, at all. There is, on the other hand, a tradition of environmental activism in Costa Rica which has been part of the mobilization of wide protest against liberalization that emerged at the end of the 1990s. In South Africa, the state appears to be preparing itself to adjust environmental policy demands to its industrial and trade policies, but actual implementation is still only in its very preliminary stage. In Argentina, it is hardly initiated; here public policy still has to recognize that there is a trade-off between the increase in environmental degradation and the economic benefits from expansion of export trade (Gutman, 1998).

Implications for theory

We have argued and found support in favour of what is now referred to as synthesizing utilitarian perspectives, mainly neo-realist and neo-liberal institutionalist theories, and of supplementing the synthesis with contributions from non-utilitarian perspectives. In this book the latter position is in particular argued by Vale and Swatuk within their deconstructivist approach. Contrary to Ruggie (1998), we hold the position that it should be possible to combine the neo-neo approaches with not only cognitivist, but even constructivist approaches. Our case studies give various degrees of support for this point, some of them perhaps weak. But for Vale and Swatuk (on South Africa) the role of ideological shift and the form and content of public policy debate over issues are important in explaining policy outcomes.

In a mostly utilitarian perspective, Joan Nelson has suggested a list of factors which are decisive for whether policy adjustment occurs at all, and if it does whether it occurs fast or slowly (Nelson, 1996). The set of factors that she has developed for a comparative perspective on policy change represents a useful checklist, the limitations of which, however, are that it basically represents utilitarian or rational choice theory.

We have found support for the view that the two-level model should be developed to put less emphasis on the unitary actor perspective and more on the complexity in the way international and domestic processes interact and coalitions form. In particular, the role and influence of transnational alliance formations needs to be reflected in the model. Our study supports the suggestion we have made that the two-level model be developed into a multilevel model. This model needs to encompass the role of ideas in shaping the strategy of state negotiators, as well as taking into account the roots of political competition and conflict and the forming of alliances or policy communities across national entities.

Neo-liberal economic ideas, very much because they form an elaborated, fairly internally consistent and much publicized package of policies, have been the dominant, or hegemonic, ideology for many years. As this decade advances, in the aftermath of the Mexican, East-Asian, Brazilian and (the rather different) Russian crises, there are indications that the power of that ideology is peaking or has already peaked. Whether that prognosis is actually true or not has not yet been ascertained, and – if it is – what comes after is impossible to say. Moreover, globalization carries a tremendous potential for innovation and growth that, if it is reconciled with the need to distribute its positive effects equally, may save the basic elements in the ideology. And since there is an amount of inertia in political systems no matter what type they are, an ideology once adopted may stay in power well beyond the point in time where its foundation has become seriously questioned.

The neo-liberal package thus has a basic message which has a strong universal appeal – that of the market being a useful institution for allocating resources and, provided it works, of preventing unproductive rent-seeking. There should be no doubt that parts of that package are economically beneficial from an efficacy point of view and that they may also be harmonized with environmental protection concerns. But the problems seen after the economic crises, and indications that socioeconomic marginalization appears to go in tandem with market-based economic growth (low-paid employment in the United States), and globalization (as documented in UNDP and UNCTAD reports), point towards a growing need to reintegrate both economy and society in any debate about optimal macroeconomic policies that give outcomes that are not only socially equitable, but also ecologically sustainable.

Notes

1. Drafts of the chapter were presented at the Roskilde University Centre, Department of Geography and International Development Studies research workshop in Gilleleje, Denmark on 9 December 1998 at a seminar co-sponsored by the Department of Political Science and the Centre on Development and the Environment at the University of Oslo on 22 April 1999. Particular thanks are due to John Degnbold Martinussen, Benedicte Bull and an anonymous referee for their useful comments and suggestions. The contents of the chapter are, however, the sole responsibility of the authors.
2. The classification into these three perspectives on globalization has been adopted from Held *et al.*, 1999.
3. For a similar argument, see Haggard, 1990.
4. For further discussion and conceptualization of 'state' and state – market relationships, see Martinussen, 1997.
5. According to the World Bank and in terms of what percentage of the GNP had to be allocated to bank rescue financing and to debt servicing.
6. Cameroon was originally selected as the case representing West Africa, but had to be cancelled in favour of the Ivory Coast.
7. These were, respectively, the Enron project and the Cogentrix project.

References

Acuña, Carlos and William Smith (1994) 'The Political Economy of Structural Adjustment: the Logic of Support and Opposition to Neoliberal Reform', in *Latin American Political Economy in the Age of Neoliberal Reform* (New Brunswick and Oxford: Transaction Publishers).

Adamolekun, Ladipo, Guy de Lusignan and Armand Atomate (eds) (1997) *Réforme de la fonction publique en Afrique francophone*. Technical Document 357F (Washington, DC: The World Bank).

Adams, Jan (1997) 'Environmental Policy and Competitiveness in a Globalised Economy: Conceptual Issues and a Review of the Empirical Evidence', OECD Proceedings, *Globalisation and Environment: Preliminary Perspectives* (Paris: OECD).

Alvares, Claude (1979) *Homo Faber: Technology and Culture in India, China and the West* (Bombay: Allied Publishers).

Amjadi, Azita and Alexander J. Yeats (1995a) *Nontariffs Barriers Africa Faces: What Did the Uruguay Round Accomplish, and What Remain to be Done?* Policy Research Working Paper 1439 (Washington, DC: The World Bank).

Amjadi, Azita and Alexander J. Yeats (1995b) *Have Transport Costs Contributed to the Relative Decline of Sub-Saharan Exports? Some Preliminary Empirical Evidence*, Policy Research Working Paper 1559 (Washington, DC : The World Bank).

Amjadi, Azita, Ulrich Reinicke and Alexander Yeats (1996) *Did External Barriers Cause the Marginalization of Sub-Saharan Africa in World Trade?* Discussion Paper no. 348 (Washington, DC: The World Bank).

Amsden, Alice H. (1989) *Asia's Next Giant: South Korea and Late Industrialization* (Oxford: Oxford University Press).

Amsden, Alice H. (1992) 'A Theory of Government Intervention in Late Industrialization', pp. 53–84 in Louis Putterman and Dietrich Rueschemeyer (eds) *State and Market in Development: Synergy or Rivalry?* (Boulder and London: Lynne Rienner).

Anyang' Nyong'o, P. (1987) 'The Development of Agrarian Capitalist Classes in the Ivory Coast', in Paul Lubeck (ed.) *The African Bourgeoisie: Capitalist Development in Nigeria, Kenya and the Ivory Coast* (Boulder, CO: Lynne Rienner).

Arias Sánches, Oscar (1971) *Grupos de Presión en Costa Rica* (San José, Costa Rica: Editorial Costa Rica).

Asamblea Legislativa (1997) *Leyes y Decretos sobre medio ambiente* (San José, Costa Rica).

Assadi, M. (1995) 'The Politics of Cogentrix', *Economic and Political Weekly*, 10 October.

Assidon, Elsa (1989) *Le commerce captif: les sociétés commerciales françaises de l'Afrique Noire* (Paris: L'Harmattan).

Austen, Ralph (1987) *African Economic History* (London and Portsmouth: James Currey and Heinemann).

Axelrod, Robert (1984) *The Evolution of Cooperation* (New York: Basic Books).

Azam, Jean-Paul (1993) 'The "Côte d'Ivoire" Model of Endogenous Growth', *European Economic Review*, vol. 37, 566–576.

Azam, Jean-Paul and Christian Morrisson (1994) *La faisabilité politique de l'ajustement en Côte d'Ivoire et au Maroc* (Paris: OECD, Development Centre).

Bach, Daniel (1982) 'L'insertion ivoirienne dans les rapports internationaux', in Yves André Fauré and Jean-François Médard (eds) *Etat et bourgeoisie en Côte d'Ivoire* (Paris: Karthala).

Balasubramaniam, Vejai (1998) 'Environment and Human Rights – a New Form of Imperialism?', *Economic and Political Weekly*, 21 February.

Barahona Montero, Manuel (1999) 'El Desarrollo Económico', pp. 97–149 in Quesada Camacho, Juan Rafael *et al. Costa Rica Contemporánea: raíces del estado de la nación* (San José, Costa Rica: Editorial de la Unviersidad de Costa Rica).

Barbier, Jean-Pierre (1993) 'L'industrialisation de l'Afrique, mythe d'hier, pari réaliste pour demain?', in Serge Michaïlof (ed.) *La France et l'Afrique, vade mecum pour un nouveau voyage* (Paris: Karthala).

Bartels, Frank and Barry H. Pavier (1997) 'Enron in India: Developing Political Capability', *Economic and Political Weekly*, 22 February.

Bayart, Jean-Francois (1993) *The State in Africa. The Politics of the Belly* (London: Longman).

Beare, Mark and Paul Bell, 'For All We Know', *Leadership* (Cape Town), July 1997, pp. 136–41.

Bennell, Paul (1996) *Privatisation in Sub-Saharan Africa: Progress and Prospects During the 1990s*, Working Paper 41 (University of Sussex: Institute of Development Studies).

Berg, Elliot J. (1971) 'Structural Transformation versus Gradualism: Recent Economic Development in Ghana and the Ivory Coast', in Philip Foster and Aristide R. Zolberg (eds) *Ghana and the Ivory Coast: Perspectives on Modernisation* (Chicago, IL: Chicago University Press).

Berg, Elliot J. and Mary Shirley (1987) *Divestiture in Developing Countries*, Discussion Paper no. 11 (Washington, DC: The World Bank).

Berg, Elliot J., Patrick Guillaumont, Jacky Amprou and Jacques Pégatiénan (2001) 'Côte d'Ivoire', in Shantayanan Devarajan, David Dollar and Torgny Holmgren (eds) *Aid and Reform in Africa: Lessons from Ten Case Studies* (Washington, DC: The World Bank).

Berthélémy, Jean-Claude and François Bourguignon (1996) *Growth and Crisis in Côte d'Ivoire* (Washington, DC: The World Bank).

Bethlehem, Lael (1996) 'An Evaluation of the Impact of International Environmental Pressures on South African Exporters', in Lael Bethlehem and Michael Goldblatt (eds) (1996) *The Bottom-line: Industry and the Environment in South Africa* (Cape Town: University of Cape Town Press).

Bethlehem, Lael and Michael Goldblatt (eds) (1997) *The Bottom Line. Industry and the Environment in South Africa* (Cape Town: University of Cape Town Press).

Bhatt, V.V. (1994) 'Understanding the East Asian Miracle', *Economic and Political Weekly*, 19 February.

Bhattacharya, Amar, Peter J. Montiel and Sunil Sharma (1997) *Private Flows to Sub-Saharan Africa: an Overview of Trends and Determinants*, mimeo (Washington, DC: International Monetary Fund and the World Bank).

Bhattacharya, Rina (1997) 'Pace, Sequencing and Credibility of Structural Reforms', *World Development*, vol. 25, no. 7 (July), 1045–61.

Biggs, Tyler, Margaret Miller, Caroline Otto and Gerald Tyler (1996) *Africa Can Compete! Export Opportunities and Challenges for Garments and Home Products in the European Market*, Discussion Paper no. 300 (Washington, DC: The World Bank).

Blackhurst, Richard, Alice Enders and Joseph F. François (1995) 'The Uruguay Round and Market Access: Opportunities and Challenges for Developing Countries', in Will Martin and L. Alan Winters (eds) *The Uruguay Round and the Developing Economies*, Discussion Paper no. 307 (Washington, DC: The World Bank).

Blackhurst, Richard, Bill Lyakurwa and Ademola Oyejide (2000) 'Options for Improving Africa's Participation in the WTO', *World Economy*, vol. 23, no. 4 (April), 491–510.

Boone, Catherine (1994) 'Trade, Taxes, and Tribute: Market Liberalization and the New Importers in West Africa', *World Development*, vol. 22, no. 3 (March), 453–67.

Bourguignon, François, Jaime de Melo and Akiko Suwa-Eisenmann (1995) 'Dévaluation et compétitivité en Côte d'Ivoire', *Revue Economique*, vol. 46, no. 3 (May), 739–49.

Bouton, Lawrence and Mariusz A. Sumlinski (2000) *Trends in Private Investment in Developing Countries: Statistics for 1970–98* (Washington, D C: International Finance Corporation).

Bramble, Barbara J. and Gareth Porter (1992) 'Non-Governmental Organizations and the Making of US International Environmental Policy,' in A. Hurrell and B. Kingsbury (eds) *The International Politics of the Environment: Actors, Interests, and Institutions* (New York: Oxford University Press).

Bratton, Michael and Nicolas van de Walle (1997) *Democratic Experiments in Africa: Regime Transitions in Comparative Perspective* (Cambridge: Cambridge University Press).

Brooks, Ray, *et al.* (1998) *External Debt Histories of Ten Low-Income Developing Countries: Lessons from Their Experience*, Working Paper no. WP/98/72 (Washington, DC: International Monetary Fund).

Bull, Benedicte (1996) *Political Structures and Sustainable Development – a Case from the Costa Rican Tourism Industry*, Dissertations and Theses, no. 6. (Oslo: Center for Development and the Environment, University of Oslo).

Bull, Benedicte (1999) '"New" Regionalism in Central America', *Third World Quarterly*, vol. 20, no. 5, 957–70.

Bulmer–Thomas Victor (1994) *The Economic History of Latin America Since Independence* (Cambridge: Cambridge University Press).

Business India (10.07.95).

Calipel, Stéphane and Sylviane Guillaumont-Jeanneney (1996) 'Dévaluation, chocs externes et politique économique en Côte d'Ivoire: analyse de leurs effets respectifs à partir d'un modèle d'équilibre général calculable', *Revue d'Economie du Développement*, no. 3 (septembre), 65–94.

Callaghy, Thomas M. (1989) 'Toward State Capability and Embedded Liberalism in the Third World: Lessons for Adjustment', pp. 115–38 in Joan M. Nelson (ed.) *Fragile Coalitions: the Politics of Economic Adjustment* (New Brunswick and Oxford: Transaction Publishers).

Cardoso, Fernando Henrique and Enzo Faletto (1979) *Dependency and Development in Latin America* (Berkeley and Los Angeles, CA: California University Press).

Carrière, Jean (1991) 'The Crisis in Costa Rica: an Ecological Perspective,' pp. 184–204 in David Goodman and Michael Redclift (eds) *Environment and Development in Latin America: the Politics of Sustainability* (Manchester: Manchester University Press).

Casaburi, Gabriel (1997) 'Comparative Study of East Asia and Latin America' (Santiago: CEPAL), CEPAL project mimeo.

Casaburi, Gabriel and Diana Tussie (1997) 'Governance and the New Lending Strategies of the MDBs', *Documentos e Informes de Ivestigación FLACSO* (Buenos Aires: FLACSO).

Casaburi, Gabriel, M. P. Riggirozzi, M. F. Tuozzo, and Diana Tussie (2000) 'Multilateral Development Banks, Governments and Civil Society: Chiaroscuros in a Triangular Relationship', in Tussie, D. (ed.) Special Issue on Civil Society and Multilateral Development Banks, *Global Governance*.

Cerdas, Rodolfo (1979) 'Del Estado Intervencionista al Estado Empresario', *Anuario de Estudios Sociales*, vol. 15, no. 1, 81–97.

Cerdas, Rodolfo (2000) 'Los Apsectos Políticos de la Reforma Económica', pp. 221–36 in Jiménez Ronulfo (ed.) *Los retos políticos de la reforma económica en Costa Rica, San José* (Costa Rica: Academia de Centroamerica).

Cerny, Phil (1995) 'Globalization and the Changing Logic of Collective Action', *International Organization*, vol. 49, no. 4.

Chamley, Christophe (1991) 'Côte d'Ivoire: the Failure of Structural Adjustment', in Vinod Thomas, Ajay Chhibber, Mansoor Dailami and Jaime de Melo (eds) *Restructuring Economies in Distress: Policy Reform and the World Bank* (Washington DC: The World Bank and Oxford University Press).

Chang, Ha-joon (1998) 'Korea. The Misunderstood Crisis', *World Development*, vol. 26, no. 8.

Chevassu, Jean-Marie and Alain Valette (1975) *Les industriels de la Côte d'Ivoire: qui et pourquoi?* (Abidjan: ORSTOM), mimeo.

Chudnovsky, Daniel, Fernando Porta, Andrés López and Martina Chidiak (1996) *Los límites de la apertura. Liberalización, reestructuración productiva y medio ambiente* (CENIT – Alianza Editorial).

Claeys, Anne-Sophie and Alice Sindzingre (2001) *L'intégration régionale dans l'UEMOA: les limites du modèle européen* (Paris: Editions Complexe) (forthcoming).

Clark, Mary (1993) 'Transnational Alliances and Development Strategies: the Transition to Export-Led Growth in Costa Rica, 1983–1990', unpublished PhD dissertation (University of Wisconsin-Madison).

Clark, Mary (1997) 'Transnational Alliances and Development Policy in Latin America: Nontraditional Export Promotion in Costa Rica', *Latin America Research Review*, vol. 32, no. 2, 71–97.

Clément, Jean A.P., with Johannes Mueller, Stephane Cossé and Jean Le Dem (1996) *Aftermath of the CFA Franc Devaluation*, Occasional Paper no. 138 (Washington DC: International Monetary Fund).

Cock, Jackie and Eddie Koch (eds) (1991) *Going Green – People, Politics and the Environment in South Africa* (Cape Town: Oxford University Press).

Coetzee, Henk and David Cooper (1991) 'Wasting Water', in Cock and Koch (eds) op. cit.

Collier, Paul (1991) 'Africa's External Economic Relations, 1960–1990', *African Affairs*, vol. 90, 339–56.

Collier, Paul (1993) 'Higgledy-Piggledy Liberalisation', *World Economy*, vol. 16, no. 4 (July), 503–11.

Collier, Paul (1997) *Ugandan Trade Policy: Liberalization in an Environment of Limited Credibility*, mimeo, April (Oxford: Centre for the Study of African Economies).

Collier, Paul and Jan Willem Gunning (1997a) *Explaining Economic Performance*, Working Paper WPS/97-2 (Oxford: Centre for the Study of African Economies).

Collier, Paul and Jan Willem Gunning (1997b) *Policy Commitment Arrangements for Africa: Implications for Aid, Trade and Investment Flows*, mimeo (Oxford: Centre for the Study of African Economies and Amsterdam: Free University).

Collier, Paul, Patrick Guillaumont, Sylviane Guillaumont and Jan Willem Gunning (1997c) 'Redesigning Conditionality', *World Development*, vol. 25, no. 9, 1399–407.

Collier, Paul, Patrick Guillaumont, Sylviane Guillaumont and Jan Willem Gunning (1997d) 'The Future of Lomé: Europe's Role in African Growth', *World Economy*, vol. 20, no. 3 (May), 285–305.

Collier, Paul and Catherine Patillo (eds) (2000) *Investment and Risk in Africa* (London: Macmillan and Oxford: Centre for the Study of African Economies).

Comisión Nacional de Comercio Exterior (CNCE), Argentine Republic (1995) *Informe Anual 1994*.

Contamin, Bernard and Yves–André Fauré (1990) *La bataille des entreprises publiques en Côte d'Ivoire: l'histoire d'un ajustement interne* (Paris: Karthala).

Conte, Bernard (1984) *La division internationale du travail et le développement interne: le cas de la Côte d'Ivoire* (Toulouse: Université de Toulouse I), Thèse.

Conte, Bernard (1984–85) 'Côte d'Ivoire: réorientation de la stratégie industrielle', *Jeune Afrique Economie*, Dec. 1984–Jan 1985, 123–24.

Conte, Bernard (1995) *Eléments d'analyse de l'efficacité de la dévaluation du franc CFA*, CED, DT/7/1995 (Bordeaux: Université Montesquieu-Bordeaux IV).

Conte, Bernard (1997) *Dévaluation du franc CFA et équilibre des paiements courants*, CED, DT/20/1997 (Bordeaux: Université Montesquieu-Bordeaux IV).

Coquet, Bruno and Jean-Marc Daniel (1992) 'Quel avenir pour la zone franc?', *Observations et Diagnostics Economiques*, no. 41 (July), 241–91.

Cotton, James (1989) 'From Authoritarianism to Democracy in South Korea', *Political Studies*, vol. 37, no. 2, 244–59.

DAC (Development Aid Committee) (1998) *Development Cooperation, 1997 Report* (Paris: OECD).

DAC (Development Aid Committee) (2000) *Development Cooperation, 1999 Report* (Paris: OECD).

Daniel, John (1996) 'A Response to Guelke: The Cold War Factor in South Africa's Transition', *Journal of Contemporary African Studies*, vol. 14, no.1, 101–04.

Dantwala, M.L. (1970) 'From Stagnation to Growth', *Indian Economic Journal*, XVIII, Oct–Dec.

Dantwala, M.L. (1991) 'Strategy of Agricultural Development Since Independence', in Dantwala (ed.) *Indian Agricultural Development Since Independence* (Mumbai: Indian Society of Agricultural Economics).

Das Gupta, Biplab (1997) 'The New Political Economy: a Critical Analysis', *Economic and Political Weekly*, 25 January.

Das, Arvind N (1994) 'Brazil and India: Comparing Notes on Liberalisation', *Economic and Political Weekly*, 19 February.

Davenport, Michael, Adrian Hewitt and Antonique Koning (1995) *Europe's Preferred Partners? The Lomé Countries in World Trade* (London: Overseas Development Institute).

De Miras, Claude (1982) 'L'entrepreneur ivoirien ou une bourgeoisie privée de son état', in Yves – A. Fauré and Jean-François Médard (eds) *Etat et bourgeoisie en Côte d'Ivoire* (Paris: Karthala).

Dean, Judith M., Seema Desai and James Riedel (1994) *Trade Policy Reform in Developing Countries since 1985: a Review of the Evidence*, Discussion Paper no. 267 (Washington, DC: The World Bank).

Deccan Herald (09.03.95) 'Statement of a Group of Thirteen Economists'.

Deccan Herald (02.05.97).

Deccan Herald (06.05.97).

Demery, Lionel (1994) 'Côte d'Ivoire: Fettered Adjustment', in Ishrat Husain and Rashid Faruqee (eds) *Adjustment in Africa: Lessons from Country Case Studies* (Washington, DC: The World Bank).

Devarajan, Shantayanan and Jaime de Melo (1987) 'Evaluating Participation in African Monetary Unions: a Statistical Analysis of the CFA Zones', *World Development*, vol. 15, no. 4 (April), 483–96.

Devarajan, Shantayanan and Jaime de Melo (1991) 'Membership in the CFA Zone: Odyssean Journey or Trojan Horse?' in Ajay Chhibber and Stanley Fischer (eds) *Economic Reform in Sub-Saharan Africa* (Washington, DC: The World Bank).

Dollar, David (1992) 'Outward-Oriented Developing Economies Really Do Grow More Rapidly: Evidence From 95 LDCs, 1976–85', *Economic Development and Cultural Change*, vol. 40, no. 3 (April), 523–44.

Dubresson, Alain (1989) *Villes et industries de Côte d'Ivoire: pour une géographie de l'accumulation urbaine* (Paris: Karthala).

Duruflé, Gilles (1988) *L'ajustement structurel en Afrique: Sénégal, Côte d'Ivoire, Madagascar* (Paris: Karthala).

Economic Times (01.05.97).

Economic Times (27.03.98).

Edwards, Sebastian (1984) 'The Order of Liberalization of the External Sector in Developing Countries', *Essays in International Finance no. 156* (Princeton, NJ: Princeton University).

Edwards, Sebastian (1989) *Real Exchange Rates, Devaluation and Adjustment* (Cambridge, MA: MIT Press).

Ekanza, Simon–Pierre (1997) 'Pillage, fraude et corruption sur la filière du bois', in Bernard Contamin and Harris Memel-Fotê (eds) *Le modèle ivoirien en question* (Paris: Karthala).

Englebert, Pierre (2000) 'Solving the Mystery of the AFRICA Dummy', *World Development*, vol. 28, no. 10, 1821–35.

Esty, Daniel C. and Robert Mendelsohn (1998) 'Moving from National to International Environmental Policy', *Policy Sciences*, vol. 31, 225–35.

Evans, Graham and Jeffrey Newnham (1992) *The Dictionary of World Politics. A Reference Guide to Concepts, Ideas and Institutions* (London: Harvester Wheatsheaf), pp. 301–02.

Evans, Peter (1993) 'Building an Integrative Approach to International and Domestic Politics: Reflections and Projections', in Peter B. Evans, Harold K.

Jacobson and Robert Putnam (eds) *Double Edged Diplomacy. International Bargaining and Domestic Politics* (Berkeley, CA: University of California Press).

Evans, Peter B. (1995) *Embedded Autonomy: States and Industrial Transformation* (Princeton, NJ: Princeton University Press).

Evans, Peter B. (1997) 'The Eclipse of the State? Reflections on Stateness in an Era of Globalization', *World Politics*, vol. 50, no. 1 (October), 62–87.

Evans, Peter B., Harold K. Jacobson and Robert D. Putnam (eds) (1993) *Double-Edged Diplomacy: International Bargaining and Domestic Politics* (Berkeley, CA: University of California Press).

Evans, Peter B. *et al.* (1998) *State–Society Synergy. Government and Social Capital in Development*, Research Series no. 94, International and Area Studies (Berkeley, CA: University of California).

Evans, Trevor, C. Castro, C. and J. Jones (1995) *Structural Adjustment and the Public Sector in Central America and the Carribean* (Managua: CRIES).

Eyssen, Hans (1996) *Are West–African Immigrants Discriminated in Côte d'Ivoire?* RPED paper no. 75, December (Washington, DC: The World Bank).

Far Eastern Economic Review (19.09.91) 'Focus: Environment in Asia 1991'.

Fédération Nationale des Industries de Côte d'Ivoire (1997) *Chiffres-clés et indicateurs de tendances*, juin (Abidjan: FNICI).

Fernandez, Raquel and Dani Rodrik (1991) 'Resistance to Reform: Status Quo Bias in the Presence of Individual–Specific Uncertainty', *American Economic Review*, vol. 81, no. 5, 1146–55.

Ferreira, Rubio Delia and Goretti Matteo (1996) 'Cuando el Presidente Gobierna Solo. Menem y los Decretos de Necesidad y Urgencia hasta la Reforma Constitucional (Julio 1989 – Agosto 1994)' *Desarrollo Económico. Revista de Ciencias Sociales*, vol. 36, no. 141, 443–74.

Fielding, David (1993) 'Determinants of Investment in Kenya and Côte d'Ivoire', *Journal of African Economies*, vol. 2, no. 3 (December), 299–328.

Fields, Karl (1997) 'Strong States and Business Organization in Korea and Taiwan', in S. Maxfield and B. Schneider (eds) *Business and the State in Developing Countries* (Ithaca, NY: Cornell University Press).

Financial Times (25.10.95).

Foster, Philip and Aristide R. Zolberg (eds) (1971) *Ghana and the Ivory Coast: Perspectives on Modernisation* (Chicago, IL: Chicago University Press).

Fowler, Michael Ross and Julie Marie Bunck (1996) 'What Constitutes the Sovereign State', *Review of International Studies*, vol. 22, no. 4 , 381–405.

Fuchs, Jean–Paul (1995) *Pour une politique de développement efficace, maîtrisée et transparente*, Rapport au Premier Ministre (Paris: La Documentation Française).

Furlong, William (2000) *Costa Rican Politics in Transition*. Paper presented at the Latin American Studies Association Meeting, Miami, Florida, March 15–18, 2000.

Gang, Man-ok and Geun-ho Cha (1997) 'Hwangyeonggijun ganghwaga gyeongjaengryeoke michineun yeonghyang? (Tightening of Environmental Standard and National Competitiveness)' *Jeongchaek* (policy) 97-15-053 (Seoul: SERI).

Gang, Moon-gyu (1997) 'Minganhwangyeongundong (Nongovernmental Environmental Movement)', Korea Environmental Technology Research Institute (KETRI), (ed.) *Hangookui Hwangyeong 50nyunsa* (The Fifty Years of the Environment in Korea) (Seoul: KETRI).

Gang, Mun-gu (1996) 'Hanguksahoeui minjuhwawa hwangyeongundong (Democratization and Environmental Movements in Korean Society)' *Hangukjeongchihakhoe* (The Korean Political Science Association), 140–59.

Gastellu, Jean-Marie and S. Affou Yapi (1982) 'Un mythe à décomposer: la "bourgeoisie de planteurs"', in Yves-A. Fauré and Jean-François Médard (eds) *Etat et bourgeoisie en Côte d'Ivoire* (Paris, Karthala).

GATT (1992) *Trade Policy Review Mechanism: Argentina* (Geneva: GATT).

Gerchunoff, Pablo and Torre Juan Carlos (1996) 'La Política de la Liberalización en la Administración de Menem', *Desarrollo Económico. Revista de Ciencias Sociales*, vol. 36, no. 143, 733–68.

Ghosh, Arun (1994) 'Structural Adjustment and Industrial and Environmental Concerns', *Economic and Political Weekly*, 19 February.

Ghosh, Arun (1996) 'Role of Planning in a Globalised Economy', *Economic and Political Weekly*, Special Number (September).

Gim, Byeong-wan (1994) *Hangukui hwangyeongjeongchaekgwa noksaekundong* (Korean Environmental Policy and Green Movements) (Seoul: Nanam).

Godeau, Rémi (1995) *Le franc CFA: pourquoi la dévaluation de 1994 a tout changé* (Paris: Editions Sépia).

Goo, Do-wan (1996) *Hanguk hwangyeongundongui sahoehak* (Sociology of Korean Environmental Movements) (Seoul: Munhakgwa jiseong).

Good, Kenneth (1997a) 'Accountable to Themselves: Predominance in Southern Africa', *Journal of Modern African Studies*, pre-publication draft.

Good, Kenneth (1997b) *Realizing Democracy in Botswana, Namibia and South Africa* (Pretoria: Africa Institute of South Africa).

Goreux, Louis M. (1995) *La dévaluation du franc CFA: un premier bilan en décembre 1995*, rapport, December (Washington, DC: The World Bank).

Gouffern, Louis (1982) 'Les limites d'un modèle? A propos d'Etat et bourgeoisie en Côte d'Ivoire', *Politique Africaine*, vol. 2, no. 6 (May), 19–34.

Gourevitch, Peter (1986) *Politics in Hard Times* (Ithaca, NY: Cornell University Press).

Greenaway, David, Wyn Morgan and Peter Wright (1997) 'Trade Liberalization and Growth in Developing Countries: Some New Evidence', *World Development*, vol. 25, no. 11 (November), 1885–92.

Group for Environmental Monitoring (GEM) (1994) *People and Parks Project 1994: National Conference Proceedings* (Johannesburg).

Guelke, Adrian (1996) 'The Impact of the End of the Cold War on South African Transition', *Journal of Contemporary African Studies*, vol. 14, no. 1, 87–100.

Guillaumont, Patrick, Sylviane Guillaumont and Patrick Plane (1988) 'Participating in African Monetary Unions: an Alternative Evaluation', *World Development*, vol. 16, no. 5, 569–76.

Guillaumont, Patrick and Sylviane Guillaumont-Jeanneney (1997) 'De l'effectivité de la dévaluation des francs CFA: quelques enseignements tirés du Cameroun et de la Côte d'Ivoire', *Revue Economique*, vol. 48, no. 3 (May), 451–60.

Gutman, Graciela (2000) 'Agriculture and the Environment: the Challenge of Trade Liberalisation', in Diana Tussie (ed.) *The Environment and International Trade Negotiation* (London: Palgrave Macmillan).

Gwak, Il-cheon (1997) 'OECD gaipgwa hangukui hwangyeonjeongchaek byeonhwa (OECD Member and Change of Korean Environmental Policy)', *Gyegan hwangyeonggwa gonghae (Quarterly Environment and Pollution)*, 29.

Gwak, Il-cheon (1999) 'Hwangyeongbojeonui gukjehwawa jibanghwa (Globalization and Decentralization of Environmental Conservation)'. Hangookhwangyeongjungchaekhakhoi (Korean Environmental Policy Acamedic Association) (ed.) *Hwangyeongjungcheakron* (Theory of Environmental Policy) (Seoul: Singwangmoonhwasa).

Hadjimichael, Michael T. and Michel Galy (1997) *The CFA Franc Zone and the EMU*, Working Paper WP/97/156 (Washington, DC: International Monetary Fund).

Haggard, Stephan (1990) *Pathways from the Periphery* (Ithaca, NY: Cornell University Press).

Haggard, Stephan and Steven B. Webb (1993) 'What Do We Know About the Political Economy of Economic Policy Reform?' *World Bank Research Observer*, vol. 8, no. 2, 143–68.

Haggard, Stephan and Steven B. Webb (eds) (1994) *Voting for Reform: Democracy, Political Liberalization, and Economic Adjustment* (Washington, DC: The World Bank and Oxford University Press).

Haggard, Stephan and Maxfield, Sylvia (1996) 'The Political Economy of Financial Internationalization in the Developing World', in Robert O. Keohane and Helen Milner (eds) *Internationalization and Domestic Politics* (Cambridge: Cambridge University Press).

Hallowes, David (1993) *Hidden Faces. Environment, Development, Justice: South Africa in the Global Context* (Cape Town: Earthlife Africa).

Han, Taek-whan (1996) 'Trade and Environment: a Korean Perspective', in Jong-Soo Lim (ed.) *Trade and Environment: International Issues and Policy Option* (Seoul: Korea Environmental Technology Research Institute).

Hanson, A.H. (1966) *The Process of Planning* (Oxford: Oxford University Press).

Harrison, Ann (1995) *Openness and Growth: a Time-Series, Cross-Country Analysis for Developing Countries*, Working Paper no. 5221 (Cambridge, MA: National Bureau of Economic Research).

Harrold, Peter (1995) *The Impact of the Uruguay Round on Africa*, Discussion Paper no. 311 (Washington, DC: The World Bank).

Heilman, Bruce and John Lucas (1997) 'A Social Movement for African Capitalism? A Comparison of Business Association in Two African Cities', *African Studies Review*, vol. 40, no. 2 (September), 141–71.

Held, David and Anthony McGrew, David Goldblatt and Jonathan Perraton (1999) *Global Transformations. Politics, Economics and Culture* (Cambridge: Polity Press).

Heo, Jang (1997) *Politics of Policy-Making: Environmental Policy Changes in Korea*, unpublished PhD dissertation (University of Wisconsin-Madison).

Herrera, Javier (1998) *Flux frontaliers, marchés parallèles et compétitivité dans les échanges entre le Nigeria et ses voisins depuis la dévaluation du FCFA*, mimeo (Paris: DIAL).

Hesselberg, Jan and Helge Hveem (eds) (1998) *Production and Trade – Environment and the Development*, SUM Report no. 8 (Oslo: Centre for Development and the Environment, University of Oslo).

Hirst, Paul and G. Thompson (1996) *Globalization in Question* (Cambridge: Polity Press).

Hobbs, Jonathan and Karin Ireton (1996) '*South Africa: a State of Change*', *UNEP Industry and Environment*, vol. 19 (March).

Hoekman, Bernard and Pierre Sauvé (1994) *Liberalizing Trade in Services,* Discussion Paper no. 243 (Washington, DC: The World Bank).

Honey, Martha (1994) *Hostile Acts. U.S. Policy in Costa Rica in the 1980s* (Gainesville, FL: University Press of Florida).

Hong, Sang-u (2000) 'Hwangyeonghyeopryeokgwa gihubyeonhwahyeopyak mit Kyoto uijeongseo' (Convention on Climate Change and Kyotyo Protocol), 2000-05-30 (http://www.mofat.go.kr/main/top.html).

Hopkins, Anthony G. (1973) *An Economic History of West Africa* (Harlow: Longman).

Hveem, Helge (1991) *Hegemonic Rivalry and Bilateralism in International Trade* (Oslo: Centre for Development and the Environment, University of Oslo).

Hveem, Helge (1994) *Internasjonalisering og politikk* (Oslo: TANO).

Hveem, Helge (1995) *Power, Promises and the Potential of the WTO: The Uruguay Round and the Developing Countries* (Oslo: Centre for Development and the Environment, University of Oslo).

Hveem, Helge (1996) *Makt og velferd. Teorier i internasjonal politikk. (Power and Welfare. Theories in International Political Economy)* (Oslo: Universitetsforlaget).

Hveem, Helge (2000) 'Explaining the Regional Phenomenon in the Globalisation Era', in Richard Stubbs and Geoffrey Underhill (eds) *Political Economy and the Changing Global Order,* 2nd edn. (London and Toronto: Oxford University Press).

IDB (2000) *Integration and Trade in the Americas,* Periodic Note, Department of Integration and Regional Programs (Washington, DC: The Inter–American Development Bank).

Im, Jong-su (1996) 'Gukjehwangyeong, muyeokyeongye nonui donghyanggwa daeeungbangan (Trends of Global Environment, Trade Issues and Its Plan)'.

Inglehart, Ronald (1989) *Culture Shift in Advanced Industrial Society* (Princeton, NJ: Princeton University Press).

International Development Research Centre (IDRC) (1995) *Building a new South Africa: Environment, Reconstruction and Development* (Ottawa: IDRC).

International Monetary Fund (1997) 'IMF Adopts Guidelines Regarding Governance Issues', *News Brief,* no. 97/15.

International Monetary Fund (1998) *Côte d'Ivoire: Selected Issues and Statistical Appendix,* May (Washington, DC: International Monetary Fund).

International Monetary Fund (2000) *Côte d'Ivoire: Selected Issues and Statistical Appendix,* August (Washington, DC: International Monetary Fund).

Jadot, Yannick and Jean-Pierre Rolland (1996) *Les contradictions des politiques européennes à l'égard des pays en développement* (Paris: Solagral).

Jang, Jae-hyun (1980) *Hwangyungoyeome gwanhan gochl (The Study on Environmental Pollution)* (Graduate School of Management and Administration, Seongkyunkwan University).

Jenkins, Robert (1995) 'Liberal Democracy and the Management of Structural Adjustment in India: Conceptual Tensions in the Good Government Agenda' *IDS Bulletin,* April.

Jiguhwangyeongjeongbo (Earth Environmental Information) (1998) '99 je 2cha.

Johnson, Omotunde E. G. (1994) 'Managing Adjustment Costs, Political Authority, and the Implementation of Adjustment Programs, with Special Reference to African Countries', *World Development,* vol. 22, no. 3, 399–411.

Johnson, Phyllis and Munyaradze Chenje (eds) (1994) *State of the Environment in Southern Africa* (Harare: Zimbabwe Publishing House for SADC/SARDC/IUCN).

Jones, Laura, Laura Griggs and Liv Fredricksen (2000) 'Environmental Indicators', 4th edn. *Critical Issues Bulletins* (The Fraser Institute).

Jones, Tom (1997) 'Globalisation and Environment: Main Issues,' OECD Proceedings, *Globalisation and Environment: Preliminary Perspectives* (Paris: OECD).

Julius, DeAnne (1990) *Global Companies and Public Policy: The Growing Challenge of Foreign Direct Investment* (London: Pinter Publishers).

Jung, Hoi-sung (1994) 'Hwangyeonghyeomosiseol Ypjijuhanggwa geukbokbangan (The Location of Environmentally Hazardous Waste Facilities and its Solution)', *Hwangyung Report* 11, 5–6.

Jung, Hoi-sung and Lee Sung-woo (1994) 'Urinara Hwangyeongundongui baldalgwajunggwa jungcheakp deahan gochal (A Study on the Development of the Green Movement and Its Policy Impact in Korea)', *Journal of Environmental Policy and Administration,* vol. 2, no. 1, 85–101.

Jung, Jin-seung (1997) 'Gyeongjegaebalgwa Hwangyeong (Economic Development and Environment', Korea Environmental Technology Research Institute(KETRI) (ed.) *Hangookui Hwangyeong 50nyunsa* (The Fifty Years of the Environment in Korea) (Seoul: KETRI).

Kabra, Kamal Nayan (1996) 'Indian Planing and Liberalisation', *Economic and Political Weekly,* 5 October.

Kahler, Miles (1992) 'External Influence, Conditionality, and the Politics of Adjustment', in Stephan Haggard and Robert R. Kaufman (eds) *The Politics of Economic Adjustment: International Constraints, Distributive Conflicts, and the State* (Princeton, NJ: Princeton University Press).

Kahler, Miles (1993) 'Bargaining with the IMF: Two-Level Strategies and Developing Countries', pp. 363–94 in Evans, Jacobson and Putnam (eds) op. cit.

Katzenstein, Peter J. (1985) *Small States in World Markets. Industrial Policy in Europe* (Ithaca, NY: Cornell University Press).

KETRI/1999/RE-09 yeongu bogoseo. Hangukhwangyeonggisulgaebalwon (Korea Environmental Technology Research Institute).

Kim, Hyeokrae and Young Rae Kim (1999) 'Hanguk NGOsui Hyeonhwanggwa Gwaje (The Present Situation and Task of Korean NGOs)' (Seoul: National Assembly Conference, Korean Political Science Association).

Kim, Samuel S. *Korea's Globalization* (New York: Cambridge University Press).

Kim, Sunhyuk (1996) 'Civil Society in South Korea: From Grand Democracy Movements to Petty Interest Groups?' *Journal of Northeast Asian Studies,* vol. 15, no. 2, 81–97.

Korea National Statistical Office (2000), http://www.nso.go.kr/report/data/svgg2000.html. Segye mit hangukui inguhyeonhwang(yoyak)? 2000.7. Tonggyecheong ingubunseok.

Keohane, Robert O. and Helen Milner (eds) (1996) *Internationalization and Domestic Politics* (Cambridge: Cambridge University Press).

Kothari, Rajni (1990) 'Environment, Technology and Ethics', in J.R. Engel and J.G. Engel, (eds) *Ethics of Environment and Development – Global Challenge, International Response* (Tuscon, AZ: University of Arizona Press).

Kouadio Bénié, Marcel (1991) 'Restructuration et évolution de l'emploi dans le secteur public et parapublic en Côte d'Ivoire', *Tiers-Monde,* vol. 32, no. 126 (avril–juin), 451–64.

Krishnaswamy, K.S. (1998) 'Patents – Long-term Strategy Needed' *Deccan Herald*, 27–28 March.

Kumar, Nagesh (1996) 'India. Industrialization, Liberalization and Inward and Outward Foreign Direct Investment', in John H. Dunning and Rahneesh Narula (eds) *Foreign Direct Investment and Governments* (London: Routledge).

Kurien, C.T. (1996) *Economic Reforms and the People* (New Delhi: Public Interest Research Group).

La zone franc, rapport annuel (diverses années) (Paris: Banque de France).

Lawrence, Robert Z. (1996) 'Competition Policies and the Developing Countries', in Robert Z. Lawrence, Dani Rodrik and John Whalley, *Emerging Agenda for Global Trade: High Stakes for Developing Countries*, Policy Essay no. 20 (Washington, DC: Overseas Development Council).

Le Dem, Jean (1994) 'Dévaluation du franc CFA: un commentaire critique', *Economie Internationale*, no. 58, 2è trimestre, 27–32.

Leconte, Nicole (1989) *Côte d'Ivoire: l'après-Houphouët* (Paris: Nord-Sud Export Consultants).

Lee, Chung (1992) 'The Government, Financial System and Large Private Enterprises in the Economic Development of South Korea', *World Development*, vol. 20, 187–97.

Lee, Manwoo (1990) *The Odyssey of Korean Democracy: Korean Politics, 1987–1990* (New York: Praeger).

Lee, Si-jae (1998) 'Hangukui siminsahoewa hwangyeongundong (Civil Society and Environmental Movents in Korea,' Im, Hui-seop, Yang, Jong-seop eds,. *Hangookul Siminsahoiwa Sinsahoi Udong* (Civil Society and New Social Movements in Korea) (Seoul: Nanam).

Lee, Su-Hoon (1993) 'Transitional Politics of Korea, 1987–1992: Activation of Civil Society', *Pacific Affairs*, vol. 66, no. 3, 351–67.

Lijphart, Arend (1977) *Democracy in Plural Societies: a Comparative Exploration*. (New Haven, CT: Yale University Press).

Lizano, Eduardo (1994) *Notas Sobre el PAE III*, Estudios 10 (San José, Costa Rica: Editorial Academia de Centroamerica).

Lizano, Eduardo (2000) 'Política Económica y Desarrollo Nacional', pp. 179–215 in Jiménez Ronulfo (ed.) *Los retos políticos de la reforma económica en Costa Rica* (San José, Costa Rica: Academia de Centroamerica).

López, Alvaro (1995) *Apertura comercial, libre mercado y proteccionismo en el sector agrícola centroamericano* (Heredia, Costa Rica: Editorial Fundación Universidad Nacional).

López, Alvaro and Aguilar, Guillermo (1985) *Cómo lograr una mejor utilizaciónd e la Iniciativa para la Cuenca del Caribe* (San José, Costa Rica: MINEX).

Lopez, Ramon (1998) 'The Tragedy of the Commons in Côte d'Ivoire Agriculture: Empirical Evidence and Implications for Evaluating Trade Policies', *World Bank Economic Review*, vol. 12, no. 1 (January), 105–31.

Low, Patrick (ed.) (1993) *International Trade and the Environment*, Discussion Paper (Washington, DC: The World Bank).

Lyman, Princeton (1996) 'South Africa's Promise', *Foreign Policy*, no. 102 (Spring), 105–19.

Mahler, Vincent A. (1994) 'The Lomé Convention: Assessing a North-South Institutional Relationship', *Review of International Political Economy*, vol. 1, no. 2 (Summer), 233–56.

Mani, Muthukumara, and David Wheeler (1998) 'In Search of Pollution Haven? Dirty Industry in the World Economy, 1960 to 1995', *Journal of Environment & Development*, vol. 7, no. 3, 215–47.

Manor, James (1995) 'Democratic Decentralization in Africa and Asia', *IDS Bulletin*, April.

March, James G. and Johan P. Olsen (1976) *Ambiguity and Choice in Organizations* (Oslo: Universities Press).

Marchand, Yves (1996) *Une urgence: l'afro-réalisme: Pour une nouvelle politique de l'entreprise en Afrique sub-saharienne*, Rapport au Premier Ministre (Paris: La Documentation française).

Marchat, Jean-Michel (1997a) *The Impact of Tax Regulations on Enterprise Entry in Côte d'Ivoire*, RPED paper no. 79 (Washington, DC: The World Bank).

Marchat, Jean-Michel (1997b) *Concurrence et structure du marché intérieur des produits manufacturés en Côte d'Ivoire*, RPED paper no. 82 (Washington, DC: The World Bank).

Marchés Tropicaux et Méditerranéens (1997) *Côte d'Ivoire*, numéro hors-série, novembre.

Markandya, A. (1994) 'Reconciliation of Environmental and Trade Policies: Synthesis of Country Case Studies', mimeo, draft paper (Geneva: UNCTAD).

Martinussen, John D. (1997) *Society, State, and Market* (London: Sage).

Martinussen, John D. (2001) *Policies, Institutions and Industrial Development. Coping with Liberalization and International Competition in India* (London: Sage).

Mathew, George (1994) *Panchayat Raj – From Movement to Legislation* (New Delhi: Concept).

Maxfield, Sylvia and Ben Ross Schneider (1997) *Business and the State in Developing Countries* (Ithaca, NY: Cornell University Press).

Mazrui, Ali A. (1995) 'The African State as a Political Refugee', *International Journal of Refugee Law* (Special Issue – Summer).

McKay, Andrew, Oliver Morrissey and Charlotte Vaillant (1997) 'Trade Liberalisation and Agricultural Supply Response: Issues and Some Lessons', *European Journal of Development Research*, vol. 9, no. 2 (December),129–47.

Mckenzie, Craig and Simon Foster (1995) *International Trade and the Environment: a South African Perspective*, (DBSA Environmental and Natural Resources Policy Programme).

Menzel, Ulrich (1985) *In der Nachfolge Europas* (Munich: Simon & Magiera).

Menzel, Ulrich (1992) 'The Experience of Small European Countries with Late Development: Lessons from History', pp. 96–161 in Lars Mjøset (ed.) *Contributions to the Comparative Study of Development: Proceedings from Vilhelm Aubert Memorial Symposion 1990* (Oslo: Institute of Social Research).

Michailof, Serge (1994) *La dévaluation du franc CFA: une décision incontournable – une opportunité de relance économique*, Document de travail, 20 avril (Washington, DC: The World Bank).

MIDEPLAN (1987) *Plan Nacional de Desarrollo 1986–1990* (San José: Costa Rica).

MIDEPLAN (1992) *Costa Rica en Cifras 1950–1992* (San José: Costa Rica).

MIDEPLAN (1993) *Documentos fundamentales del Tercer Programa de Ajuste Estructural (PAE III)* (San José: Costa Rica).

Mitra, Ashok (1997) *Deccan Herald*, 9 April.

Monga, Celestin (1997) 'A Currency Reform Index for Western and Central Africa', *World Economy*, vol. 20, no. 1 (January), 103–25.

Moon, Chung-in (1998) 'Hankookui Minjoohwa, Segyehwa, Jungbu-giup gwangye (Democratization and Globalization and Government-Business Relations in Korea', in Moon (ed.) *Minjoohwasidaeui Jungbuwa giup* (Government and Business in the Democratic Era) (Seoul: Oreum).

Moon, Chung-in (2000a) 'In Shadow of Broken Cheers: South Korea's Globalization Strategy', in A. Prakash and J. Hart (eds) *Responding to Globalization* (New York: Routledge).

Moon, Chung-in (2000b) 'Workers and Globalization', Samuel in S. Kim (ed.) *Korea's Globalization*. Cambridge: Cambridge University Press.

Moon, Chung-in and Rashemi Prasad (1994) 'Beyond the Developmental State: Networks, Politics, and Institutions', *Governance: an International Journal of Policy and Administration*, vol. 7, no. 4 (October), 360–86.

Moon, Chung-in and O Kyeong-taek (1999) 'Dongasiaul Saengtaeanbowa Hanbando (The Crisis of Northeast Asian Ecosystem and Korean Peninsula)', *Tongil Yeogu (Korean Unification Studies)* vol. 3, no. 1, 179–219.

Moon, Chung-in and Jongryn Mo *The Politics of Structural Changes in South Korea* (Washington, DC: The Economic Strategy Institute) (forthcoming).

Morello, J. and B. Marchetti (1995) 'Fuerzas socioeconomicas condicionantes de cuatro proesos de degradación', Comisión Economica para America Latina y el Caribe (CEPAL), *Document CEPAL, DLC/R/1545* (Santiago: CEPAL).

Mori, Antonella (1996) 'The Impact of the Uruguay Round on International Commodity Agreements: the Case of Coffee', in Meine Pieter van Dijk and Sandro Sideri (eds) *Multilateralism versus Regionalism: Trade Issues after the Uruguay Round*, EADI Book Series 19 (London: Frank Cass).

Mosley, Paul, Jane Harrigan and John Toye (1991) *Aid and Power: the World Bank and Policy-based Lending*, vol. 1 (London: Routledge).

Moyo, Sam *et al.* (1994) *The Southern African Environment* (London: Earthscan).

Muda, Mohammed (1996) 'Malaysia-South Africa Relations and the Commonwealth, 1960–95', *The Round Table*, no. 340 (October), 423–40.

Muller, J.J. (Kobus) (1997) 'A Greener South Africa? Environmentalism, Politics and the Future', *Politikon*, vol. 42, no. 1.

Mundt, Robert J. (1997) 'Côte d'Ivoire: Continuity and Change in a Semi-Democracy', in John F. Clark and David E. Gardinier (eds) *Political Reform in Francophone Africa* (Boulder, CO: Westview Press).

Murray, Martin J. (1996) 'The South African Transition: More Trouble Than it Looks', *Southern African Report*, vol. 12, no. 1 (November).

Mytelka, Lynn (1984) 'Foreign Business and Economic Development in the Ivory Coast', in I. William Zartman (ed.) *The Political Economy of Ivory Coast* (New York: Praeger).

Mytelka, Lynn (1992) 'Ivorian Industry at the Cross-Roads', in Frances Stewart, Sanjaya Lall and Samuel Wangwe (eds) *Alternative Development Strategies in Sub-Saharan Africa* (London: Palgrave Macmillan).

Nagaraj, R. (1997) 'What has happened since 1991? – Assessment of India's Economic Reforms', *Economic and Political Weekly*, 8 November.

Nandy, Ashis (1980) *Alternative Sciences* (New Delhi: Allied Publishers).

Natraj, V.K. (1995) 'Marketing Liberalisation – India's Quest', *The European Journal of Development Research*.

Naudet, David (1996) *Le marché régional ouest-africain: les obstacles liés au franchissement des frontières*, Document de travail 1996-01/T (Paris: DIAL).

Nelson, Joan M. (1996) 'Promoting Large-Scale Institutional Change: Social Service Reforms in Developing and Post-Communist Countries', Paper for the 1996 Annual Conference of the Norwegian Association for Development Research, Chr. Michelsen Institute, Bergen.

Newman, John L., Victor Lavy, Raoul Salomon and Philippe de Vreyer (1990) *Firms' Responses to Relative Price Changes in Côte d'Ivoire: the Implications for Export Subsidies and Devaluations*, WPS 550 (Washington, DC: The World Bank).

Ng, Francis and Alexander Yeats (1996) *Open Economies Work Better! Did Africa's Protectionist Policies Cause its Marginalization in World Trade?* Policy Research Working Paper no. 1636 (Washington, DC: The World Bank).

Norval, Aletta (1996) *Deconstructing Apartheid Discourse* (London: Verso).

O'Meara, Dan (1996) *Forty Lost Years: the Apartheid State and the Politics of the National Party, 1948–1994* (Johannesburg: Ravan).

Onselen, Charles van (1996) *The Seed is Mine: the Biography of Kas Maine, a South African Sharecropper 1894–1985* (Cape Town: David Philip).

Oshikoya, Temitope (1996) 'The Uruguay Round of Trade Negociations: Implications for Africa', in Oladeji O. Ojo (ed.) *Africa and Europe: the Changing Economic Relationship* (London and Abidjan: Zed Books and African Development Bank).

Oyejide, Ademola, Ibrahim Elbadawi and Paul Collier (eds) (1997) *Regional Integration and Trade Liberalization in Subsaharan Africa*, vol. 1 (Basingstoke and London: Macmillan).

Page, Sheila with Michael Davenport (1994) *World Trade Reform: Do Developing Countries Gain or Lose?* (London: Overseas Development Institute).

Palermo Vicente & Novaro Marcos (1996) *Política y poder en el gobierno de Menem* (Grupo Editorial Norma).

Papageorgiou, Demetrios, Armeane M. Choksi and Michael Michaely (eds) (1991) *Liberalizing Foreign Trade* (Oxford: Basil Blackwell).

Patel I.G. (1992) 'New Economic Policies: A Historical Perspective', in R.K. Sinha (ed.) *Economic Crisis Management and Challenges: Restructuring the Indian Economy* (Deep and Deep Publishers).

Patnaik, Prabhat and C.P. Chandrashekhar (1995) 'Indian Economy Under Structural Adjustment', *Economic and Political Weekly*, November 25.

Patnaik, Utsa (1996) 'Export – Oriented Agriculture and Food Security in Developing Countries and India', *Economic and Political Weekly*, Special Number (September).

Patterson, Mathew (1995) 'Institutions for Global Environmental Change,' *Global Environmental Change*, vol. 7, no. 2, 175–77.

Pégatiénan, Jacques (1988) *Stabilisation and Adjustment Policies and Programmes, Country Sudy: Côte d'Ivoire* (Helsinki: World Institute for Development Economics Research (WIDER).

Pégatiénan, Jacques and Bakary Ouayogode (1997) 'The World Bank and Côte d'Ivoire', in Devesh Kapur, John P. Lewis and Richard Webb (eds) *The World Bank: its First Half Century, vol. 2: Perspectives* (Washington, DC: Brookings Institution Press).

Pettman, Jan Jindy (1996) *Worlding Women: a Feminist International Politics* (New York: Routledge).

Plane, Patrick (1997) 'La privatisation de l'électricité en Côte d'Ivoire: évaluation et interprétation des premiers résultats', *Tiers-Monde*, tome XXXVIII, no. 152 (octobre-décembre), 859–78.

Porter, Gareth (1999) 'Trade Competition and Pollution Standards: 'Race to the Bottom' or 'Stuck at the Bottom'?' *Journal of Environment & Development*, vol. 8, no. 2, 133–51.

Ports, Donatella Dells and Mario Diani (1999) *Social Movements: an Introduction* (Oxford & Malden, MA: Blackwell).

Przeworski, Adam *et al.* (1995) *Sustainable Democracy* (Cambridge: Cambridge University Press).

Putnam, Robert D. (1988) 'Diplomacy and Domestic Politics. The Logic of Two-Level Games', *International Organization*, vol. 42, no. 3, 427–60.

Putnam, Robert D. (1993a) 'Diplomacy and Domestic Politics: the Logic of Two-Level Games', in Peter B. Evans, Harold Jacobson and Robert D. Putnam (eds) *Double-Edged Diplomacy: International Bargaining and Domestic Politics* (Berkeley, CA: University of California Press).

Putnam, Robert D. (1993b) *Making Democracy Work* (Princeton, NJ: Princeton University Press).

Ragin, Charles C. (1987) *The Comparative Method: Moving Beyond Quantitative and Qualitative Strategies* (Berkeley, CA: University of California Press).

Rapley, John (1993) *Ivoirien Capitalism: African Entrepreneurs in Côte d'Ivoire* (Boulder, CO: Lynne Rienner).

Reddy, Amulya K.N. & Gladys D. Sumithra (1997) 'Karnataka's Power Sector: Some Revelations', *Economic and Political Weekly*, 22 March.

Representación Social, Comisión Especial Mixta del ICE (2000) *Informe final ¡Construyamos juntos un nuevo ICE!* (San José, Costa Rica).

République de Côte d'Ivoire, Institut National de la Statistique, *Banque des Données Financières*, Données 1990–1996.

Riddell, Roger (1992) 'Manufacturing Sector Development in Zimbabwe and the Côte d'Ivoire', in Frances Stewart, Sanjaya Lall and Samuel Wangwe (eds) *Alternative Development Strategies in Sub-Saharan Africa* (London, Macmillan).

Risse-Kappen, Thomas (ed.) (1995) *Bringing Transnational Relations Back In* (Cambridge: Cambridge University Press).

Rodrik, Dani (1989) 'Credibility of Trade Reform: A Policy Maker's Guide', *World Economy*, vol. 12, no. 1 (March) 1–16.

Rodrik, Dani (1992a) 'Political Economy and Development Policy', *European Economic Review*, vol. 36, no. 2–3, 329–36.

Rodrik, Dani (1992b) 'The Limits of Trade Policy Reform in Developing Countries', *Journal of Economic Perspectives*, vol. 6, no. 1, 87–105.

Rodrik, Dani (1996) 'Why is There Multilateral Lending?' pp. 167–93 in Michael Bruno and Boris Pleskovic (eds) *Annual World Bank Conference on Development Economics 1995* (Washington, DC: The World Bank).

Rodrik, Dani (1997) *Has Globalization Gone Too Far?* (Washington, DC: Institute for International Economics).

Rosecranze, Richard (1986) *The Rise of the Trading State* (New York: Basic Books).

Rosenberg, Christoph B. (1995) *Fiscal Policy Coordination in the WAEMU After the Devaluation*, Working Paper WP/95/25 (Washington, DC: International Monetary Fund).

Rovira Mas, Jorge (1986) *La crisis de Costa Rica* (San José, Costa Rica: Instituto Centroamericano de Documentación y Investigación Social).

Roy, Bunker (1996) 'Foreign Funds and Threat to Voluntary Sector: An Open Letter to Home Minister', *Economic and Political Weekly'*, 7 December.

Rueda-Sabater, Enrique and Andrew Stone (1992) *Côte d'Ivoire: Private Sector Dynamics and Constraints*, WPS no. 1047 (Washington, DC: The World Bank).

Rueschemeyer, Dietrich and Peter B. Evans (1985) 'The State and Economic Transformation: Towards an Analysis of the Conditions Underlying Effective Intervention', pp. 45–77 in Peter B. Evans, Dietrich Rueschemeyer and Theda Skocpol (eds) *Bringing the State Back In* (Cambridge: Cambridge University Press).

Ruf, François (1995) *Booms et crises du cacao* (Paris: Karthala, CIRAD and Ministère de la Coopération).

Ruf, François (1997) 'Les cycles du cacao en Côte d'Ivoire: la remise en cause d'un modèle?', in Bernard Contamin and Harris Memel-Fotê (eds) *Le modèle ivoirien en question* (Paris: Karthala).

Sa, Deuk-hwan (1997) *Hanguk hwangyeongjeongchaekui ihae* (Understanding of Korean Environmental Policies) (Seoul: Bibongchulpansa).

Sahai, Suman (1998) 'Protecting Basmati', *Economic and Political Weekly'*, 28 February.

Salazar, Roxana, Jorge Cabrera Medaglia, and Alvaro López Mora eds (1994) *Biodiversidad, políticas y legislación a la luz del desarrollo sostenible* (Heredia, Cost Rica: Fundación Ambio y Escuela de Relaciones Internacionales, Universidad Nacional).

Salom Echeverría (1992) *Costa Rica: deuda Externa y Soberanía* (San José, Costa Rica: Ediorial Porvenir).

Salomon, J.J. and A. Lebeau (1993) *Mirages of Development* (Boulder).

Sand, Peter H. ed. (1992) *The Effectiveness of International Environmental Agreements: a Survey of Existing Legal Instruments* (Cambridge: Grotius Publications).

Sandbrook, Richard (1986) 'The State and Economic Stagnation in Tropical Africa', *World Development,* vol. 14, no. 2.

Sapir, André (1993) 'Regionalism and the New Theory of International Trade: Do the Bells Toll for the GATT? A European Outlook', *World Economy*, vol. 16, no. 4 (July) 423–38.

Saul, John S. (1993) *Recolonization and Resistance in Southern Africa in the 1990s* (Toronto: Between the Lines), p. 109.

Schifter, Jacobo (1978) 'La Democracia en Costa Rica como producto de neutralización de clases', in Chester Zelaya (ed.) *Democracia en Costa Rica. Cinco opiniones polemicas* (San José, Costa Rica: Editorial Universidad Estatal Distancia).

Schneider, Hartmut *et al.* (1992) *Ajustement et équité en Côte d'Ivoire* (Paris: OECD, Development Centre).

Scott, Alan (1990) *Ideology and the New Social Movement* (London: Routledge).

Segura, Olman (1998) 'Una mezcla necesaria: comercio-ambiente' (Heredia, Costa Rica: Centro Internacional de Política Económica (CINPE), Universidad Nacional).

Senghaas, Dieter (1982) *Von Europa Lernen* (Frankfurt: Suhrkamp).

Shefter, Martin (1977) 'Party and Patronage: Germany, England and Italy', *Politics & Society*, vol. 7, no. 4, 403–51.

Sindzingre, Alice (1991) 'L'ajustement au-delà de l'économie: contraintes institutionnelles et effets sociaux' *Marchés Tropicaux et Méditerranéens*, no. 2380, juin, special issue Côte d'Ivoire, 1549–51.

Sindzingre, Alice (1995) *Economie politique et démocratie en Afrique de l'ouest francophone: l'exemple de la Côte d'Ivoire*, mimeo, International Meeting on Democratisation in Africa (Zaria: Ahmadu Bello University).

Sindzingre, Alice (1996a) *L'ajustement structurel en Afrique francophone: les limites de l'orthodoxie*, mimeo, 8th Conference on Socio-Economics, July (Geneva: Society for the Advancement of Socio-Economics).

Sindzingre, Alice (1996b) *Industrie, ajustement et 'entrepreneurship' en Côte d'Ivoire et au Ghana*, Politics and Economics no. 2 (Leipzig: University of Leipzig Papers on Africa).

Sindzingre, Alice (2000a) 'Le contexte économique et social du changement politique en Côte d'Ivoire', *Afrique Contemporaine*, no. 193 (January–March) 27–37.

Sindzingre, Alice (2000b) *Competitiveness, Trade Arrangements and Political Economy: the Case of ECOWAS*, Working Paper (Oslo: University of Oslo, Centre for Development and the Environment).

Singh, Manmohan (1992) 'Managing the Economic Crisis' in R.K. Sinha (ed.) op. cit.

Skålnes, Tor (1993) 'The State, Interest Groups and Structural Adjustment in Zimbabwe', *The Journal of Development Studies*, vol. 29, no. 3, 401–28.

Smith, Jackie (1998) 'Global Civil Society?' *American Behavioral Scientist*, vol. 42, no. 1, 93–107.

Sogodogo, Alassane (1997) 'Dévaluation, croissance et équilibres macroéconomiques: le cas de la Côte d'Ivoire', in Bernard Contamin and Harris Memel-Fotê (eds) *Le modèle ivoirien en question* (Paris, Karthala).

Sojo, Carlos (1992) *La mano visible del mercado: La asistencia de Estados Unidos al sector privado costarricense en la década de los ochenta* (Managua: Ediciones CRIES/CEPAS).

Sojo, Carlos (1995) *Gobernabilidad en Centroamérica: la sociedad después del ajuste* (San José, Costa Rica: FLACSO).

Son, Byeong-seon (1996) 'Hangukul Hwankyeongdanche (Environmental Organizations in Korea),' Kim Jae-yeong et al (eds) *Hwaneongjeonchiwa Hwangeongjeongchak* (Environmental Politics and Environmental Policy (Seoul: Samusa).

Song, Byongrak (1994) *The Korean Economy* (Hong Kong: Oxford University Press).

Sorsa, Piritta (1997) 'The Uruguay Round and Subsaharan Africa's Trade Policies', in Ademola Oyejide, Ibrahim Elbadawi and Paul Collier (eds) *Regional Integration and Trade Liberalization in Subsaharan Africa*, vol. 1 (Basingstoke and London: Macmillan).

Southall, Roger (1996) 'Regionalization and Differentiation in South Africa: Some Policy Implications for Canadian Aid', in Larry A. Swatuk and David R. Black (eds) *Canada and Southern Africa After Apartheid: Foreign Aid and Civil Society* (Halifax: Centre for Foreign Policy Studies).

Stary, Bruno (1995) *Dévaluation du CFA et flux transétatiques en Afrique de l'Ouest: exemple de la frontière entre la Côte d'Ivoire et le Ghana*, Travaux et Documents no. 47 (Bordeaux: Centre d'Etude d'Afrique Noire).

Stasavage, David (1997) 'The CFA Franc Zone and Fiscal Discipline', *Journal of African Economies*, vol. 6, no. 1 (March) 132–67.

Steel, William F. and Leila Webster (1992) 'How Small Enterprises in Ghana Have Responded to Adjustment', *World Bank Economic Review*, vol. 6, no. 3 (September) 423–38.

Stevens, Candice (1993) 'The Environmental Effects of Trade' *World Economy*, vol. 16, no. 4 (July) 439–51.

Stevens, Christopher (1996) 'The Single European Market: Opportunities and Challenges in Trade', in Oladeji O. Ojo (ed.) *Africa and Europe: the Changing Economic Relationship* (London and Abidjan, Zed Books and African Development Bank).

Stiglitz, Joseph E. (1989) 'Markets, Markets Failures, and Development', *American Economic Review*, vol. 79, no. 2 (May) 197–203.

Stopford, John and Susan Strange (1991) *Rival States, Rival Firms* (Cambridge: Cambridge University Press).

Strange, Susan (1996), *The Retreat of the State: the Diffusion of Power in the World Economy* (Cambridge: Cambridge University Press).

Sunday (03.05.97).

Suttner, Raymond and Jeremy Cronin (1986) *30 Years of The Freedom Charter* (Johannesburg: Ravan Press).

Swatuk, Larry (1996) 'Learning the Hard Way: Environmental Policy Making in Southern Africa', in Gordon J.F. Macdonald *et al.* (eds) *Environmental Policy Making in Latin America in International Perspective* (Boulder: Westview).

Söderbaum, Fredrik (1996) *Handbook of Regional Organizations in Africa* (Uppsala: Nordiska Afrikainstitutet).

Sørensen, Georg (1991) *Democracy, Dictatorship and Development* (London: MacMillan).

Sørensen, Georg (1993) 'Democracy, Authoritarianism and State Strength', *The European Journal of Development Research*, vol. 5, no. 1, 6–34.

Taranga (14.02.97).

The Bank of Korea (http://www.bok.or.kr) *Economic Statistics Yearbook 1997*.

The Citizen's Movement Communication Center, *Hangukmingand anchechongram* (Directory of Korean NGOs) (http://www.kngo.net/new/pds/pds-cmcc.html).

The Economist (2000) 'Argentina's Struggle for Confidence and Growth', Nov. 18th:89.

Thomas, Rosalind H. (1997) *The WTO and Trade Cooperation Between the ACP and the EU: Assessing the Options*, Working Paper no. 16 (Maastricht, ECDPM).

Thompson, Peter and Laura A. Strohm (1996) 'Trade and Environmental Quality: A Review of the Evidence', *Journal of Environment & Development*, vol. 5, no. 4, 363–88.

Thornton, Robert (1996) 'The Potentials of Boundaries in South Africa: Steps Towards a Theory of the Social Edge', in Richard Werbner and Terence Ranger (eds) *Postcolonial Identities in Africa* (London: Zed Press).

Times of India (30.04.97).

Trigo, E., D. Kaimowitz and R. Flores (1991) "Bases para una agenda de trabajo para el dessarrollo agropecuario sostenible", Instituto Interamericano de Cooperación para la Agricultura (IICA), *Serie Documentos de Programas, 25.* (San Jose, Costa Rica).

Tussie, Diana (1993) 'Bargaining at a Crossroads: Argentina', in D. Tussie and D. Glover *The Developing Countries and World Trade: Policies and Bargaining Strategies* (Boulder, CO: Lynne Rienner).

Tussie, Diana (ed.) (1997) *El BID, el Banco Mundial y la Sociedad Civil: Nuevas Formas de Financiamiento Internacional* (FLACSO-Oficina de Publicaciones del CBC).

Tussie, Diana and Botzman Mirta (1989) 'Sweet Entanglement: the IMF and the World Bank', *Development Policy Review*, vol. 8, no. 4, 393–409.

Tussie, Diana and M.F. Tuozzo (2001) 'Opportunities and Constraints for Civil Society Participation in Multilateral Lending Operations: Lessons from Latin America', in M. Edwards and J. Gavanta (eds) *Global Citizen Action* (Boulder: Lynne Rienner).

UNCTAD (1995a) *Foreign Direct Investment in Africa* (Geneva: United Nations).

UNCTAD (1995b) *Trade and Development Report 1995* (Geneva: United Nations).

UNCTAD (1998) *World Investment Report* (Geneva: United Nations).

UNCTAD (1999) *World Investment Report 1999* (New York: United Nation).

UNCTAD (several years) *Trade and Development Report* (Geneva: United Nations).

UNDP (2000) *Human Development Report 2000* (New York: United Nations Development Programme/Oxford University Press).

UNDP (several years) *Human Development Report*.

UNEP (1999) *Global Environmental Outlook 2000* (London: Earthscan Publication Ltd).

Van de Walle, Nicolas (1991) 'The Decline of the Franc Zone: Monetary Politics in Francophone Africa', *African Affairs*, no. 90, 383–405.

Van de Walle, Nicolas and Timothy A. Johnston (1996) *Improving Aid To Africa*, Policy Essay no. 21 (Washington, DC: Overseas Development Council).

van der Lugt, Cornelius (1996) *Introductory Notes and Policy Considerations Concerning the Issue of Trade and the Environment,* issued by the Directorate: Environment and Marine, Multilateral Branch, (SA) Department of Foreign Affairs (October).

Verdier, Isabelle (1996) *Côte d'Ivoire: cent hommes de pouvoir* (Paris: Indigo Publications).

Villa, Pierre (1994) 'Dévaluation du Franc CFA et profitabilité à l'exportation', *Economie Internationale*, no. 58, 2è trimestre, 33–51.

Von Brokowski, Gabrielle (1997) 'Sous le signe du développement partagé', *Le Courrier*, no. 166, novembre–décembre, 54–7.

Waterbury, John (1989) 'The Political Management of Economic Adjustment and Reform', pp. 39–56 in Joan M. Nelson ed. *Fragile Coalitions: The Politics of Economic Adjustment* (New Brunswick/Oxford: Transaction Books).

Weiss, Linda (1995) 'Governed Interdependence: Rethinking the Government-Business Relationship in East Asia', *The Pacific Review*, vol. 8, no. 4, 589–616.

Weiss, Linda (1998) *The Myth of the Powerless State* (Ithaca: Cornell University Press).

Weiss, Linda and John Hobson (1995) *States and Economic Development: a Comparative Historical Analysis* (Cambridge, UK: Polity Press).

Whalley, John (1996) 'Trade and Environment, the WTO, and the Developing Countries', in Robert Z. Lawrence, Dani Rodrik and John Whalley (eds) *Emerging Agenda for Global Trade: High Stakes for Developing Countries*, Policy Essay no. 20 (Washington, DC: Overseas Development Council).

Widner, Jennifer (1993) 'The Origins of Agricultural Policy in Ivory Coast, 1960–86', *Journal of Development Studies*, vol. 29, no. 4 (July) 25–59.

Williamson, John (1994) 'In Search of a Manual for Technopols', in John Williamson (ed.) *The Political Economy of Policy Reform* (Washington, DC: Institute for International Economics).

Wilson, Bruce M. (1994) 'When Social Democrats Choose Neoliberal Economic Policies: The Case of Costa Rica', *Comparative Politics*, vol. 26, no. 2, 149–68.

Wilson, Bruce M. (1998) *Costa Rica. Politics, Economics, and Democracy* (Boulder, CO: Lynne Rienner Publishers).

Wilson, Bruce M. (1999) 'Leftist Parties, Neoliberal Policies, and Reelection Strategies. The Case of the PLN in Costa Rica', *Comparative Political Studies*, vol. 32, no. 6, 752–79.

Woods, Dwayne (1994) 'Elites, Ethnicity and 'Home Towns' Associations in the Côte d'Ivoire: an Historical Analysis of State-Society Links', *Africa*, vol. 64, no. 4, 465–83.

Woods, Ngaire (1997) 'Governance in International Organisations: The Case for Reform in the Bretton Woods Institutions', Paper prepared for the G-24 Technical Group, mimeo.

World Bank (1994) *Republic of Côte d'Ivoire: Private Sector Assessment*, Report no. 12885-IVC (Washington, DC: The World Bank).

World Bank (1995) *Argentina. Managing Environmental Pollution: Issues and Options* (Washington DC: Environmental and Urban Development Division).

World Bank (1997a) *Poverty in Côte d'Ivoire: A Framework for Action*, Report no. 15640-IVC (Washington DC: the World Bank).

World Bank (1997b) *African Development Indicators* (Washington, DC: The World Bank).

World Bank (2001) www.worldbank.org/sprojects.

World Resources Institute (1998) *World Resources 1998–99* (Washington, DC: World Resources Institute).

Woronoff, Jon (1972) *West African Wager: Houphouet Versus Nkrumah* (Metuchen: The Scarecrow Press).

WTO (1995) *Examen des Politiques Commerciales: Côte d'Ivoire, vol. 1: Rapport du Secrétariat de l'OMC; vol. 2: Remarques récapitulatives, Rapport du Gouvernement de la Côte d'Ivoire, Compte-rendu* (Genève: OMC).

WTO/(CTE) (1999) (The Second WTO/CTE) 34:5 (1999.08).

Wynberg, Rachel (1993) *Exploring the Earth Summit*, (Johannesburg: Penrose Press).

Yearley, Steven (1996) *Sociology, Environmentalism, Globalization: Reinventing the Globe* (London: Sage Publications).

Yoo, Pal-moo (1995) 'Siminsahoiui Sungjanggwa Siminundong (The Development of Civil Society and Civil Movement),' in Yoo P. and Kim Hogi (eds) *Siminsahoiwa Siminundong* (Civil Society and Civil Movement) (Seoul: Hanul).

Yoon, Seo-sung (1999) 'Hwangyeongjungchaekul uiui mit gyeongjunggujo (The Meaning of Environmental Policy and Decision-Making Structure.' Hangookhwangyeongjungchaekhakhoi (Korean Environmental Policy Acamedic Association), (ed.) *Hwangyeongjungcheakron* (Theory of Environmental Policy) (Seoul: Singwangmoonhwasa).

Zolberg, Aristide R. (1964) *One-Party Government in the Ivory Coast* (Princeton, NJ: Princeton University Press).

Index